PRAISE FOR
MONEY FOR LIFE

"I urge you to do something special for others and those you love—read *Money for Life*. The responsible planning of your time, talents and treasure will allow you to finish well and leave a legacy that blesses future generations."

Dan Miller, Life Coach and Author *48 Days to the Work You Love*
48Days.com

"As a financial coach I often hear my clients say, 'I wish I had learned more about money sooner.' Don't let this happen to you. *Money For Life* provides financial information that you'll refer to again and again. The author explains complex topics in a way that non-financially minded people can understand. This is one of those books that you will wish you had read years ago."

Derek C. Olsen, Author of *The Four-Week Financial Turnaround*
HisPlusHersEqualsOurs.com

"If you could read one book that could teach you how to live with more abundance, joy, and wealth, would you try it? What would life look like for you if your finances weren't a worry? *Money for Life* takes readers through SIMPLE and EASY steps to finding financial freedom."

Jen McDonough (aka "The Iron Jen"), Motivational Storyteller and Author
TheIronJen.com

MONEY
FOR
LIFE

FINANCIAL PRINCIPLES FOR BECOMING FINANCIALLY SAVVY!

MARILYNN E. HOOD

Money for Life

30 Minute Living
PO Box 10381
College Station, TX 77842
30minuteliving.com

DISCLAIMER:
The stories and anecdotes presented in this publication are based on true experiences. The names have been changed, and certain situations may have been altered to protect the privacy of any individuals mentioned. This publication is designed to provide accurate and authoritative information with regard to the subject matter covered. It is presented with the understanding that neither the author nor the publisher is engaged in rendering financial, accounting, legal or other professional advice. Individual situations are unique, and the services of a competent professional person should be sought if personal financial, accounting, legal or other professional assistance is required. The author and publisher specifically disclaim any liability or loss which may be incurred as a consequence, either directly or indirectly, of the use and application of any of the contents of this publication.

ISBN 13 TP: 978-1-939255-01-3
ISBN 13 Ebook: 978-1-939255-00-6

Library of Congress Control Number: 2013940732

Front cover by Imagine! Studios, LLC

This book is dedicated to the many thousands of students
who have taught me so much.

CONTENTS

Introduction

Why Do Financial Planning?

While grocery shopping several years ago, I happened to overhear the conversation of two little ladies who were slowly pushing their buggy down the aisle of the supermarket. As they were discussing what to buy and carefully going over the items on their list, one of the ladies reached over and picked up a two-liter bottle of soda. Turning to her friend, she asked, "Shall we get this or not?" The other lady replied, "Well, it'll be O.K. if we have enough money left over when we're through."

My heart sank as the meaning of their dialog soaked in. I thought, how much does that two-liter bottle of soda cost—maybe $1.25 at most? Their grocery budget was so tight that the decision whether to buy a bottle of soda was a major consideration!

Granted, there are people who choose to live very frugally while they may have thousands or even millions socked away in various investments. Those people, however, are by far the exception and not the norm. Too many people find themselves counting pennies, wondering if they'll ever be able to retire, or if they have already retired, hoping they won't live longer than their money will last.

Where do you want to be financially when you retire? Wouldn't you rather be faced with tough decisions like—do we spend the winter in the mountains at our condo skiing or at our beach house on the coast with our toes in the sand—rather than worrying if you can afford a bottle of soda?

If you want to end up financially in a different spot from those who are fearful of outliving their money, then you'll have to consciously do something differently.

It's called Financial Planning, and it's not hard—it just takes a little bit of thought.

But why wait until you retire? Why not start right now on the road to financial independence? Begin putting the financial resources in place so that you can call the shots yourself—no matter what your age. Financial Planning can help you achieve that as well, and probably sooner than you think.

Note:
This book is for general informational purposes only and is not meant to provide legal, financial, accounting, or otherwise professional advice. No representations are made as to the truth and validity of the contents.

"The art of living easily as to money is to pitch your scale of living one degree below your means."

~Sir Henry Taylor

CHAPTER 1
Overview of the Financial Planning Process

How can you live within your means if you don't know what your means are? Many people honestly don't know. Personal finance is not a subject that's widely taught, yet countless parents of my college students have told me this is the one course they wish they could have taken when they were in school. It would have saved them years of having to learn things the hard way—from the School of Hard Knocks.

Financial Planning—
Foundation for Achieving Financial Independence

The purpose of this book is to provide a foundation of knowledge in personal finance. It's not meant to turn you into a millionaire overnight, but to help you gain something even more valuable—your financial independence.

Financial independence means you have breathing room. You're not constantly being pushed to the wall by financial matters. You have reserves to handle the smaller misfortunes of life and plenty of unused credit capacity to deal with the big ones.

Gaining financial independence depends not so much on the *amount* of money you make, but more on the *way you handle whatever you do have.*

People of relatively modest means can and do achieve financial independence. They are people who think through what they truly want and systematically work toward achieving their goals. Yet, there are others who make a lot of money who always manage to keep themselves financially strapped by chasing after the appearance of wealth. They consistently spend more than they make, no matter how much they make.

Financial planning can help you achieve financial independence. It's an ongoing process that you will refine and adjust as your needs and circumstances in life change. In a nutshell, you will:
- Determine the financial goals that you want to achieve—your goals point you in the direction you need to take.
- Create the plans for achieving your goals—your plans define the pathway for reaching your goals.
- Carry out your plans—your follow through will help you build momentum and propel you toward your goals even faster than you had imagined.

Fail to plan and you'll find yourself adrift like so many others, always at the mercy of whatever wind that blows. Determine instead to set your own sail and harness the winds to take you where you want to go in life.

Steps in the Financial Planning Process

The following provides a brief overview of the financial planning process:

1. Define your financial goals

What do you wish to accomplish financially? Search your own self—your goals need to be yours and not someone else's. You need to know where you want to go so that your financial plans can help you chart the course to get there. And remember, the more specific your goals, the more likely you are to attain them.

2. Evaluate your current position

Where are you now financially, and what are you doing with your money? Gain insight into your current situation by tracking your expenses over a period of several months and by creating your balance sheet and income statement. When you understand your spending habits and know where your money is going, you can better control your expenses and measure your progress toward your goals.

3. Plan your future expenditures

Does the mere mention of the word budget make you break out in a cold sweat? In truth, budgets can help make your dreams come true, so start thinking of them instead as enablers. A budget is a simple but powerful tool to help you plan your future expenses and channel your money toward the things that are important to you. A budget can actually liberate you AND provide you with a pathway for reaching your financial goals!

4. Fund your cash accounts

Liquid assets, such as checking or savings accounts, can be turned into cash pretty rapidly without significant loss of value. These are the types of assets you'll need for goals you wish to achieve during the next year or so. You also need liquid assets for the financial emergencies that are bound to occur (at the worst possible times, of course). Without enough cash-type assets to cover at least three months of living expenses, you're likely to have to charge up your credit cards or beg your loved ones for help—not a pleasant thought!

5. Manage your debt

Speaking of credit cards, do you carry a balance on yours from one period to the next? If so, paying off your credit card debt should be one of your top priorities. Debt used wisely can be a very useful tool. Too much debt or the wrong type of debt can be like a noose tightening around your neck. Controlling debt is an important key to building wealth.

6. Insure your valuables

What would you do if your assets were destroyed or stolen? What would your family do without your earning capacity if you became disabled? Insurance helps protect the value you have in your property, your life, your health, and your ability to work. But be aware that you want just enough. Too much insurance or the wrong type of insurance drains away dollars that could be used to create wealth.

7. Invest for your future

Investments (such as stocks, bonds or real estate) are assets that are meant to be left alone for a longer period of time—at least a year or more. They are used to fund your longer-term goals, such as saving for college or retirement. Your choice of investments will depend on your level of risk tolerance and how long before you need the money. Investments help build wealth and create financial independence.

8. Plan for your estate

Without proper planning, taxes can absorb a large portion of what you leave behind. Or worse, your assets can go to the wrong people! Take steps now to ensure that what you do leave behind will be maximized and distributed in the manner that you desire. Even more important than your assets are your minor children or other dependents. Don't leave it up to the courts to determine who will care for them.

Define Your Financial Goals

Your goals drive the entire financial planning process, because where you want to go determines the course you should plot to get there. The worksheet below shows a few examples of various goals designed simply to stimulate your thought process and get you going on creating your own goals.

Your list should be a "living" document that you mark all over, revise and rewrite as you live your life. Check things off when you accomplish them or scratch them out when they're no longer relevant. Just remember that the goals should be yours and/or your family's, and not necessarily what everyone else seems to be striving for.

(Examples of financial goals – yours will vary according to your needs and what you wish to accomplish.)

Goal	Time Frame	How I plan to attain it:
Organize my financial records	Now	Set aside 1 hour each Tuesday evening to pay bills and balance my checkbook; learn to use the money management program I purchased last year.
Fund my cash reserve account with enough money to cover at least 3 months of living expenses	Beginning with my next paycheck	In a separate savings account set aside at least $50 per month until I reach my goal.
Pay off student loans	Within 5 yrs. of graduation	Pay an extra $200 on my loans each month from money saved by eating out less.
Start my own business	Within the next 10 yrs.	Research businesses that I'm interested in; explore various financing options; set aside $300 per month in a separate account.
Become financially independent	Within the next 20 yrs.	Fully fund all available retirement accounts; invest 10% of my take-home pay each month.

In writing each of your financial goals, you should:
- Be specific in defining your goal.
- Set a time frame.
- Map out a pathway for attaining your goal.

Whether you write them on paper or on your computer, keep your goals where you can see them and think about them. Maybe tack a copy to the wall over your desk. Goals help you *focus your efforts and keep you on track!* And remember:

You will be much more likely to attain any goal that you COMMIT IN WRITING! Additionally, if you SHARE YOUR GOALS with a supportive friend who helps hold you accountable, you're virtually assured to reach your goals.

Use this goal sheet to begin planning for your own financial goals. You may reproduce this page and update your goals as often as you like.

My Financial Goals Worksheet

Goal	Time Frame	How I plan to attain it:

Track Your Expenses

No, you can't skip this step (blank forms are waiting patiently for you on the next few pages). While some people really *do* understand how they spend every cent, they're probably in the minority. Most of us are able to gain a much better understanding of our spending habits and a much clearer picture of our finances by tracking our expenses over a period of time.

Whether you use a pencil and paper, a little notebook that you carry with you, or a computer program, here's what you need to do:

> *Step 1:* Record every cent you spend for at least a month (three to six months would be even better, but hey — even a week is better than nothing!).

> *Step 2:* Separate your expenses into "Necessary" and "Discretionary" categories and total each group.

> *Step 3:* Evaluate both types of expenses.

Your "Discretionary" expenses offer the greatest opportunities. Capture these dollars instead of allowing them to drain out of your pocket on things that don't particularly mean anything to you or that don't enhance the quality of your life. *Beginning today*, you can start channeling some of these expenditures toward attaining your financial goals.

Then take a look at your "Necessary" expenses. Remember, even though they're necessary for now, they're not set in stone. What can you reshuffle in this category? You have to pay your phone bill, but do you really need and use all the extra features you're paying for? You need to eat, but how much are you spending on sodas, snacks, and eating out? With planning and forethought, you'll be able to rearrange or reduce your necessary expenditures over time and redirect the funds you've freed up toward your financial goals as well.

Who defines "Necessary" and "Discretionary?" You do! Each person has different needs, different resources, and different abilities. What one person may regard as totally frivolous may be exactly what another person needs in order to function. Ask yourself what would happen if you did not incur a certain expense — how would it affect your life?

For people who have never had to discern between necessary and discretionary, this becomes a very important exercise!

The information you glean from tracking your expenses is truly the cornerstone of your financial planning. If you do not understand what you're doing with your money at this most basic level, you cannot plan effectively. You will use this information throughout the financial planning process. It will prove particularly useful for taking the next steps covered in Chapters 2 and 3: preparing your balance sheet, which shows your current financial position; preparing your income statement, which shows where you've been; and planning your budget, which plots the course for where you would like to go.

Step 1: Record Your Expenses
Write down every cent you spend for a month (or more).

My Spending Diary

(Use the small box to left of Expense column to label your expense N for necessary or D for discretionary.)

	Expense	Amount		Expense	Amount

(You may reproduce this page and repeat this process as often as you like.)

Step 2: Categorize Your Expenses
Separate the expenses from your Spending Diary into Necessary or Discretionary.

Categorized Expenses

Necessary Expenses	Amount	Discretionary Expenses	Amount

(You may reproduce this page and repeat this process as often as you like.)

Step 3: Evaluate Your Expenses

What Will You Change?

Now it's time to mark all over your lists. What changes do you wish to make? Which discretionary expenses can you reduce or eliminate entirely? Which necessary expenses can you alter or renegotiate? *Right now*, incorporate these changes into your budget!

If you had reservations about even starting this exercise, realize that you are in the company of thousands of others! Many people are doubtful, even to the point of being skeptical, that they have extra money. They just don't believe they'll be able to change any of their expenses.

Having assigned this exercise to my students for years, I can tell you that those who take it seriously usually come back wide-eyed after they've completed it. Some are truly disgusted when they see the total of what they've spent on beer, lottery tickets, coffee, sodas, snacks from the vending machine, etc. Many are able to make small changes that really add up, and remember, these were mostly college-age students — not people who generally make serious money! If they can find money that's dribbling through their fingers, it's a good bet you can too.

Darren Hardy admits in his book, *The Compound Effect*[1]. "I learned about the power of tracking the hard way, after I'd acted like a colossal idiot about my finances." When his accountant informed him he owed over $100,000 in taxes, Darren got serious about tracking his expenses. This worked so well that he began applying the technique to other areas of his life in order to bring about transformational change. Today Darren is a multi-millionaire who associates with and interviews other highly successful people on a daily basis and has been able to positively impact the lives of thousands of others.

Small amounts of money truly add up through time, and larger amounts regularly invested can change your life, even more rapidly than you might imagine. The graph which follows shows the growth of a *single $1,000 investment* at various interest rates, compounded annually. Note that the growth pattern is not linear, but exponential. The longer the money stays invested and the higher the interest rate, the faster those growth lines start to shoot straight up!

---

[1] Find information on Darren Hardy's book at www.30minuteliving.com.

Growth of a Single $1,000 Investment

This graph shows a single one thousand dollar investment left to grow over time. Just think what you could accumulate with regular deposits year after year! Time is a powerful ally, and over time, small amounts can grow into substantial sums.

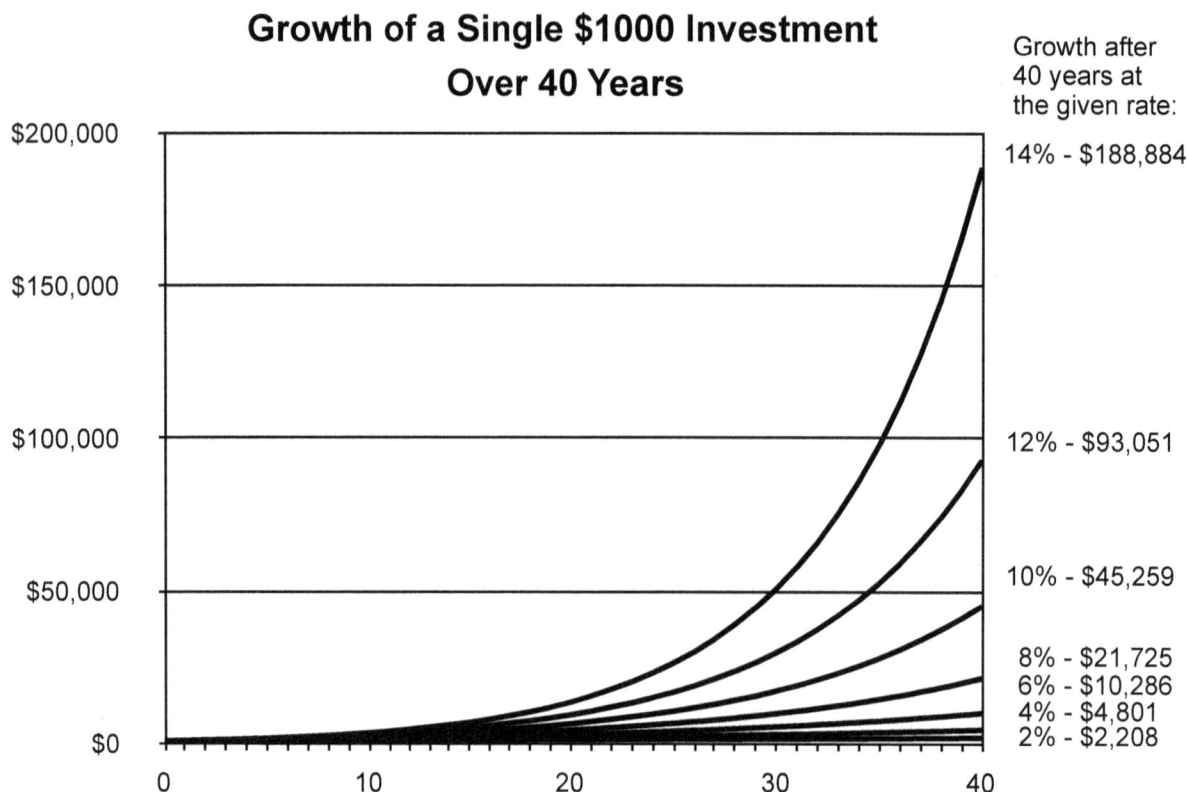

Growth of a Single $1000 Investment Over 40 Years

Growth after 40 years at the given rate:

14% - $188,884
12% - $93,051
10% - $45,259
8% - $21,725
6% - $10,286
4% - $4,801
2% - $2,208

Note that with every 2% increase in return, your investment results more than double over a 40-year period. If you can increase your return from 4% to 6%, instead of $4,801 you'll have $10,286. And if you can increase your return to 8%, you'll end up with $21,725, more than twice what you would have with a 6% return.

Two percent is the equivalent to two measly cents on a dollar. So every time you find a couple of pennies on the sidewalk, let them remind you of this graph and the power of compound growth over time.

30 Minute LIVING

Suggested Action Plan

- *Think about the future.* Review the steps in the financial planning process and start thinking about how the overall process applies to your life.

- *Determine your financial goals.* Be sure to make one of your goals (if it's not already) the accumulation of a cash cushion of at least 3 months of living expenses. Even several hundred dollars in savings is a start. Put your goals in writing, and share your goals with a supportive friend who will help hold you accountable.

- *Track your expenses.* Just the act of having to write things down makes you stop and think before you spend. You need to know where your money is going and for what purposes. Otherwise, you cannot plan effectively. (This information will be used in creating your personal financial statements in Chapter 2: Evaluating Your Current Position, and your budget in Chapter 3: Planning Your Future Expenditures.)

- *Make changes.* Use the information you have learned about your spending to start making changes. Any amount saved can be funneled immediately toward your financial goals. You may want to open separate savings accounts for certain goals. (More about managing your cash accounts in Chapter 4: Understanding your Cash Accounts, and Chapter 5: Funding Your Cash Accounts.)

- *Work on your personal development.* Read books on financial topics or listen to CDs, particularly while you're stuck in the car driving. Not only will you expand your knowledge of finance, but you'll also be encouraged and inspired as well. A good place to start would be with Darren Hardy's book, *The Compound Effect* (referenced previously). Short, concise and easy to read, this book (also available with audio or as an e-book) shows you how small actions build upon one another in almost every area of your life. This book, written from a multi-millionaire's viewpoint, is truly a primer for success.

CHAPTER 2
Evaluating Your Current Position

How many times have you looked at the map in a shopping mall or an airport and searched for the "You are here" marker? Knowing where you are now allows you to go more directly toward your destination. Otherwise, you're stuck wandering around, wasting valuable time and resources, hoping to happen upon it somehow.

It's the same with financial planning. Your goals focus your sights toward *where you want to go*, your destination. But like a global positioning system (GPS), you need to know *where you are now* in order to plot the course to get you there. Preparing your financial statements will give you a better handle on your current position so that you can more effectively plan how to proceed. In this chapter you will: 1) measure your net worth using a balance sheet, and 2) find your cash surplus or deficit using an income statement.

1. Measure Your Net Worth

Your net worth is a measure of your current financial position, and *over time you would like for this number to increase!* A personal balance sheet is a simple but powerful tool that you can use to help you determine your net worth. (A blank form is provided for you following this exercise, or you can create a spreadsheet on your computer.)

To create a balance sheet, list everything you own and everything you owe. **Assets** are things you own, and you will need an estimate of their fair market value. **Liabilities** are debts you owe, and for them you will need their payoff amount. Add up both categories and subtract your total liabilities from your total assets. The difference between the two sums is your **Net Worth**. A very simple example of a balance sheet follows:

BALANCE SHEET			
Prepared for: Samantha Smith		As of: June 30, 20XX	
Assets		**Liabilities**	
Checking account (current balance)	$1,000	Credit card 1 (current balance)	$1,500
Savings account (current balance)	3,000	Credit card 2 (current balance)	600
XYZ Mutual Fund (current balance)	4,000	Student loan (current payoff amount)	10,000
Auto (fair market value)	18,000	Auto loan (current payoff amount)	16,000
		Total Liabilities	$28,100
		Net Worth	($2,100)
Total Assets	$26,000	**Total Liabilities + Net Worth**	$26,000

The parentheses around the Net Worth amount indicate a negative number—Samantha owes more than she owns, an unfortunate but common problem. A student once showed me his balance sheet with a negative net worth. Thinking he had made a mistake, he said, "You can't have a negative net worth, can you?" Oh, if only that were true!

Notice that the numbers at the bottom of each column are the same—that's why it's called a "balance" sheet. Getting your personal balance sheet to balance is no big deal, because you find your net worth by subtracting your liabilities from your assets. So unless your math is wrong, it's a given that the amount you get when you add your liabilities to your net worth is the same as the total of your assets. *The crucial number is the Net Worth.*

This all looks and sounds pretty simple, but a little further explanation may prove helpful. The following sections on Terminology and Frequently Asked Questions address issues which commonly arise.

Balance Sheet Terminology

Asset—something you own, that you have the title to or can call your own, whether it's completely paid for or not. If you've bought a home, you have a title to the property and you own it even though it may be years before it's paid for. Students frequently ask if their cars, which their parents have bought for them, should be considered assets. The answer is yes—if it's yours to keep. If you have to give it back, then it's not.

You'll notice on the example balance sheet above that no personal assets are listed, like furniture, jewelry, computer equipment, etc. Certainly, you can list whatever you own that you feel has value, but be cautious in the amount you assign to such items. Are these items you would actually consider selling? If you could find a market for these items, what could you realistically sell them for? One young woman who had been a beauty pageant contestant listed her formal gowns as an asset item worth $20,000. When asked about the market for used gowns, she admitted she could realistically expect to sell them for only a fraction of what she paid for them and lowered her valuation amount dramatically.

Fair market value—this is how much you would expect to receive for an asset if you sold it, not how much you paid for it. An example of fair market value would be a vehicle's "Blue Book" value, or what you could reasonably expect to receive for your vehicle if you were to sell it today.

Cash basis of accounting—those with an accounting background may be thinking that assets should be listed at historical cost and then depreciated through time, as is usually the case in corporate accounting. Valuing assets is one of the areas in which personal accounting and corporate accounting methods differ, and it all goes back to—you guessed it—the tax code. In general, individuals are to use the "cash basis" of accounting and corporations the "accrual basis." [For those who are concerned about the differences in personal and corporate accounting methods and why these differences matter, please see the frequently asked question below, Why can't I prepare my personal financial statements using corporate accounting methods?]

Liabilities — are debts that you owe, like on your credit card, your home mortgage, or your auto loan. This is a pretty straightforward category for most people except in areas such as a leased vehicle or cell phone service for which you would be charged a penalty for early termination. Such leases and agreements have various terms and conditions in the contracts, so it's hard to make a generalization. However, if you feel there is at least a certain amount you would be stuck with, regardless of whether you continue the lease or terminate it today, then you would probably want to list that amount as a liability.

Payoff amount — this is the amount at which you will list each of your liabilities. As an example, let's say you won the lottery and wanted to pay off your car loan today. If you could march into the bank with a fist full of dollars, how much money would you have to slap on the counter to pay off that loan? That's the payoff amount. It is NOT your monthly payment times how many months are left to pay on the loan, which almost assuredly includes the future interest you will owe. Remember, a balance sheet shows your *current* financial position — your position as of *today*.

Net Worth — on a personal balance sheet, this is simply the difference between the total of your assets and the total of your liabilities. It is the residual or leftover amount. The counterpart to net worth on a corporate balance sheet would be the equity or ownership section, and a number of items would be listed, such as common stock, excess paid-in capital, retained earnings, etc. A corporation has many owners with each owning a small portion, so the equity section of a corporate balance sheet must reflect the different forms of ownership and how it's divided. However, each of us as individuals has only one owner — ourself — so there is no division of ownership to show.

Frequently Asked Questions for Balance Sheets

Why even create a personal balance sheet?

Simply put, a balance sheet shows you what would be left if you were forced to liquidate your assets to pay off your debts. Preparing a personal balance sheet can help you in several ways:
- Listing everything together on one page allows you to view your entire financial scene at once.
- Preparing your balance sheet means you have to check your current account balances, which in itself helps you to keep up with them.
- Calculating your net worth provides you with a single number, which then serves as a comparison point for future measurements of your net worth.

The personal balance sheet and income statement (discussed later) serve as tools that allow you to put dollar amounts on your finances. They are measuring rods with which you can track your progress toward your financial goals. They also make you face reality, which in itself is a huge hurdle for some people, because *you cannot deal with a situation that you refuse to face.*

I have a life insurance policy. Should I list the death payout as an asset?

Only policies which build cash value should be listed as assets, and then only the cash value portion, not the death benefit amount. Term life insurance policies do not build cash value, so they would not be listed on your balance sheet. Other types of policies which do build cash value tend to build it fairly slowly. Look at your latest statement to see if the cash value is shown. Remember, what you are trying to determine with your balance sheet is this: if the worst case scenario occurred and I were forced to liquidate my assets today, what would I have left? (More about insurance in later chapters.)

If I have a negative net worth, will I go bankrupt?

Even though a negative net worth is usually not desirable, it doesn't necessarily signal that you will need to declare bankruptcy or that you are mishandling your finances. For example, many students have a negative net worth—they may have assets consisting of their calculator, books and maybe a bicycle, while they have $20,000 (or more) in student loans.

In such cases, the determining factor becomes the terms of how you are required to repay your debt. If your required payments are low enough that you are able to pay them when due each period, then you won't go bankrupt. When the payments become too great for your income to support or you lose your income—that's when you'll be in danger of having to declare bankruptcy.

If you are past the student stage and find yourself with a negative net worth, you need to carefully consider every aspect of your finances in order to determine what has caused you to be in this position. Which contributing factors are within your control, and which are not? What steps do you need to take to change your situation? Do you need to seek outside help?

Finally, remember that declaring bankruptcy is not a cure-all by any means! Some debts cannot be erased by bankruptcy, such as student loans, child support payments, or taxes owed the IRS. In fact, recently passed legislation has made it more difficult to even obtain debt forgiveness. Also to be considered is the damage that bankruptcy does to your credit rating, making future credit both more difficult and more costly to obtain. A negative net worth is definitely a concern, and those who find themselves in this position need to handle their finances with extreme care. More on debt in later chapters.

I paid a lot of money for my car, so it's an investment, right?

No. For the vast majority of us, our vehicles are depreciating assets (assets which decline in value over time) and not investments. Investments are purchased with the expectation that their values will appreciate through time (even though their current values may fluctuate). Unless you are a car collector or purchase old cars to restore, you are probably painfully aware that your vehicle's value will decrease. In fact, many people who purchase new cars find themselves "upside down" on their auto loans for several years—meaning if they sold their car now, they would not receive enough to pay off the loan amount.

Why can't I prepare my personal financial statements using corporate accounting methods?

In general, personal accounting and corporate accounting procedures are similar, but there are some notable differences. Several of these are addressed below:

- *Historical cost and depreciation of assets*—Corporations are allowed to expense the purchase of certain items used in producing income. They record such items on their balance sheets at historical cost (what they paid for them), and then depreciate a portion of those costs year by year. The amount depreciated each year is counted against their income, which in turn lowers the amount of income taxes owed for the year.

  In general, individuals are not afforded a tax break for the depreciation of their assets (unless they are business owners or contract workers with Schedule C income). So when individuals are preparing their personal balance sheets to determine their current net worth, the fair market value of their assets is what they need to know. However, it is wise to keep a record of what you paid for your assets, *particularly for investments*. (Investments will be discussed in a later chapter.)

- *Prepaid items vs. expenses and the cash vs. accrual basis of accounting*—Corporations typically use the *accrual basis* of accounting. When a corporation pays an expense up front, like their insurance premium for the next year, only the portion that is considered used up for a given time period will be listed as an expense on their income statement, and the unused amount will be listed on their balance sheet as a prepaid asset.

  This is typically *not* done on personal financial statements, because individuals will, in general, use the *cash* basis of accounting (discussed earlier). When you mail the check or pay your bill online, the money is considered gone and the whole amount becomes an expense at that time. Conversely, money is considered income when you actually have it at your disposal. If someone owes you money and has promised to pay it in the future, it doesn't count as income yet, because it may never show up.[2]

2. Determine Your Cash Surplus or Cash Deficit

A personal income statement measures your cash surplus or deficit over a given time period, and over time you would like to consistently have cash surpluses! If more cash flowed in than flowed out, you have a cash surplus. Conversely, if more cash flowed out than in, you have a cash deficit. With cash surpluses, you will be able to build up your resources and work toward attaining your financial goals. Cash deficits, however, use up your existing resources and may cause significant financial distress. An example of a personal income statement is shown on the next page.

In preparing your own income statement, use the information you gathered in tracking your expenses (in Chapter 1) or go back through your checkbook or whatever records you have of your income and expenses. Then list all the money that came in during the last time period in the income section.

Our example is for one month, but definitely you will also want to prepare a yearly income statement as you progress in your financial planning. Next, list your expenses for the same time period. Subtract the total of your expenses from the total of your income to determine your cash surplus or deficit.

[2]This information is meant to be general in nature and not for providing specific income tax advice.

INCOME STATEMENT		
Prepared for: _Samantha Smith_	For the month ending: _June 30, 20XX_	
Income		
Paycheck (take-home pay)	$ 3,000	
Investment income	100	
	Total Income	$ 3,100
Expenses		
Rent	$ 800	
Utilities	100	
Phone	50	
Food	300	
Clothing	50	
Personal care, misc.	50	
Auto insurance	80	
Gasoline & maintenance	200	
Auto loan payment	350	
Student loan payment	250	
Credit card 1 payment	35	
Credit card 2 payment	25	
XYZ Mutual Fund (purchase of additional shares)	100	
	Total Expenses	$ 2,390
Cash Surplus (Deficit)		$ 710

Fortunately, even though Samantha had a negative net worth on her balance sheet (shown in the previous section), she has a cash surplus on her income statement. She has enough to pay her expenses for the month with money left over. She can use her cash surplus to build up her savings, pay down her debt, or do a combination of both.

If Samantha had a cash deficit instead, that would mean that she couldn't pay all of her month's expenses with her earnings from this month. She would have to cover her deficit in one of two ways: 1) use up some of her assets, like dip into her savings account, or 2) increase her liabilities, like charge more stuff on her charge cards. (Please note that failing to pay some of the bills is not a viable option for those who are serious about improving their financial situation and preserving their credit rating!)

Now that we have covered both the balance sheet and income statement, you may have questions as you prepare your own financial statements. Usually these questions concern how to list various items, so check out the FAQs section which follows.

Frequently Asked Questions for Income Statements

Why does "XYZ Mutual Fund" show up on both the balance sheet and the income statement?

Usually, items are listed on either the balance sheet or the income statement, but not on both. In this case, the specific entries for XYZ Mutual Fund reflect different things. The balance sheet entry shows the current balance, and Samantha now owns a total of $4,000 worth of XYZ Mutual Fund as of the date on her balance sheet.

The income statement entry shows activity, and during the month shown, Samantha purchased an additional $100 worth of XYZ Mutual Fund. You'll notice that the purchase of the $100 in additional shares of the mutual fund is not recorded on the balance sheet, but this amount will be part of the total value of her ownership in XYZ Mutual Fund at the end of the given time period.

This brings us to an important consideration: if we were to put the balance sheet and income statement entries on a time line, for a given time period, the income statement entries occur first. Then, at the end of the given time period, time stops. You take a reading (i.e., prepare the balance sheet), and then time continues on to the next time period, as shown in the illustration which follows:

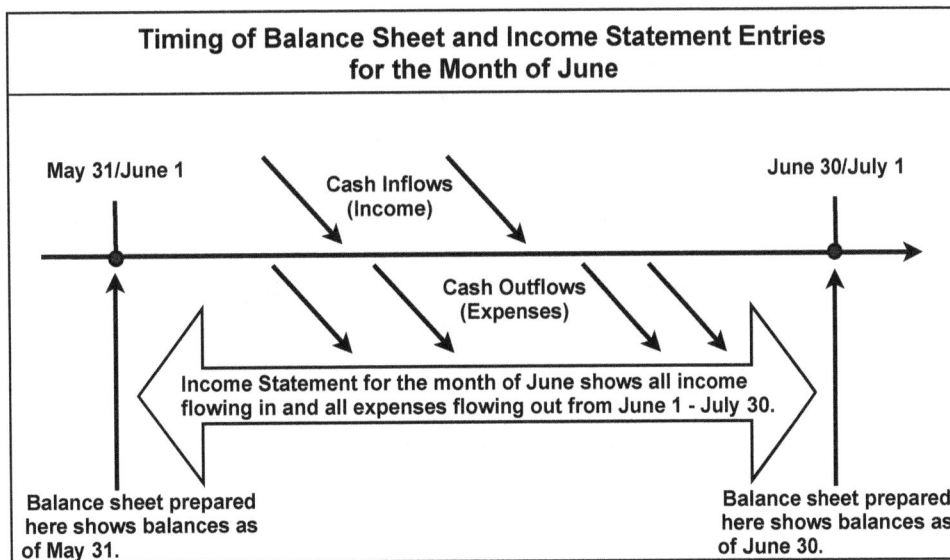

Timing of Balance Sheet and Income Statement Entries for the Month of June

May 31/June 1 — Cash Inflows (Income) — June 30/July 1

Cash Outflows (Expenses)

Income Statement for the month of June shows all income flowing in and all expenses flowing out from June 1 - July 30.

Balance sheet prepared here shows balances as of May 31.

Balance sheet prepared here shows balances as of June 30.

So here's a quick question for you: if Samantha purchased $100 worth of XYZ Mutual fund shares during the month of June, and her balance in her account was $4,000 at the end of June, what was the balance in her account at the end of May (assuming the mutual fund shares did not fluctuate in value)? Looking at the time line above, it would be easy to work backward and determine that she had $3,900 worth of XYZ Mutual Fund at the end of May (or first of June) before she made her June purchase.

Why is the purchase of an investment considered an expense?

Often, the term "expense" means something that is consumed and gone when the time period is over, like the monthly rent or utility payments. But definitely, you can also use up part of your income to purchase an asset. When preparing your personal income statement, it may help you to think of the expense section as merely a listing of how you allocated your income during the given time period. In the example given, Samantha used part of her monthly income to purchase an additional $100 worth of XYZ Mutual Fund, so she added to one of her assets.

Shouldn't I list my paycheck as an asset on my balance sheet?

No, your paycheck is income which you used during the given time period to pay your bills and make purchases. What's left of it (if there is any), will show up in the balance of an asset(s), probably your checking account.

What is the difference between "net" and "gross"?

Gross means big or entire, so your gross pay is the big number on your pay stub, the entire amount you earned for the period. Your net pay is what's left after the various taxes and deductions have been taken out. Be careful when preparing your income statement that you don't list your net pay and then subtract taxes as an expense. If you want to list out all the items deducted from your paycheck as expenses, then you would use the gross pay for income rather than the net. Just be consistent from one time period to the next.

I just took out a loan. Should I list that as income on my income statement?

A loan is not considered income because it's something you have to pay back. Let's say you get a loan to purchase a car. On your balance sheet you will list the car as an asset at fair market value and the loan payoff amount as a liability. Then on your income statement, you would list your monthly payment as an expense.

However, if you used the loan to purchase something consumable, like your honeymoon to Tahiti, then you won't have an asset to list on your balance sheet, but you'll still have the liability and expense entries.

If you have money that you didn't spend left over from a loan, then the residue will show up in another asset, like in the balance of your checking account.

Prepare your financial statements monthly and use them to track your progress. Be extra vigilant if:
- Your income and/or expenses vary widely from month to month.
- You're considering a big purchase or a big change in your life.
- Your budget is really tight.

Forms that you can use in preparing your personal financial statements follow.

Determining Your Net Worth

(You may reproduce this form as needed to use in preparing your personal financial statements.)

BALANCE SHEET			
Prepared for: _____		As of: _____	
Assets		**Liabilities**	
		Total Liabilities	
		Net Worth	
Total Assets		**Total Liabilities + Net Worth**	

Determining Your Cash Surplus or Cash Deficit

(You may reproduce this form as needed to use in preparing your personal financial statements.)

INCOME STATEMENT		
Prepared for: _____ For the month ending: _____		
Income		
Total Income		
Expenses		
Total Expenses		
Cash Surplus (Deficit)		

30 Minute LIVING

Suggested Action Plan

- *The first time you prepare your personal balance sheet and income statement, be sure you're thorough and accurate.* Of course, you want to be thorough and accurate every time, but these first statements will serve as your anchor points to refer back to in the future so you can measure your progress toward your goals. If you're not consistent from one time to the next, then it's harder to tell how you're doing.

- *Be like The Millionaire Next Door!* The authors of this modern-day classic have spent 20 years interviewing millionaires trying to learn how they are different from people who have not accumulated much wealth. They found that most millionaires today made their money themselves, and they did it by consistently spending less than they made over a long period of time. In other words, they had cash surpluses time after time on their income statements.

So go back and look at the income statement you just prepared. Do you have a cash surplus for this time period? If so, you have already started to build wealth! If you have a cash deficit, realize that for most people, deficits are bound to happen occasionally. Try to determine *why you have a cash deficit* this period and think about *what you can do* to eliminate having a deficit next time.

- *Plan ahead for your surpluses.* Leaving extra money in your checking account makes it too easy to spend. Set up a savings account or some other investment account now so that you already have a spot waiting when those surpluses arrive.

- *Pay yourself first.* You've probably heard this sage advice before. If you wait to see what's left over before setting your money aside, usually there won't be anything left. For many of us, our "must have" list automatically expands to absorb whatever extra we have.

On the other hand, if you skim money off the top of your paycheck, you'll probably never even miss it! It's helpful to set up an automatic draft for a certain amount to go into savings or an investment shortly after you get your paycheck. If it's on autopilot, you don't even have to think about it — it's just done! (More on managing your cash accounts and how to fund them in Chapters 4 and 5.)

CHAPTER 3
Planning Your Future Expenditures

It's tempting to think that people who succeed financially are just plain lucky or were born wealthy. In reality, the great majority of people who gain financial independence are *Regular People* who planned carefully. In this chapter, we will discuss using a budget to create a master plan for allocating your future income.

The balance sheet and income statement were addressed in Chapter 2. These important financial tools help you better understand your current financial position and how you spend your money. However, these instruments provide *historical* information; they show you what occurred in the recent past.

A budget looks *forward*. You use the knowledge provided by the historical information you've gathered to help you plan and plot your course for the future. Budgets are powerful—they help turn your goals into realities!

Considerations in Preparing Your Budget

With your spending diary from Chapter 1 and income statement from Chapter 2 in hand, sit down and begin preparing your budget. (A blank form is provided for you at the end of this chapter, or you can create one on your computer.)

Of course, the future may not be exactly like the past, so as you begin preparing your budget, think about:
- What will be different going forward?
- How should I make allowances for these differences in my budget?

Remember, as the time period that you have budgeted for unfolds, *you may need to alter your budget in midstream*—redo your budget from a certain point forward. What you may expect to happen and what actually happens don't always align!

For those so inclined, a computer spreadsheet or financial management program can help streamline the budgeting process. If you have entered your checkbook or downloaded your account transactions into a financial management program, such as Quicken, Microsoft Money, or Moneydance, the program itself may help you construct a budget. However, if you prefer to do a budget by hand, that's great. The main thing is to get it done in a way that works for you.

A sample budget follows on the next two pages. (It has been broken apart in order to fit the space better.)

BUDGET						
Prepared for: Samantha Smith						
	Jan.	Feb.	Mar.	Apr.	May	June
Income						
Paycheck – take home pay	$ 3,000	$ 3,000	$ 3,000	$ 3,000	$ 3,000	$ 3,000
Investment income						100
Contract work			500			
Total Income	3,000	3,000	3,500	3,000	3,000	3,100
Expenses						
Rent	800	800	800	800	800	800
Utilities	100	100	100	100	100	100
Phone	50	50	50	50	50	50
Food	300	300	300	300	300	300
Clothing	50	50	50	50	200	50
Personal care	50	50	50	50	50	50
Auto insurance	80	80	80	80	80	80
Gas & maintenance	200	200	200	200	200	250
Auto loan payment	350	350	350	350	350	350
Student loan pmt.	250	250	250	250	250	250
Credit card 1 pmt.	35	35	35	35	35	35
Credit card 2 pmt.	25	25	25	25	25	25
XYZ Mutual Fund	100	100	100	100	100	100
Savings	100	100	100	100	100	100
Vacation						
Entertainment	50	50	50	50	50	50
Total Expenses	2,540	2,540	2,540	2,540	2,690	2,590
Cash Surplus or (Deficit) For Each Month	460	460	960	460	310	510
Cumulative Surplus or (Deficit) Running Total	$460	$920	$1,880	$2,340	$2,650	$3,160

On our sample budget, you'll notice that the format follows this order:

1. List income items first, followed by expenses. Total each section separately.
2. At the bottom on the next-to-last line, subtract each month's expenses from its income. This gives the expected budget surplus or deficit for each given month.
3. On the last line, calculate the running total or the cumulative surplus or deficit. For each month, take the expected surplus or deficit from the previous month and add it to the expected surplus or deficit for the given month.
4. When you finish, the cumulative surplus or deficit at the end of December (on the bottom row) should equal the end number in the "Total" column, i.e., the two shaded cells on the bottom right corner should be equal.

BUDGET (Con't)							
					For the year ending: _December 31, 20XX_		
	July	Aug.	Sept.	Oct.	Nov.	Dec.	Total
Income							
Paycheck	$ 3,000	$ 3,000	$ 3,000	$ 3,000	$ 3,000	$ 3,000	$ 36,000
Investment income						100	200
Contract work				1,000			1,500
Total Income	3,000	3,000	3,000	4,000	3,000	3,100	37,700
Expenses							
Rent	800	800	800	800	800	800	9,600
Utilities	175	175	175	150	100	100	1,475
Phone	50	50	50	50	50	50	600
Food	300	300	300	300	300	300	3,600
Clothing	50	50	50	50	200	50	900
Personal care	50	50	50	50	50	50	600
Auto insurance	80	80	80	80	80	80	960
Gas & maintenance	600	200	200	200	200	350	3,000
Auto loan payment	350	350	350	350	350	350	4,200
Student loan pmt.	250	250	250	250	250	250	3,000
Credit card 1 pmt.	35	35	35	35	35	35	420
Credit card 2 pmt.	25	25	25	25	25	25	300
XYZ Mutual Fund	100	100	100	100	100	100	1,200
Savings	100	100	100	100	100	100	1,200
Vacation	1,000						1,000
Entertainment	50	50	50	50	50	50	600
Total Expenses	4,015	2,615	2,615	2,590	2,690	2,690	32,655
Cash Surplus or (Deficit) For Each Month	(1,015)	385	385	1,410	310	410	5,045
Cumulative Surplus or (Deficit) Running Total	$2,145	$2,530	$2,915	$4,325	$4,635	$5,045	

Samantha's Budget

In our example shown, Samantha expects a deficit for the month of July when she goes on vacation. However, she will easily be able to cover this deficit with surpluses from previous months.

If she hadn't written down her budget and planned for her vacation, do you think she would have had enough surplus to cover it? Or do you think the extra from the previous months might have dribbled out of her pocket and she would have ended up charging her vacation expenses instead? Who knows what a pretend person would do, but out in the real world, it's often so much easier to spend than to save.

Remember, the simple act of writing down the numbers helps you to formulate a plan. You'll make more of a commitment toward attaining your goals!

While you can't know every major expense that lies ahead, you can certainly plan for the ones that you do know are coming. If you see that you will not be able to pay for the expense entirely *within a few months,* you might want to find ways to **scale back** if possible. For something like a vacation, you can definitely have an enjoyable and memorable time without breaking the bank.

If you see that you're going to run a deficit for an *extended period of time,* you may need to **adjust your lifestyle.** Depending on your situation, you may need to earn some extra money on the side, find a cheaper place to live, or cut other expenses where possible. Whether the expense is optional or unavoidable, it can be dealt with in a more thoughtful and rational manner when you plan ahead.

Thinking Ahead: Plan for the Unexpected

What about the expenses that you don't know about ahead of time, that just crop up and you have to deal with on the spot? Right now, before the next emergency occurs, spend some time just thinking about how you might handle a financial blow.

Do you have savings or other assets that you could tap?
If not, you need to start building up your savings with any monthly budget surpluses you may have. (Chapters 4 and 5 discuss cash accounts and savings strategies.)

Do you have credit that you could use?
If not, do you need to establish credit, or have you already maxed out your credit sources? Handling credit wisely is another basic building block in successful financial planning. (Chapters 6 and 7 discuss managing debt.)

Beyond your two choices of depleting your assets or increasing your debt load, you are left with: prevailing upon family or friends to bail you out, defaulting on the expense and ruining your credit rating, or declaring bankruptcy, which won't do your credit rating much good, either.

Put some thought into how you would handle an unexpected expense by filling out your own "Thinking Ahead" chart, using the example which follows for ideas (a blank form is provided for you at the end of this chapter).

Example: Thinking Ahead—Unexpected Expenses	
What would I do if faced with an unexpected expense of $100?	Pay for it out of current earnings.
What would I do if faced with an unexpected expense of $1,000?	Pay for it out of savings or charge it and pay it off in 3 months.
What would I do if faced with an unexpected expense of $10,000?	Borrow from my retirement plan or my home equity line of credit. Apply for a personal loan at my bank or credit union. Charge it on my charge cards, possibly shopping for a card with more favorable terms.
What would I do if faced with an unexpected expense of $100,000 or more?	See if special arrangements can be made directly with the person or organization to which the money is owed. (High expenses such as this are common for people with no health insurance who must have a major surgery or treatment. Many hospitals provide financing in such cases.) Otherwise, bankruptcy is a real possibility.

Planning ahead serves as an important key to handling budget deficits. So does regularly putting money in savings so that you'll have something to fall back upon when you have unexpected expenses. And unexpected expenses *will* occur—you can count on it!

Budget Surplus

A budget surplus is so much more pleasant to deal with than a budget deficit! Your objective is to consistently have monthly surpluses, or at least more surpluses than deficits so that you can use surpluses from one month to cover deficits from another. This is called *Living Within Your Budget*, a fantastic accomplishment that means you're well on your way to financial independence!

As your surplus amount builds up in your checking account, start to shift some of it over to your savings. If you let it all stack up in checking, you may feel flush and find it easier to splurge on things that are not in your budget. On the other hand, if you separate it out to savings and don't see it in your checking account balance, you may not be as tempted to spend it.

You will also want to keep a copy of your financial goals handy to remind yourself of what you're working toward. Budget surpluses will help turn your goals into reality because these are funds you can capture and apply toward attaining your financial goals. *When you give yourself a budget surplus, you are giving yourself power — power to accomplish your goals!*

Did you notice the words—*give yourself a budget surplus?* Each of us makes a number of choices every day, and you can choose to spend less and have a surplus that in turn will bring you closer to your financial goals. Or you can choose to spend all that you have, charge up your charge cards, and thereby pledge future money that you have not yet earned to fulfill the debt obligations you make today.

Do you really expect to earn substantially more in your next paycheck? Probably not. So when the next pay period rolls around, not only must your paycheck cover your expenses for that time period, but also the debt you have encumbered yourself with from the past. *You can choose to dig your hole deeper by spending MORE than you make, or you can choose to propel yourself toward achieving your financial goals by spending LESS than you make.* The choice is yours.

At this point, you may say that you have absolutely cut your expenses to the bone and can't cut any more. Unfortunately, that is true for some who are indeed in financial straits. But most of the people who are not living within their budget have *chosen* not to live within their budget and either don't want to admit it or just don't care.

Living Within Your Budget

How can you live within your budget? Go back to Chapter 1—write down your financial goals, track every cent you spend, categorize each expense as necessary or discretionary, and keep your goals in front of you to remind you why controlling your expenses is so important to you.

The discretionary spending is the easy money, money which you can apply *now* toward achieving your financial goals. The necessary spending is not as easy, but indeed, through time you may be able to alter or renegotiate some of these items as well—or you may decide that weighed against your financial goals, some of this spending is not so necessary after all!

Here are some actual examples from former students:
- One young couple discovered that all they had to do in order to afford to enroll their son in a certain program (and I am not making this up) was for the husband to give up his snuff habit and the wife her diet sodas.
- Robert realized how much he was spending on coffee each month and started bringing a thermos from home.
- Jennifer was disgusted when she realized how much she was spending on water and sodas from the vending machines, particularly compared to how inexpensively she could purchase these items at the grocery store and put them in her lunch bag.
- Michael was spending so much living in a cool apartment complex that he never had money to go out with his friends. He found someone looking for a roommate in an apartment closer to campus, and not only did he save on his rent expense, but he was able to ride his bike to school as well. This enabled him to go out with friends occasionally as well as to start saving for a car that would actually run.

All of these examples have the same thing in common—by writing down their financial goals and tracking their expenses, these people were able to redirect money that had been spent on things that did not enhance the quality of their lives toward things that were meaningful to them.

Knowledge is power, and when you know how you are spending your money, you give yourself the power to control it!

Thinking Ahead: Plan for Extra Cash

While you're contemplating budget surpluses and finding extra money, here's another exercise designed to help you think ahead. Have you ever thought about what you would do if you suddenly came into some money? Think about it now, keeping in mind your financial goals and how you could use your windfall to fulfill them. Here are some ideas. (A blank form is provided for you at the end of this chapter.)

Example: Thinking Ahead—Extra Cash	
What would I do if I had an extra $100?	Pay extra on my credit card or put it in savings.
What would I do if I had an extra $1,000?	Pay extra on my home mortgage.
What would I do if I had an extra $10,000?	Pay off my car loan or put it toward a down payment on a home.
What would I do if I had an extra $100,000 or more?	Pay down debt and/or invest it.

[Note: When deciding whether to save and invest extra money or pay down debt, you must carefully consider what's right for your given situation, particularly the interest you pay on your debts vs. what you can earn on your savings or investments. Chapter 6 addresses, among other things, the issue of which debts to pay first.]

This exercise may seem more like wishful thinking because you don't think you're likely to ever receive a windfall. It happens more frequently than most people are aware, due to life insurance payouts or other assets received at the death of a loved one. Most payouts are made in one lump sum, and sadly, *most people let this money slip through their fingers fairly rapidly, usually leaving them no better off than before.*

Don't let this happen to you! Right now think about what you would do, should the occasion ever arise. Then you will be prepared to immediately apply the windfall directly toward your attaining your financial goals instead of blowing it!

Saving and Investing

Back in the example budget, notice that Samantha is regularly putting money into her savings and mutual fund investment. We've just talked about budget surpluses, and certainly your surpluses need to be channeled into savings. But a surplus is money you have left over, *after* you've taken care of everything else.

Another important thing you can do to help yourself more rapidly build up a financial cushion (which will be addressed further in Chapters 4 and 5) is to *make a regular spot in your budget for saving and investing* just as you would for paying the utilities. Remember, one of the greatest things you can do to propel yourself toward your financial goals is to pay yourself first!

Entertainment

You'll notice also that Samantha budgeted in money for entertainment, which is an important thing to do. While it's true that many people overindulge and could stand to cut back in this area, *by recognizing entertainment as a legitimate expense and giving it a designated spot in your budget, you will be able to control it better.*

Entertainment is definitely an area that can be scaled down when your budget is tight. If you are in financial distress, you may need to cut it out entirely or search for free alternatives, such as the public library or free concerts in the park. But for those who have a bit more leeway, give yourself some amount of entertainment money.

If you plan on living very frugally until all your bills are paid or some other financial goal is attained, you're likely to become weary of your drab lifestyle, chuck your budget and go blow your money. By budgeting in entertainment and a vacation, you give yourself something to look forward to, and *knowing that you can enjoy yourself and still stay on track financially gives you a real boost.* Try to make a budget you can truly live with.

Budget													
Prepared for: _____					For the year ending: _____								
	Jan	Feb	Mar	Apr	May	Jun	Jul	Aug	Sep	Oct	Nov	Dec	Total
Income													
Total Income													
Expenses													
Total Expenses													
Monthly Cash Surplus (Deficit)													
Cumulative Surplus (Deficit)													

Thinking Ahead—Unexpected Expenses	
What would I do if faced with an unexpected expense of $100?	
What would I do if faced with an unexpected expense of $1,000?	
What would I do if faced with an unexpected expense of $10,000?	
What would I do if faced with an unexpected expense of $100,000 or more?	

Thinking Ahead—Unexpected Cash	
What would I do if I had an extra $100?	
What would I do if I had an extra $1,000?	
What would I do if I had an extra $10,000?	
What would I do if I had an extra $100,000 or more?	

You may reproduce these forms as needed.

30 Minute LIVING

Suggested Action Plan

- *Change your thinking about budgets.* If the thought of making a budget and trying to stick to it fills you with dread, rethink your thinking. Budgets are actually enablers. They put the power in your hands. When you know what you want to accomplish financially, a budget can help you stay on track and on target to reach your goals.

- *Be realistic.* One of the main reasons people find it difficult to stick to a budget is because they didn't create a realistic budget in the first place. Go back over the past year and find expenses that only happen occasionally—the ones that sneak up on you. Also, unless you're currently in financial distress, allow yourself and your family some amount of entertainment expense. Deciding that you'll never eat out again is probably not realistic.

- *Be creative.* Renting a movie and popping popcorn for a movie night at home can be a lot of fun for the whole family. Declare a halt on all things electronic (no television, computer games, etc.) and work a jigsaw puzzle or play a board game. With the money you save, you'll be able to schedule a few special weekends throughout the year.

- *Plan for the worst.* By putting in some thought now as to what you would do should unexpected expenses occur, you'll be in a better position to handle whatever comes your way. Financially, you can work now on building your savings account. Psychologically, you won't be so overwhelmed—such events can be almost paralyzing.

- *Expect the best!* The actions you take build upon one another. When you deliberately start plotting and then actually taking positive steps toward your financial goals, the compound effect will begin to kick in. You're likely to attain your goals even more quickly than you had imagined!

Chapter 4
Understanding Your Cash Accounts

Budget Hero!

Cash accounts are the unsung heroes of your budget. They help you stay the course and keep you on target to reach your financial goals. By serving as a cushion, your cash accounts pad against the financial shocks that are bound to come your way. It's not a matter of *if* such shocks will occur, but rather, *when*.

By having something in reserve, you can take care of the smaller unexpected expenses outright. For larger unexpected expenses, even if you don't have enough money set aside to handle them entirely, you're still better off than you would be without a cash reserve. You're likely to have *more* options when you have *something* in reserve versus *nothing*.

How much should you try to accumulate in cash reserves?

Funding your cash accounts is covered in Chapter 5, but as a general rule of thumb, you need enough to cover at least three months of living expenses. However, if you have more uncertainty in your life, such as with your job or your health, you might want to try to save enough for six to nine months. If your job is in a cyclical industry, such as real estate, you might want to save enough for a year of living expenses.

Of course, how much is right for you will depend on your other assets and the resources available to you. With too little in cash reserves, you can rapidly find yourself in financial distress. On the other hand, if you hold too much in cash accounts, then you're giving up more growth than is necessary. Also, the return received on cash accounts is often less than the rate of inflation, which means that you're losing buying power on what you hold in cash. So, what you're trying to find is the balance that's right for you.

This chapter discusses the types of cash accounts that are available, their various features, and when they may be appropriate to use.

Types of Cash Accounts

The term "cash" means liquid assets, or *assets which can be turned into money for spending in a reasonable time period without a significant loss in value*. Usually **one year** is considered the cut-off time period for an asset being labeled "liquid" or "short-term," but if you're just now building up your cash cushion, start with assets you can get your hands on almost immediately. We'll call this your *"first tier" of liquid assets*, and it includes accounts such as checking and savings.

Later, after you have a decent amount in savings (at least $1,000 or perhaps a month's worth of living expenses, depending on your personal situation), you may want to start putting a portion into assets with a little longer maturity. These usually offer a little higher return. This *"second tier" of liquid securities* includes money market accounts, money market mutual funds, asset management accounts, savings bonds, short-term certificates of deposits, and short-term marketable securities, such as Treasury bills.

FIRST TIER ACCOUNTS

Checking

Your checking account is your most basic cash account. It's your operating account into which you likely deposit your paycheck and from which you pay your bills. Most people are very familiar with checking accounts.

Not all checking accounts are created equally, however. Some have all sorts of fees, and many offer no interest on your money. Consider this: if your checking account charges you fees and offers no interest, you are getting a negative return on the money held in that account. If, instead, you could find a no-fee checking account that pays no interest, the return on your money would then increase to zero. At least you wouldn't be losing money on your account.

What if you could find a no-fee checking account that also pays interest?
While such offerings are not all that popular with banks, they are fairly common with credit unions. Called "share draft" accounts at credit unions or at other mutually owned banking institutions, these accounts function in a similar manner to checking accounts at banks. If you qualify for membership at a credit union, check out the accounts available. However small it might be, a positive return beats a zero or negative return any day. Types of banking institutions will be discussed further in Chapter 5: Funding Your Cash Accounts.

Savings

Savings accounts usually offer higher returns than do checking accounts (which admittedly is not hard to do, considering many checking accounts offer no interest). Usually it's a simple matter to open a savings account to accompany your checking account, but be sure to check on fees, minimum balances and returns offered.

Internet banks may offer higher returns.
In recent years, the returns offered by many banking institutions on savings accounts have been abysmally low. But if you are comfortable with the idea of Internet banking, there are several well-established banks which offer very competitive savings rates through their Internet banking divisions.[3]

Once you open an online savings account, it's usually connected to your existing account with your current bank. Then you go online and upload money into the Internet savings account. Be aware, though, that when you download money back into your checking account

---

[3] Make sure it's FDIC insured and that it's chartered in the U.S. Refer to the Bank Find page below.

the process may take several days, so allow plenty of time. And, because of the Federal Reserve Board's Regulation D [Section 204.2(d)(2)][4] you may be limited to only six transfers per month or statement cycle, so be sure to inquire about limits on your account.

Use savings accounts to manage your money.

Savings accounts are a wonderful tool for financial management. Even if the returns are low, they offer an easy way to segment funds. Having excess funds in checking causes some of us to feel rather flush, which in turn may prompt overspending. It's just easier to leave money alone if it's separated out and earmarked for a certain purpose that's attached to a financial goal—for instance, to build up $3,000 in emergency reserves.

SECOND TIER ACCOUNTS

Six types of accounts or short-term investments will be discussed in this section. While all still fall in the liquid asset category, they are generally not where you would start when building cash reserves. They are usually more appropriate for when you already have some amount built up in your checking and savings.

Accounts That Combine Functions

The first three types perform many of the same functions as would a checking and savings account combined into one. Given an individual's financial resources and needs, these accounts might prove to be appropriate choices.

The first two in this category deal with money market offerings. Although they may sound similar, there are fundamental differences. Banks that also offer brokerage services often have both types available, so you need to understand what it is you're getting.

Money Market Deposit Account

- Offered by banking institutions (bank side of institution, not brokerage side)
- FDIC insured (make sure your bank is FDIC insured—most are)[5]

Money market deposit accounts (MMDAs) offer some amount of return coupled with check writing privileges. Such accounts are intended to correspond to those offered by money market mutual funds, although there can be wide variations in the required minimums, returns offered, and check writing features. If your bank is federally insured, these accounts will be insured as well.

On the negative side, the returns tend to be low and the required minimum balances high. Also, there are usually limits on the check writing, such as a maximum number of checks per period, with each check being for at least a minimum amount, such as $100.

---

[4] Examine the Federal Reserve Board regulations at: www.fdic.gov/regulations/laws/rules/7500-500.html
[5] Banking institutions are discussed in Chapter 5. Find out if your bank is insured at the FDIC's Bank Find page: www2.fdic.gov/idasp/main_bankfind.asp Credit unions are insured by their own federal agency. Research credit unions at this site: researchcu.ncua.gov/Views/FindCreditUnions.aspx Many banks that are chartered in other countries are not FDIC insured—be sure to find out, particularly if it's an Internet bank!

Money Market Mutual Fund

- Offered by mutual fund companies (may be offered through the brokerage side of a banking institution)
- Not FDIC insured[6]

Money market mutual funds (MMMFs) offer similar features to MMDAs. You earn a return on your funds, and you usually have check writing privileges, within certain limits. Mutual funds will be discussed more in the chapter on investments, but a brief overview will be presented here also in order to better highlight the characteristics and risks of MMMFs.

Features of Money Market Mutual Funds

Mutual funds are offered by investment companies, such as Fidelity, Vanguard, T. Rowe Price, American, etc. Each mutual fund is its own separate company within its family, and each is comprised of a collection of securities (financial investments such as stocks, bonds, commercial paper, etc.). That collection can vary widely, depending on the investment objective of the individual mutual fund.

Special regulations (discussed later) dictate what can be held in a fund that is designated as a *money market* mutual fund. The return on any mutual fund fluctuates and depends on the returns of the securities that are held in the fund.

> It is important for the investor to understand that the return on a money market mutual fund (MMMF) is NOT guaranteed and that mutual funds, even *money market* mutual funds, can go DOWN in value as well as up. This is in contrast to a money market deposit account (MMDA), which offers a rate of return and is held at a banking institution. Even though the returns on MMDAs are often variable rates, you should not lose principal.

Capital markets versus money markets

The securities held in mutual funds are traded in the secondary markets (the New York Stock Exchange and the NASDAQ are examples of secondary securities markets). One way the securities markets can be segmented further is into capital markets and *money markets.*

> In general, the capital markets are designed for investment purposes, while the money markets are designed for stability and preservation of principal.

Most mutual funds are designed for the *capital* markets, meaning that the majority of the securities held in their funds (for example, stocks or corporate bonds) are traded in the capital markets. *Money market* mutual funds, on the other hand, are designed for the money markets. The securities held in MMMFs consist of short-term, high-quality debt instruments of corporations and/or the government.

---

[6] The U.S. Dept. of the Treasury opened its Temporary Guarantee Program for Money Market Funds in Sept. 2008, but allowed it to expire on Sept. 18, 2009. www.treasury.gov/press-center/press-releases/Pages/tg293.aspx

Features of money market mutual funds

MMMFs are considered fairly low-risk because of the special regulations which determine what can be traded in the money markets.[7] However, even within this low-risk environment, there are still varying degrees of risk. An MMMF made up of U.S. Treasury securities would have a very low risk and correspondingly low return, while an MMMF containing corporate debt would offer a little higher return but at a little higher risk.

But LOW risk does not mean NO risk. It is possible for money market mutual funds to experience losses.

MMMFs usually offer limited check-writing privileges, similar to those on the MMDAs mentioned previously. A drawback would be the annual fees mutual funds charge, and if you make purchases through a broker, you may have transaction fees as well. Nevertheless, MMMFs usually offer somewhat higher returns than do MMDAs, and often require much lower minimum investments to open an account.

Asset Management Account

Offered by brokerage firms, asset management accounts consolidate your checking, saving and investing functions into a single account. You can think of this type of account as a holding tank. When the account holder is ready to make an investment, it's a simple matter to make the purchase from this account because the money is already at the brokerage firm. Then when it's time to sell an investment, it's likewise a simple matter for the brokerage firm to deposit, or sweep, the proceeds from the sale into their client's asset management account.[8]

These accounts are similar to money market mutual funds in that they often pay a small amount of interest and allow check-writing privileges (usually with some restrictions as noted on money market deposit accounts). The accounts at most brokerage firms are insured by the SIPC (Securities Investor Protection Corporation), but this insurance does not guarantee a certain value for your securities, only to replace the securities in the event a brokerage fails.[9] (For example, if you had 100 shares of XYZ security, you get 100 shares of XYZ back. Their value will depend on the current price per share.)

Accounts That Are for Growth

You can think of the next three items as short-term investments. While all of them can be held for longer periods of time than one year, those which are a year or less away from maturity would still fall into the liquid or cash category. They are a good place to stash what you hope you won't need but want to have available just in case. These usually offer a little higher rate of return than other accounts but do not have check-writing privileges.

---

[7] Visit the Securities and Exchange Commission Web site for general information on money market mutual funds. sec.gov/answers/mfmmkt.htm

[8] Find the rates of return currently being offered on money market mutual funds at iMoneyNet's Web site. www.imoneynet.com

[9] Learn more about SIPC insurance for brokerage firms at: www.sipc.org

Certificates of Deposit

- *Certificates of deposit*, or CDs, that mature in a year or less would fall into the liquid category. A certificate of deposit represents an amount of money that you place on deposit with your banking institution and pledge to leave alone for a given time period. In return, the bank usually offers you a little higher rate of return than on a savings account.[10]

  At the end of the given time period, you can either take your money out or renew your CD. If you take your money out before the maturity date, you will likely forfeit some of the interest, and if you take your money out too soon after putting it into the CD, you could even lose some of your principal.

- *Jumbo CDs* usually offer an even higher rate of return but usually require a deposit of $95,000-100,000. This brings up the question of FDIC coverage on such large amounts. In the past, this insurance only went to $100,000 for each ownership category (such as single ownership, joint ownership, or an IRA) at any one banking institution. However, Congress has increased FDIC coverage to $250,000 (per depositor, per insured depository institution for each account ownership category), and made this limit permanent as of July 21, 2010.[11]

  So if you happen to have enough for a jumbo CD, you need to determine if FDIC will cover it completely (given any other assets you may have at that bank). You also need to consider if you want to tie up thaacet much money all at one time in one instrument at one institution.

- *Brokered CDs* are sold through brokerage firms rather than banking institutions. If you must cash out of your CD early, the broker will sell it on the market, much as he or she would sell shares of stock. While the broker doesn't penalize you for early withdrawal, you may indeed suffer a loss, depending on how much the buyer of your CD is willing to pay. Brokered CDs present greater complexities than do regular CDs, and the FDIC's Web site provides a great deal of information on what to look for in choosing a brokered CD.[12]

CDs in general are not as liquid as some of the other cash-type items mentioned in this chapter. You would not want to start your emergency reserve account with a CD. But if you already have some amount of money tucked away in savings and wish to have an even greater cash cushion, certificates of deposit may be a good choice if you really don't believe that you will need the money during the given time period.

Because of the penalty for early withdrawals, CDs provide a built-in incentive to leave the money alone, something many of us need! Depending on the terms of any given CD, even if you do have to pull your money out early and forfeit some of the interest, you may still be better off than if you had settled for a checking or savings account with a lower return.

---

[10] Pull up www.bankrate.com to research the current CD rates offered locally and around the country.

[11] The Federal Deposit Insurance Corporation (FDIC) Web site explains how bank accounts are insured. Find out if your bank has FDIC coverage and the limits that are currently in effect. www.fdic.gov/deposit/deposits Pull up this page to find a listing of the recent changes that have been made in FDIC Deposit Insurance coverage: www.fdic.gov/deposit/deposits/changes.html Read the press release concerning the new FDIC coverage limits: www.fdic.gov/news/news/press/2010/pr10161.html

[12] More information can be found on CDs at: www.fdic.gov/deposit/deposits/certificate/index.html
This article explains more about brokered CDs. www.fdic.gov/consumers/consumer/news/cnfall00/BankCD.html

Treasury Bills

Treasury bills, notes and bonds are all direct debt obligations of the U.S. government.[13] Treasury *bills* mature in one year or less, *notes* in greater than one year up to ten years, and *bonds* in greater than ten years. They are all *marketable* securities, meaning that once the government issues them, the buyers can sell them before maturity to someone else if they so desire. For all Treasury securities (bills, notes, bonds and TIPS[14]), the minimum purchase amount is $100, and incremental purchases must also be in multiples of $100.[15]

Treasury bills are sold at a discount.

Treasury bills (or T-bills) are different from T-notes and T-bonds in that they are sold at a discount and do not pay interest while you hold them. (Treasury notes and bonds are similar to corporate bonds in that they pay interest semi-annually. Bonds will be covered in the investments chapter.)

When a security is sold at a discount, you purchase it for less than its face value, and then at maturity you receive the face value. The difference between the purchase price and face value is the interest you receive, which seems to be an efficient way of paying interest on securities that investors hold for such a short period of time.

For example, say that you purchased a $10,000 T-bill directly from the Treasury for $9,900. If you held it until maturity, you would receive $10,000, with the $100 difference being your interest earned for that time period. The amount of the purchase discount is determined by the length of time until maturity and the going rate on T-bills at the time of issue—the longer the time until maturity and the higher the rate, the greater your discount and the less you will pay for the purchase price, and vice versa.

Even though the rates of return offered on Treasury securities are usually low compared to that of other types of investments, Treasuries are considered to be safe from default because they are backed by the U.S. government. While the interest earned on Treasury securities is subject to federal income taxes, it is exempt from state and local income taxes. For investors who live in states and/or cities with income taxes, this is an important consideration.

Treasury bills are highly marketable.

The marketability feature of T-bills makes them highly liquid securities. Not only can they be bought and sold on the secondary markets, but you're extremely likely to find many people or institutions ready to trade with you at the moment you're ready to buy or sell.

Original issues of T-bills can be purchased directly from the Treasury and are currently offered in maturities of 4, 13, 26 and 52 weeks. They can also be bought on the secondary markets through brokers and dealers. This allows you to choose from a wide range of maturity dates, including Treasuries that may have originally been issued with longer maturities but are now within the short-term range.

---

[13] Visit the Web site of the United States Government Accountability Office to find this booklet dealing with various aspects of the federal debt. www.gao.gov/new.items/d04485sp.pdf

[14] TIPS are Treasury Inflation-Protected Securities. They are issued in 5, 10 and 30 year terms.

[15] The previous minimum purchase and transfer amount of $1,000 was changed to $100 on April 7, 2008. www.treasurydirect.gov/indiv/research/faq/faq_100mktmin.htm

Many investors simply buy and hold their T-bills to maturity, often in a Treasury Direct account.[16] Those who wish to sell their securities before maturity must go through a brokerage firm, bank or dealer. If held in a TreasuryDirect account, they would have to first be transferred to a bank, broker or dealer before they could be sold.[17]

While you generally don't go buy groceries with T-bills, they are nevertheless one of the most marketable of securities, aside from the greenback dollar. U.S. Treasury securities are traded in the securities markets virtually around the world. Their liquidity and high level of safety make them popular with individual and institutional investors alike.

Savings Bonds

The U.S. Treasury also issues Series I (i for inflation) and EE Savings Bonds. Both must now be held for a minimum of one year before they can be redeemed, so they barely fall within the definition of short-term securities. But because they are such widely held securities, it's a good bet that many people have some amount of savings bonds already in their possession which would qualify to be redeemed on short notice if needed.

Savings bonds are owned exclusively by one person.
Like Treasury bills, notes, and bonds, Savings Bonds are also direct debt obligations of the U.S. government and are considered safe from default. However, they are *not* marketable securities, meaning that you can't sell your bonds to someone else. You can only redeem them at a banking institution that is authorized as a paying agent by the Treasury Department. They are also *registered* securities, which means they are owned exclusively by the person in whose name they are issued.

Features of Savings Bonds
Savings bonds come with many and varied rules and regulations, depending on when they were issued. Some of the high points are listed below. For more extensive information, please refer the Treasury's Web site.

Rates of return
Both the I and EE Savings Bonds offer savings rates that are comparable to the other securities discussed in this section. The I Bond is indexed to inflation, which means the rate of return that you earn will fluctuate, depending on the cost of living. This tracking feature is designed to prevent inflation from eroding your earnings. The Series EE Savings Bonds have been earning a market-based rate keyed to five-year Treasury securities, but beginning in May 2005, newly issued EEs will earn a fixed rate of return.[19]

Taxation
Like the Treasury securities mentioned previously, the earnings on Savings Bonds are exempt from state and local income taxes. While you do have to pay federal income taxes on

---

[16] Learn more about Treasury bills and how to buy them from Treasury Direct.
http://treasurydirect.gov/indiv/research/indepth/tbills/res_tbill.htm
[17] Learn more about selling Treasuries. www.treasurydirect.gov/indiv/research/indepth/tips/res_tips_sell.htm
[18] Learn more about U.S. Treasury products at: www.treasurydirect.gov/indiv/research/indepth/indepth.htm
[19] Research rates of return for savings bonds here:
www.treasurydirect.gov/indiv/research/indepth/ebonds/res_e_bonds_eeratesandterms.htm

the earnings, you can defer taxation until the bonds reach final maturity or until you redeem them.[20] If you use the bonds to pay for qualified higher education expenses, your earnings may be exempt from federal income taxes, but definitely some restrictions apply (see the points listed at the end of this chapter).

Affordability

Savings bonds are very affordable. You purchase a paper EE bond at half its face value, and its denominations go as low as $50. This means you pay $25 to purchase a $50 face value bond, and then it will accrue interest such that within at least 20 years it will reach its face value of $50. If you redeem your bond before it reaches its face value, you will receive your $25 plus the interest that it has earned up to that time.

Paper bonds

The Treasury has begun phasing out paper savings bonds and eventually will issue only electronic savings bonds to be held on account. As of September 30, 2010, federal employees were no longer able to purchase paper savings bonds through a payroll deduction plan. For all other (non-federal) employees, that date was January 1, 2011. As of January 1, 2012, paper savings bonds are now no longer sold at financial institutions.

Electronic bonds

Electronic EE savings bonds do not come in denominations, but can be purchased for specific amounts as low as $25, in one-penny increments. For example, you could purchase an electronic savings bond for $27.23 if you so desired. As with paper EE savings bonds, your investment is guaranteed to double in least 20 years.

Inflation-indexed savings bonds

Concerning the inflation-indexed I bonds, they are purchased at face value (that is, you pay $50 for a $50 face value bond) and accrue interest through time. I bonds do not guarantee a certain level of earnings. When you redeem them, you receive back the face value plus any interest earned. Denominations for paper I bonds go as low as $50, but the paper bonds have been phased out and are no longer sold at financial institutions as of January 1, 2012. The electronic form of I bonds can be purchased in amounts of $25 or more, to the penny.[22]

Redeeming your bonds

You must hold your savings bonds for at least 12 months before redeeming them (until February 2003 you only had to hold them for six months). However, if you redeem a savings bond earlier than five years from its issue date, you pay an early redemption penalty equal to the last three months of earned interest. But bear in mind this is interest that you forego and not principal that you give up, so you may still be better off with savings bonds even if you do have to redeem them early, depending on your situation. For lots more information, refer to U.S. Treasury's TreasuryDirect Web site: www.treasurydirect.gov.

---

[20] You can also choose to pay taxes on the interest year by year, but once you start this method, you must continue to use it for all savings bonds and notes you own or may acquire. Refer to this page:
www.treasurydirect.gov/indiv/research/indepth/ebonds/res_e_bonds_eetaxconsider.htm Scroll down to "Methods of Reporting Interest."

[21] Visit the Treasury for more information on purchasing EE savings bonds:
www.treasurydirect.gov/indiv/research/indepth/ebonds/res_e_bonds_eebuy.htm

[22] Learn more about I bonds here: www.treasurydirect.gov/indiv/research/indepth/ibonds/res_ibonds.htm

Why Build Cash Reserves?

Back in the late 90s when the stock market was soaring and the returns on cash-type assets were only so-so, students would invariably ask—why put any money in cash when other investments are yielding so much higher returns? After the early 2000s and the fall of the stock markets, no one seems to ask that question anymore! Regardless of the current economic climate, most people will always have a need for some amount tucked away in cash reserves. Here's why:

1. *To meet financial emergencies.* This is the overriding reason for cash-type accounts. Periodically you will need to come up with cash on short notice. If you don't have adequate cash reserves, you will likely have to go into debt or liquidate other assets in order to meet the need. Even if you have accumulated a fair amount of other assets and investments, you wouldn't want to be forced to cash out early, possibly at a loss, because of a financial emergency.

2. *To use as a temporary storage place for financial needs that you are expecting in the next six months to one year.* Let's say your child will enter college in the next few months. You may want to go ahead and cash out of other investments in order to have the money ready to meet this need. Cash accounts serve as the holding place for funds that you know you are going to need in the short term.

3. *To serve as a place to accumulate funds for other investments that require a certain larger sum to purchase or to store funds while you are deciding on which investment you would like to make.* Perhaps you would like to invest in a certain mutual fund, but the minimum initial investment required is $5,000. Cash accounts serve as an excellent temporary storage place where you can accumulate these funds by setting aside a certain amount each month until you have the required minimum.

4. *To serve as investment vehicles for those people who are very risk-averse or for those who wish to lower their overall level of investment risk.* There are many people, who for whatever reason, either cannot or will not tolerate the risk of losing any of their principal. While cash-type accounts rarely earn more than what inflation and taxes take away, they are usually considered fairly safe from default or loss of principal. For people who have lived through severe economic times, such as the Great Depression of the 1930s, this level of safety may be their overriding concern.

Also, as people approach and then enter retirement, they may wish to lower their total portfolio risk by progressively investing more in cash accounts and less in other investments with a higher level of risk. Finally, people who have more than enough money to satisfy both their current and future needs may feel no need to risk losing any of their principal in order to grow their assets. Quite simply, they already have enough and are content to just coast along.

Building sufficient cash reserves is one of the most important steps in the financial planning process. Without a cash cushion, those emergencies that are bound to arise can throw your personal finances into a tailspin. Tips and strategies for funding your cash reserves will be discussed in Chapter 5.

30 Minute LIVING

Suggested Action Plan

- *Inventory your cash.* If you haven't done so already (preparing your personal balance sheet is covered in Chapter 2), now is a great time to make a list of all your cash-type accounts and assets along with their current values, where they are located, the titling of each account and the beneficiaries. You may want to create a spreadsheet on your computer to keep track.

- *Research your savings bonds.* Many people have paper savings bond squirreled away somewhere. Locate them and put them all together in a safe place. [Note: If they're in your parents' safe-deposit box because they purchased them when you were a child, you may want to ask for them. Unless your name is on their safe-deposit box account, upon their death you might not have access to the box until the estate is settled. Have them ask their bank how this would be handled.]

- *Record the date of issue of each bond, its denomination and series.* Then use the Treasury's Savings Bond Calculator to find its value as of a certain date: www.treasurydirect.gov/BC/SBCPrice [Note that even though the calculator has a box for the bond's serial number, you do not have to plug it in to calculate its value.] Find detailed instructions for using the calculator on this page: www.treasurydirect.gov/indiv/tools/tools_savingsbondcalc_instructions.htm

- *Find out if the interest is tax-exempt on any savings bonds that you wish to redeem to pay for higher education costs.* Again, you must know the date of issue of the bonds, the name in which the bonds were issued, and if that person was 24 years old or more at the time of purchase. Then the expense must be a qualified expense made at an eligible institution, and there is a limit as to how much income you can make. And yes, there are additional requirements that may apply to your specific situation! Find more information on this topic at the Treasury's Education Planning Center: www.treasurydirect.gov/indiv/planning/plan_education.htm

- *Consider converting your paper savings bonds to electronic bonds.* Particularly if you tend to move frequently or just want to simplify your finances, you may want to convert. Learn more about converting your paper bonds at: www.treasurydirect.gov/indiv/research/indepth/smartexchangeinfo.htm

Chapter 5
Funding Your Cash Accounts

What Amount of Cash Reserves is Sufficient?

None but the clairvoyant knows what the future holds, so the rest of us have to go by rules of thumb. In general, you would like to have three to six months of living expenses where you could get to the money fairly easily. However, you may need more, depending on your own situation and comfort level. For example:

- *The more uncertainty in your life,* such as in your family life or job stability, the greater the amount you should try to keep in cash reserves.

- *If you live off commission sales,* particularly in a cyclical industry such as real estate, you may wish to have a year's worth of living expenses set aside.

- *If you plan on changing jobs,* moving to another city or state, or opening your own business or professional practice, it would probably be wise to have at least six months to a year's worth of living expenses socked away.

On the other hand, if you have a substantial amount of other investments that you could liquidate if needed within the next three to six months, then that would lower your need for having so much in cash reserves.

Try to find an appropriate balance between cash and your other investments. While you need adequate cash reserves, the return you can earn on cash is often less than the rate of inflation. This means you usually lose purchasing power on cash, and you forego what you could be earning on other investments. This chapter builds on the information presented in Chapter 4: Understanding Your Cash Accounts and addresses the actual funding of your cash accounts.

Strategies for Building Cash Reserves

Avoid Fees
Whether you have already accumulated cash reserves in a bank account or are just beginning to manage your money, it's good to examine the banking options that are available to you. If you're just starting to build your reserves, a *no-fee* checking account with *no minimum balance requirement* will help you keep more of your money.

If you already have some amount built up, try to find an account that offers *interest*. However, you must be able to keep your balance above the required minimum, as fees can more than wipe out any earnings. Usually, having a checking account will enable you to then open an accompanying savings account at your banking institution. But be sure to check whether there is a *low balance fee* on the savings account or not.

> Remember, for people who don't yet have much money, fees are a bigger consideration than if the account pays interest or not. If you can only earn a few cents a month in interest, one low balance fee of $5 (or more) could wipe out a year's worth of interest! **Paying a fee is like throwing your money in the garbage can.**

You can always ask that a fee be refunded, which may work occasionally. It never hurts to try, but don't count on it. The bank's objective is to make money.

Divide and Conquer!

The next step is to not overspend the budget that you developed in Chapter 3 so that you have the surplus you planned! Start stuffing what you've allocated in your budget for savings and investments, along with anything extra, into your savings account as soon as the money is available. *If you don't see it in checking, you're not as likely to spend it!*

Even if you feel like you're going to need some of that money for a non-budgeted but necessary expense this month, go ahead and put it in savings until you really need it (assuming there are no penalties or limitations involved for transferring your money back and forth). Why? Well, you may not need the money after all, or you may be able to adjust your other budgeted expenses in order to cover the extra expense. If so, you'll be ahead!

Consider Other Types of Accounts

As discussed in Chapter 4, your checking and savings accounts typically form the first layer or tier in your wealth building. When you've accumulated a comfortable amount in those accounts and are past the danger of low balance fees, start searching for a cash-type account that offers a better return. You may want to consider these options:

- **Internet bank accounts**—accounts with Internet banks[23] typically link to existing checking accounts. These virtual banks sometimes offer a higher return on their checking and savings accounts than traditional banks do on their short-term certificates of deposit where your money is tied up for a period of time. They can be a great option, but be aware that if you need the money for an emergency, it may take several days to transfer the funds back into your checking account.

- **Short-term CDs**—these could be more appropriate for those who don't want to open an Internet bank account, or for those who need a little incentive to leave their money alone. Check out the rates available on three-, six- and nine-month CDs as well as the minimum deposits required.

- **Money market deposit accounts at banking institutions (MMDAs)**—these accounts usually offer a little higher return, but you may need a substantial amount of money (perhaps $10,000 or more) to open one, depending on your institution.

Let's say you're past your salad days. You are earning a decent amount of money and have a fair amount of cash reserves already built up. If you're ready to invest in the capital

---

[23] Find out where your bank is chartered. If it's chartered outside the U.S., it may not be FDIC insured. Use the FDIC's Bank Find site to find out if your bank is FDIC insured. www2.fdic.gov/idasp/main_bankfind.asp

markets (such as in stocks, bonds and mutual funds, which are discussed in the investments chapters), you may want to consider these options:

- **Asset management account with a brokerage firm** — some type of interest-bearing money account is available at most brokerages. This account serves as a central account from which you can purchase investments or deposit the proceeds from the sale of investments.

- **Money market mutual fund (MMMF)** — if you wish to start investing with a particular mutual fund family, you could start with its money market mutual fund. Then as you build up this account, you are usually able to transfer money over to another mutual fund within the same fund family.

As an aside, a transfer of money from one fund to another is considered a sale. The gain portion of the sale, not the return of principle portion, is a taxable event unless these funds are held in a tax-sheltered account, such as an IRA or a retirement account.

Other options for people who already have a decent amount in savings would include U.S. Treasury securities:

- **Treasury bills** — T-bills can be bought and sold in a fairly short period of time. You can hold them in a TreasuryDirect account or in a brokerage account.

- **U.S. Savings Bonds** — you must hold Savings Bonds, both EE and I Bonds, for at least a year. But because you can purchase them in amounts as low as $25, you don't have to tie up much of your money. Then after a year, with each passing month you potentially have access to more and more of your money. If you choose to purchase several small bonds each month rather than one large bond, you can cash out the amount needed and leave the rest invested.

Laddering

Laddering deals with the timing and selection of maturity dates for investments which have maturity dates, like CDs and bonds. Normally, the longer the term you select on these investments, the higher the interest rate you receive. This presents a twofold problem: you may not want to tie up your money for long periods of time, and the rates may go up after you have locked in your money.

By building a ladder, you are able to take advantage of the higher rates and potentially increase your overall return. Let's say you have $4,000. Instead of putting the entire amount in one CD, you could put $1,000 each into a three-month, six-month, nine-month and one-year CD. When the shortest-term CD comes due three months down the road, you reinvest it in a one-year CD. Soon you will have everything reinvested at the one-year rate, but you will have something coming due every three months just in case you need access to your money.[24]

---

[24] Bankrate presents an excellent Savings Guide, "Saving in a Low-Yield World." The topics include laddering, inflation, and how the rich save today. www.bankrate.com/finance/savings/saving-in-a-low-yield-world.aspx

You can customize your ladder according to your needs. If it's money that you want to keep fairly liquid but you're not likely to need, you could go out several years for the top rung on your ladder and increase your intervals to perhaps the six-month, one-year, eighteen-month, and two-year rates. Then after two years, every time you renew, it will be at the higher two-year rate, but you have something coming due each six months in case you need the money.

You can also add rungs to your ladder by saving more and investing it above your current highest rate or at other intervals. Retirees might want to have a rung for every month and use the interest for income. You could also ladder Treasury securities or bonds of any kind.

Consider the direction future interest rates are headed!

Laddering is a particularly useful technique during inflationary times when interest rates typically rise. Each rung that comes due is reinvested at the highest long-term rate on your ladder. However, if interest rates are expected to go down in the future, you might want to invest more now in the longer-term rates.

Keep an eye on the yield curve.[25] If longer-term rates are higher than shorter-term rates, stick with your laddering. On the other hand, if shorter-term rates are higher than longer-term rates, that's when you want to reconsider how you structure your ladder and possibly lock in the higher rates offered now for longer periods of time.

Which Type of Banking Institution Is Best?

Banking-type institutions include commercial banks, savings and loans, savings banks and credit unions. Most will be federally insured, but don't take it for granted—find out for sure.[26] Note that banks chartered in other countries may *not* be FDIC insured, so particularly check out an Internet bank *before* opening an account.

Current banking laws allow all banking institutions to perform pretty much the same functions—take money on deposit and make loans. One real difference among these institutions, however, lies in their *ownership structure*—whether they are stockholder held or mutually owned.[27]

---

[25] Find the current U.S. Treasury yield curve at Yahoo's Bond Center. finance.yahoo.com/bonds Investopedia explains more about the yield curve and what its shape means. www.investopedia.com/terms/y/yieldcurve. asp StockCharts presents a Dynamic Yield Curve through time in relation to the S&P 500 Index. Note how from 2005–2007 as the stock market was rising, the yield curve was flattening and then inverting. Many times an inverted yield curve indicates an upcoming recession. Note that this applet requires Java. Click Animate to start and Pause to see a specific date. stockcharts.com/charts/YieldCurve.html

[26] For more information on the FDIC, visit their Web site. www.fdic.gov To find out if your bank is FDIC insured, pull up this site: www2.fdic.gov/idasp/main_bankfind.asp To see the account coverage limits, pull up: www.fdic.gov/deposit/deposits/dis To research a credit union, go here: researchcu.ncua.gov/Views/FindCreditUnions.aspx

[27] This Securities and Exchange Commission article discusses the concept of mutual ownership in the first paragraph: www.sec.gov/investor/pubs/mutualconversion.htm For information on various types of fraud, go to the SEC home page and search on "fraud."

Differences in Ownership

- **Stockholder owned**—institutions that are stockholder held are owned by those who hold shares of the company's stock and are governed by a board of directors. The objective of stockholder-held institutions is to make a profit for the owners. Most banking institutions are stockholder held.

- **Mutually owned**—mutual institutions, on the other hand, are owned and sometimes governed by their members. The members are the depositors in the institution. To become a member, you usually have to purchase a share of ownership for perhaps $25-$100. Because mutual institutions are member owned, the account fees may be somewhat lower and the returns somewhat higher than those offered by stockholder-held institutions. Credit unions and a few banks are mutually owned.

Credit Unions

Of the various banking institutions, credit unions are different in several ways. Whereas banks may or may not be mutually owned, *all* credit unions are mutually or cooperatively owned. Also, credit unions are organized as not-for-profit institutions, and as such, do not pay federal income taxes. This gives them an inherent cost advantage over for-profit institutions which must earn more in order to pay taxes and still be left with a profit. Because of this advantage, the law limits who may join credit unions.

A credit union's charter must define its "field of membership," such as an employer, church, school, or community. To join a credit union, you must fit into the definition of its membership. Anyone working for an employer that sponsors a credit union, for example, is eligible to join that credit union.[28]

Additionally, accounts at credit unions *are* federally insured for up to $250,000,[29] but *not* by the FDIC. Rather, it's another agency of the federal government, the National Credit Union Administration, which administers the National Credit Union Share Insurance Fund (NCUSIF) for the purpose of insuring deposits at credit unions.

Importance of Building Cash Reserves

There are two very big reasons for spending so much time discussing cash accounts:

1. *Because cash-type accounts and securities are as far into investing as many people ever get.* Many people do not have the confidence, the understanding, or the trust to take any of their money from an environment pretty much safe from default and put it in market-based securities. They need to understand all the cash-type options available and maximize every little bit!

---

[28] The Credit Union National Association is the national trade association which serves most credit unions across the country. Learn more about credit unions or click on "Consumer Information" for consumer news, personal finance tips, and investor education. www.cuna.org

[29] Visit the NCUA Web site to learn more about this federal agency and its role in chartering, supervising and insuring credit unions. www.ncua.gov Find information on NCUA share insurance covering deposits up to $250,000 at: www.ncua.gov/DataApps/Pages/SI-NCUA.aspx

2. *Because small things add up through time.* Even though the returns on cash-type accounts are not high, most people will have a checking and savings account until they die or are no longer able to handle their own money. So paying unnecessary fees or forgoing interest you could have earned, however small the amount, can be quite significant when compounded over an entire lifetime!

To illustrate the importance of small amounts, the graph which follows shows how money, when compounded, grows over time. Etch this image into your mind's eye, because *Einstein is said to have called compound interest the greatest mathematical discovery of all time and the most powerful force in the universe!*[30]

Graph 5-A

Growth of $1,000 Over 40 Years

Growth after 40 years at the given rate:

8% - $21,725

6% - $10,286

4% - $4,801

2% - $2,208

Years

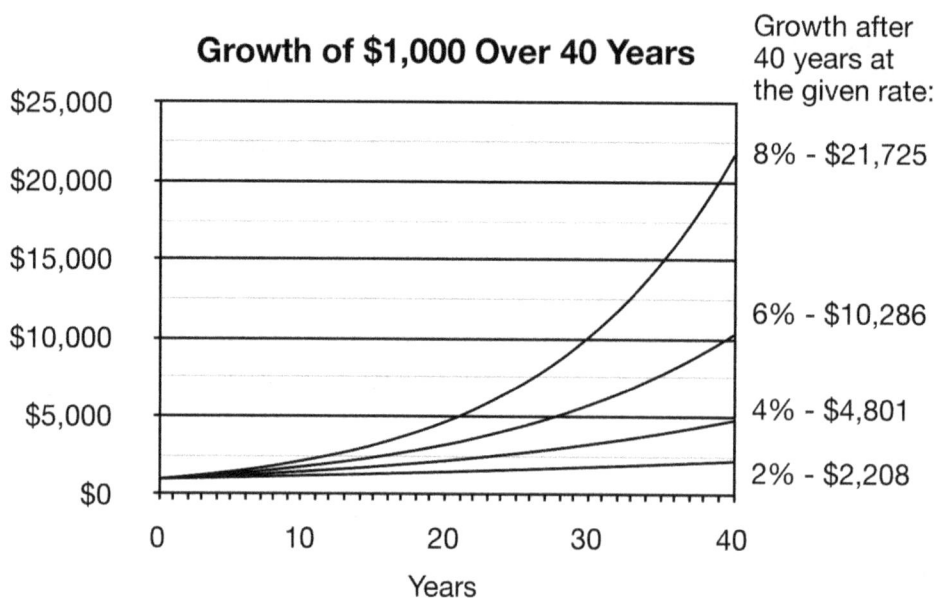

The graph above shows that if you make a one-time investment of $1,000 and let it grow at a compounded rate of 2% per year, after 40 years you will have more than doubled your money to $2,208. However, if you had instead gotten a 4% annually compounded return, you would have ended up with $4,801, which is more than double what you would have gotten at 2%. Look on up at the 6% line and then the 8% — do you see that with each 2% increment, your investment results more than double over a 40-year period?

A measly 2% difference becomes very powerful when applied over a long period of time. Two percent equates to two pennies on the dollar. How many times have you stepped over pennies lying on the sidewalk? Each time you see a penny on the ground, let it remind you of the power of compounding!

---

[30] This article from The Motley Fool quotes Einstein and discusses the advantages of reinvesting dividends. www.fool.com/news/commentary/2005/commentary05031110.htm Here's a whole page of Einstein quotes: en.wikiquote.org/wiki/Albert_Einstein

The next graph takes the same illustration and expands it further to include the annual compounded rates of return of 10%, 12% and 14% (the 2% and 4% return lines had to be omitted). Look what happens, this time over a 50-year time period!

Graph 5-B

Growth of $1,000 Over 50 Years

Growth after 50 years at the given rate:

14% - $700,233

12% - $289,002

10% - $117,391
8% - $46,902
6% - $18,420

Years

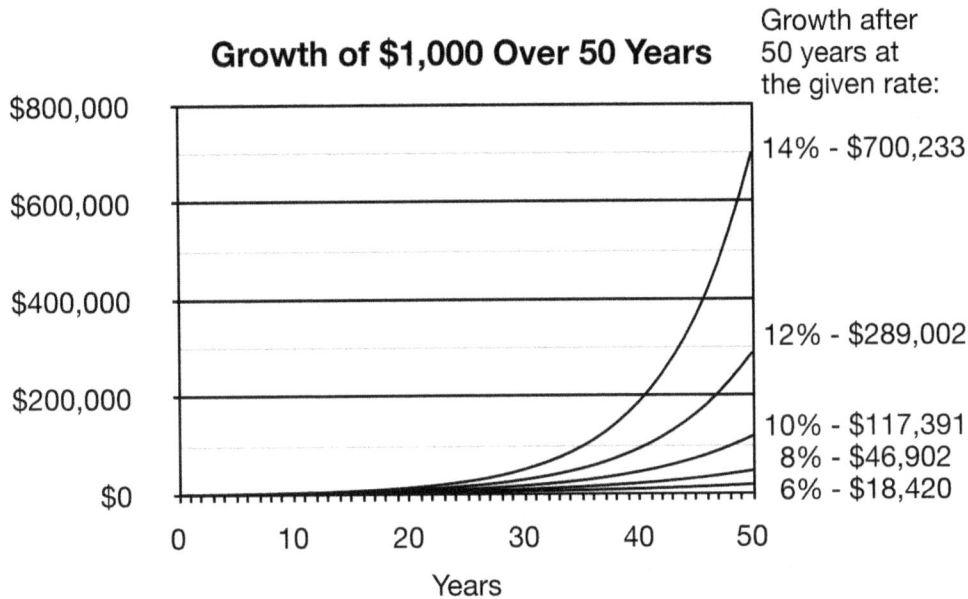

While it's highly doubtful that you will be able to average the higher rates of return on cash-type accounts over a 50-year period, it is important to note how the growth lines start to shoot straight up. That's because when money is compounded, the path of its growth is not linear but exponential.

At the lower interest rates and over shorter time periods, this growth phenomenon is not so obvious. But you can see from the graph that the higher the rate of interest, the faster the growth curve starts to turn upward, and the longer the time period, the higher those curves can go! That's what Einstein was referring to when he said compound interest is the most powerful force in the universe — the fantastic growth that occurs when money (or anything) compounds over time![31]

Now, you may be thinking it's just lovely to see the magnitude of growth that can occur over time, but we're talking cash accounts here. Compounding is not going to help that much when the annual rate of return on such accounts is typically low compared to the returns available on other assets during any given time period.

---

[31] Both of these sites help explain more about how compounding works.
www.free-financial-advice.net/compounding-effect.html
www.investopedia.com/university/beginner/beginner2.asp

Think of your cash accounts, not in isolation, but as an integral part of your total holdings, everything you own now or expect to own in the future. If you can squeeze an extra one or two percent return out of each of your holdings, or even average this extra return across all your holdings, do you see how much difference it will make in the long run? *Remember, if you can obtain an extra 2% return over a 40-year period, your investment results will more than double!* Some of you could do that just by avoiding fees alone.

Selecting no- or low-fee cash accounts that offer a little higher return is a pretty painless way to increase your overall average rate of return on your holdings. You can do this on your current budget, without having to sacrifice anything or save more. And very little, if any, risk is involved. It's not some exotic investment. It's free money that you're walking away from—just like stepping over those pennies on the sidewalk—if you don't maximize the returns on your cash accounts.

> If you don't take advantage of this found money, you will have to earn more in order to reach your financial goals, i.e., *you'll have to earn more to get to the same place!* And lest you forget—when you earn money, it gets *taxed*.

As an aside, here's a quick tax lesson: If you need one more dollar in order to reach your financial goal, how much would you have to earn to be left with that dollar on an after-tax basis? If your marginal income tax rate is 25% and you work for someone else, you'd have to earn $1.485 to be left with $1.00 after paying taxes. If you work for yourself, you'd have to earn $1.675—well over 50% extra to be left with $1.00.[32] However, if you also have to pay state and/or city income taxes, you'd have to earn even more![33, 34, 35]

To belabor the point yet again—*small amounts here and there can make a staggering difference over time.* And it's not just the fees on your checking account and the interest you could have earned on your savings. Couple these foregone amounts with the money that seeps out of your budget for clothes you bought on sale that you'll never wear, late fees on your charge card or utility bill, or overpriced lattes with more calories than a cheeseburger.

---

[32] In addition to federal income taxes which will vary according to your taxable income, your earned income is also subject to Social Security taxes of 6.2% (on income up to $110,100 in 2012) and Medicare taxes of 1.45% (no limit on income) for a total of 7.65%. If you have an employer, the employer pays 7.65% and you pay 7.65%. If you are self-employed, you get to pay both parts, for a total of 15.3%.

So here's the math if you work for someone else, assuming your average federal income tax rate is 25%:
You need to earn some larger amount, X, such that you can subtract 25% of X for federal income taxes and 7.65% of X for Social Security and Medicare taxes and be left with $1.00—
$X - 0.25X - 0.0765X = 1.00$ [and you thought you'd never need algebra!]
$X - 0.3265X = 1$; $0.6735X = 1$; $X = 1.4848$

If you are self-employed, the equation would be:
$X - 0.25X - 0.153X = 1.00$
$X - .403X = 1$; $0.597X = 1$; $X = 1.675$

[33] Find income tax information at Yahoo's Tax Center. finance.yahoo.com/taxes
[34] Find state income tax rates at the Federation of Tax Administrators Web site. www.taxadmin.org
[35] Find Social Security and Medicare tax rates and current earnings limits at Social Security's Web site. www.ssa.gov

This is money gone *forever*, money that will never have the opportunity to grow for you, and money that in order to replace, you'll have to earn about 50% more in order to get back to where you were! And you'll still be behind where you could have been if you'd invested your money instead!

Table 5-A on the following page shows how money grows over time at various interest rates. Study the numbers to see how much difference a little extra time and a little extra return can make. [The calculations reflect annual, end of year compounding using the formula for determining future value, with the present value being $1000, i being the interest rate, and n being the number of years: $FV = PV(1 + i)^n$]

When you learn to manage your cash accounts and maximize their returns, you are well on your way to managing your personal finances as a whole. And what better way to give your cash accounts a boost than to control your debt, which will be discussed next in Chapters 6 and 7!

Table 5-A: Growth of $1,000 Over Time at Various Interest Rates:

Years	2%	4%	6%	8%	10%	12%	14%
0	$1,000	$1,000	$1,000	$1,000	$1,000	$1,000	$1,000
1	$1,020	$1,040	$1,060	$1,080	$1,100	$1,120	$1,140
2	$1,040	$1,082	$1,124	$1,166	$1,210	$1,254	$1,300
3	$1,061	$1,125	$1,191	$1,260	$1,331	$1,405	$1,482
4	$1,082	$1,170	$1,262	$1,360	$1,464	$1,574	$1,689
5	$1,104	$1,217	$1,338	$1,469	$1,611	$1,762	$1,925
6	$1,126	$1,265	$1,419	$1,587	$1,772	$1,974	$2,195
7	$1,149	$1,316	$1,504	$1,714	$1,949	$2,211	$2,502
8	$1,172	$1,369	$1,594	$1,851	$2,144	$2,476	$2,853
9	$1,195	$1,423	$1,689	$1,999	$2,358	$2,773	$3,252
10	$1,219	$1,480	$1,791	$2,159	$2,594	$3,106	$3,707
11	$1,243	$1,539	$1,898	$2,332	$2,853	$3,479	$4,226
12	$1,268	$1,601	$2,012	$2,518	$3,138	$3,896	$4,818
13	$1,294	$1,665	$2,133	$2,720	$3,452	$4,363	$5,492
14	$1,319	$1,732	$2,261	$2,937	$3,797	$4,887	$6,261
15	$1,346	$1,801	$2,397	$3,172	$4,177	$5,474	$7,138
16	$1,373	$1,873	$2,540	$3,426	$4,595	$6,130	$8,137
17	$1,400	$1,948	$2,693	$3,700	$5,054	$6,866	$9,276
18	$1,428	$2,026	$2,854	$3,996	$5,560	$7,690	$10,575
19	$1,457	$2,107	$3,026	$4,316	$6,116	$8,613	$12,056
20	$1,486	$2,191	$3,207	$4,661	$6,727	$9,646	$13,743
21	$1,516	$2,279	$3,400	$5,034	$7,400	$10,804	$15,668
22	$1,546	$2,370	$3,604	$5,437	$8,140	$12,100	$17,861
23	$1,577	$2,465	$3,820	$5,871	$8,954	$13,552	$20,362
24	$1,608	$2,563	$4,049	$6,341	$9,850	$15,179	$23,212
25	$1,641	$2,666	$4,292	$6,848	$10,835	$17,000	$26,462
26	$1,673	$2,772	$4,549	$7,396	$11,918	$19,040	$30,167
27	$1,707	$2,883	$4,822	$7,988	$13,110	$21,325	$34,390
28	$1,741	$2,999	$5,112	$8,627	$14,421	$23,884	$39,204
29	$1,776	$3,119	$5,418	$9,317	$15,863	$26,750	$44,693
30	$1,811	$3,243	$5,743	$10,063	$17,449	$29,960	$50,950
31	$1,848	$3,373	$6,088	$10,868	$19,194	$33,555	$58,083
32	$1,885	$3,508	$6,453	$11,737	$21,114	$37,582	$66,215
33	$1,922	$3,648	$6,841	$12,676	$23,225	$42,092	$75,485
34	$1,961	$3,794	$7,251	$13,690	$25,548	$47,143	$86,053
35	$2,000	$3,946	$7,686	$14,785	$28,102	$52,800	$98,100
36	$2,040	$4,104	$8,147	$15,968	$30,913	$59,136	$111,834
37	$2,081	$4,268	$8,636	$17,246	$34,004	$66,232	$127,491
38	$2,122	$4,439	$9,154	$18,625	$37,404	$74,180	$145,340
39	$2,165	$4,616	$9,704	$20,115	$41,145	$83,081	$165,687
40	$2,208	$4,801	$10,286	$21,725	$45,259	$93,051	$188,884
41	$2,252	$4,993	$10,903	$23,462	$49,785	$104,217	$215,327
42	$2,297	$5,193	$11,557	$25,339	$54,764	$116,723	$245,473
43	$2,343	$5,400	$12,250	$27,367	$60,240	$130,730	$279,839
44	$2,390	$5,617	$12,985	$29,556	$66,264	$146,418	$319,017
45	$2,438	$5,841	$13,765	$31,920	$72,890	$163,988	$363,679
46	$2,487	$6,075	$14,590	$34,474	$80,180	$183,666	$414,594
47	$2,536	$6,318	$15,466	$37,232	$88,197	$205,706	$472,637
48	$2,587	$6,571	$16,394	$40,211	$97,017	$230,391	$538,807
49	$2,639	$6,833	$17,378	$43,427	$106,719	$258,038	$614,239
50	$2,692	$7,107	$18,420	$46,902	$117,391	$289,002	$700,233

30 Minute LIVING

Suggested Action Plan

- *Determine your cash goal.* If you haven't done so already, carefully consider how much you would like to build up in your cash reserves. Make it a top priority to add to this account each month.

- *Explore your banking options.* Compare the current rates available at various banking institutions, including where you currently bank. Check out national as well as local rates at Bankrate's site: www.bankrate.com/compare-rates.aspx.

- *Find credit unions in your area.* Use this tool to locate credit unions in your area: www. creditunion.coop (You'll probably need to pull up each credit union's specific site to find their membership requirements.) Then check out the rates that are posted and compare with those offered by your current banking institution.

- *Consider opening a new account.* After you have researched the rates offered by various banks and credit unions, consider whether you would like to open a new account or not. Examine all the other features offered by this account, particularly if it has free online bill pay. Research the bank itself at the FDIC web site.

  The simplest way to open a new account is to leave your existing account intact and write a check for the minimum to open the new account. That gives you the option of keeping both accounts open or later transferring all your money and automatic transactions to the new account.

- *Stamp out fees!* Go back through the last year of bank statements and jot down any fees that you paid on your accounts. Find the total amount you paid, and then determine how you can eliminate paying fees in the future. If you rationalize that this is not enough money to worry about, stop and think—if you had that much money in your hand right now, would you go throw it away just because it's not much?

Chapter 6

Managing Your Debt

So easy to get into—so hard to get out of!

It was the first day of Personal Finance class for the new semester, and the moment class was dismissed, a young man who had been sitting front row and center stepped forward to speak with the instructor. Anxiously, he explained that he could barely make the minimum payments on his credit card. Any amounts he did pay went almost entirely to interest, and his outstanding balance hardly budged from one month to the next. His part-time job didn't pay much, and being a full-time college student, he couldn't work that many hours anyway. Frustration and worry with his debt had almost consumed his life.

Financial counselors hear this same story over and over, and not just from people with limited incomes, like college students. You remember those beautiful graphs in Chapter 5 that show how money grows when compounded through time? Unfortunately, when you're in debt, that compounding is working in your *lender's* favor and *against* you, and usually at rates *much higher* than those shown on the graphs!

You can bet your bottom dollar that your lenders understand the power of compound interest and how small amounts add up through time. Bankers are renowned for never leaving a penny uninvested if at all possible! In this chapter we will discuss various aspects of debt, along with how to use it and how to control it.

The Bright Side of Debt!

Debt itself, though much maligned by the popular financial press and much abused by the American consumer, is neither good nor bad. Debt is a *tool*, and like most tools, it can be used either as an instrument of creation or of destruction.

Debt can be likened to a hammer. When placed in the right hands, it can be used to construct a beautiful home. When placed in the wrong hands, it can be used to destroy anything in its path.

With the wise use of debt, you can leverage your position to attain that which you otherwise would not be able to attain. With the unwise use of debt, you can plunge your economic situation to the depths of financial ruin!

In the United States we tend to take debt for granted, when in fact, being able to borrow money is a privilege and not an inalienable right. Visit with people from other countries around the world about this topic, and you'll soon understand the importance of a safe and efficient *financial intermediary system* (addressed below) that facilitates the borrowing of money. As one international friend explained, in her country married couples frequently live with their parents until they are well into their adult years. They must either accumulate enough money to purchase a home outright or wait until their parents die to inherit the family home.

A *financial intermediary*, such as a bank or credit union, acts as a middleman or matchmaker. It matches those who have money (the savers) with those who need money (the borrowers). Because of debt, you can purchase a car and use that car all during the time you're paying for it, to drive yourself to work and earn a paycheck to take care of yourself and your family. Because of debt, you can purchase a home and live in it while you are paying for it instead of being shoehorned into your parents' basement, attic or spare bedroom for who knows how long.

This brings us to a basic rule of thumb concerning the wise use of debt:

The item purchased should outlive the payments!

Buying a washer and dryer on credit and paying for them over a year or two is not a bad use of debt when you either don't have enough money to pay cash or you can put your cash to a better use. Your laundry duo should faithfully care for your clothes for many years to come and save you countless trips to the Laundromat.

But what if the item purchased does not outlive the payments? This brings us to —

The Dark Side of Debt!

Stop and think what you're doing when you charge up your charge card. You are pledging money you have not yet earned to pay for something you purchased today. In essence, you are attaching part of tomorrow's paycheck for today's use. When tomorrow gets here, you'll still have all the bills associated with tomorrow—your rent, utilities, food, etc.—plus the extra burden of paying for yesterday. Plus interest.

What happens if that extra burden makes you run a little short tomorrow? You charge more! And so begins the downward spiral. As mentioned earlier, that exponential curve of how money grows when compounded through time (see Chapter 5) works just beautifully—for your lender! You, on the other hand, may feel like you're in a bad sci-fi movie and about to get sucked into the vortex.

You may have seen or read illustrations concerning how much all that stuff charged in college really costs you.[36] It's no joke that some people are still paying for their pizzas years later because they keep piling on the debt and making only the minimum payments.

Continuing to charge items while making minimum payments will keep you perpetually in debt. Remember that charging consumable items on your charge card is a poor use of debt

---

[36] Use Bankrate's handy Credit Card Calculators to see how long it will take you to pay down your debt. www.bankrate.com/calculators/index-of-credit-card-calculators.aspx

unless you are —

The Convenience User of Debt

Certainly, credit cards can be used wisely and even profitably, but before you can rightfully label yourself a "convenience user," you must abide by certain guidelines:

1. *You must first be in control of your spending and confident that you can maintain control during the course of time.* If you are unable to control your spending, you cannot be a convenience user. It's as simple as that, and in the next section you'll be given a few tips on how to gain control of your spending.

2. *You must be able to stay on your budget.* If other items in your budget, such as saving and investing, are being shortchanged, you are not a convenience user! You are overspending on your charge card and are fortunate enough to make enough money to support your habit. The rest of your budget must be on target before you can label yourself a convenience user.

3. *You must make it a point to pay your balance in full every month and not incur any fees (late, over the limit, etc.).* You might have thought this would be the first guideline for being a convenience user. Actually, it should be a given that convenience users normally incur NO expenses in the use of their charge cards.

Now, to directly contradict this premise, there are occasions when rightful convenience users may carry a balance or incur some amount of expense. Remember that debt is a tool, and as different situations arise you should examine all the tools in your toolbox and pick the one that is most appropriate. Maybe you currently can obtain a low rate of interest on your charge card. Maybe you have a store's credit card that allows you to pay off your purchases in, say, 12 months without incurring interest. Such deals can be incredibly helpful when purchasing big ticket items, such as when building a home.

The point is this — *if you have your spending under control and are purchasing something that you need and it aligns with your financial goals, then charging the purchase may be your best option at that point in time.* Particularly if you can get a deal with no interest or fees, why not let your money stay in your cash account a little longer where it's earning some amount of interest?[37]

Why be a convenience user of debt?

It is decidedly to your advantage to get yourself to the convenience user level as rapidly as possible. Here's why:

- A number of businesses do not accept personal checks. If you can't allow yourself to use a credit card, you must either pay by *cash* or with a *debit card*.
- It's usually not a good idea to carry around a wad of cash. Using an ATM to get cash may incur a fee. Also, an ATM machine may not be readily available in a safe location.
- Debit cards can be a greater problem when stolen than are credit cards.
- More importantly, your credit card can serve as your *emergency backup system!*

---

[37] Before you sign up for another credit card, carefully consider your personal situation, if you really need another card or not as well as the implications, positive or negative, or your credit report.

Unexpected expenses are bound to occur, and you're not always in a position to instantly transfer funds to meet the need. Or the need may be too great for you to cover with your own funds.

Your spending needs to be under control so that you can allow yourself the privilege of carrying a credit card. Consider the plight of one young woman who found herself stranded in Madagascar while traveling for her family's business. As she related her experience, she remarked, "It was the greatest thing ever to be able to slap that credit card on the counter and buy a plane ticket home!"

NFC—Near Field Communication

Now there's a new kid on the block which may pose an even greater danger to those who are trying to budget and spend their money wisely. NFC, which stands for Near Field Communication, is the technology that allows smart phone users to simply hold their phone next to another NFC device and transfer payments. If your spending is not firmly under your control, having instant access to both debit and credit use could wreak total havoc to your budget!

If you are someone who struggles with impulse purchases, NFC is something you want to be very cautious about using.

Renting a Car Without a Credit Card

As an aside, renting a car used to be almost impossible without a credit card, but these days it can be done. Locally owned car rental companies may be more inclined to rent on a cash basis, or you may want to get a pre-paid voucher from your travel agency designed specifically for rental car purposes. Rental car companies may allow you to apply for a Cash Deposit ID Card, but you need to do this in advance to make sure you're approved so you're not stranded somewhere without a car.

You may be allowed to use a debit card to rent a car, particularly if your card has the Visa or MasterCard logo, or if you do it online ahead of time. Be aware that the rental company may put an authorization hold on an amount greater than your anticipated charges—just in case—and the company may charge you an extra deposit amount as well. That money will be unavailable to you, even though it's still in your account, until it's unblocked. This may take several days after you've returned the car. Also, if you're using a debit card, the rental company may run a credit check on you to determine the level of risk in renting to you. The credit inquiry is likely to show up on your record and could affect your credit score somewhat.

Controlling Your Spending

So how do you go about controlling your spending when your credit card is calling out, "Charge me! Charge me!" and new technology makes it easier than ever to empty your wallet?

Here's the thing—*you personally must have the desire to control your spending!* Short of sending you to jail, no one but YOU can force YOU to change your behavior.

So if you personally have the desire to control your spending, read on.

First, get out your budget and review your spending plan. Next, get out your credit card statements or other documentation of your actual spending. Then compare your *actual* spending with your *planned* spending. In what areas did you overspend? Analyze what you actually spent and determine why the overspending occurred. You might want to create a spreadsheet to help you analyze your budget variances (areas where your planned spending didn't mesh with your actual spending).

Referring back to the sample budget prepared for Samantha Smith in Chapter 3, let's assume that the first quarter of the year has passed. Samantha, realizing that her budget has not worked out as planned, would like to further examine her spending. For the sake of brevity, we'll consider only a few items as shown in the following illustration.

BUDGET ANALYSIS

Prepared for: Samantha			For the quarter ending: March 31, 20XX						Totals for Quarter		
	Planned	Actual	Variance	Planned	Actual	Variance	Planned	Actual	Variance	Planned	Actual	Variance
	Jan.			Feb.			Mar.					
Expenses												
Rent	800	800	0	800	800	0	800	800	0	2,400	2,400	0
Utilities	100	110	(10)	100	135	(35)	100	92	8	300	337	(37)
Phone	50	45	5	50	48	2	50	100	(50)	150	193	(43)
Food	300	450	(150)	300	525	(225)	300	490	(190)	900	1,465	(565)
Clothing	50	250	(200)	50	175	(125)	50	180	(130)	150	605	(455)
Total	1,300	1,655	(355)	1,300	1,683	(383)	1,300	1,662	(362)	3,900	5,000	(1,100)

Analyzing the Budget
- *Fixed expenses*, such as the rent, are expected to remain the same from month to month for at least a given time period.
- *Variable expenses* are not expected to be the same dollar amount time after time. These expenses can usually be broken apart further into either necessary or discretionary expenses.

When budgets go astray, it is usually due to the *discretionary* portion of your *variable* expenses!

Seasonal variances are bound to occur.
So let's look at Samantha's spending over the last quarter. As expected, her rent stayed the same with no variance. Her utilities did vary, but that is to be expected. On expenses such as utilities, you will spend more in some months and less in others, so you try to list an amount that averages out over the course of the year. Samantha might want to examine whether her average amount needs to be adjusted or if she can adjust the thermostat to conserve more energy, but her utilities variance is not of great concern.

Expect occasional variances due to special circumstances.

The variance on her phone bill may not be much of a concern either if her overspending in March is only an occasional happening due to travel or special circumstances. However, if she thinks her phone expenses will increase in the future due to a *change in her situation*, such as needing to use her cell phone for work, Samantha should adjust her budget now for the rest of the year. But again, her phone variance is not a major concern.

Carefully examine overages that occur frequently!

What should concern Samantha greatly is the fact that she has large overages every month for food and clothing! She needs to go through her actual expenses in these two areas in detail and separate the necessary expenditures from the discretionary. In fact, she probably needs to split food into two different expense entries on her budget—groceries and eating out (or maybe necessary food and discretionary food, because you can buy many discretionary items at the grocery store or you may find it necessary to eat out due to your work situation).

Samantha needs to determine if these overages are necessary. If so, she needs to budget more in these areas. On the other hand, if her extra spending is due to impulse purchases, she needs to understand why she is doing this and figure out how to control her spending.

Why your budget may not be working!

Overages can be due to a variety of causes. For example, when people prepare their budget, they may not have an accurate idea of what they are actually spending in certain areas (this is why the spending diary presented in Chapter 1 is so important—to confront reality head-on!). Also, situations can change or unexpected events can occur after the budget is prepared. A periodic review of the budget will help so that you can make adjustments before a situation becomes serious.

However, the unfortunate truth is that many times overspending occurs because we cannot (or do not wish to) clearly distinguish between our needs and our wants. We don't like to tell ourselves "No!"

Psychology of Spending

The psychology of overspending could be a course all its own, and probably is somewhere. People can have hang-ups from their childhood, they may be using overspending to strike back at someone else, or they may use overspending to prop up their sense of self-worth. It's up to you to analyze your own spending habits (or get someone to help you) and understand what triggers your overspending. Then you're going to have to deal with it, because no one else can deal with it for you.

Problems with plastic and virtual money.

In some people's minds, there is a disconnect during the spending process such that using plastic or their smart phone technology does not equate to real money. This is in spite of the fact that they understand they must pay money as required when they receive their statement. Many people find it much easier to overspend virtually or with plastic than with cash, even when they have plenty of cash in their wallet. If this seems to be your problem, you need to leave your plastic at home and not enable your phone's spending technology until you can work through this issue.

Don't like being denied.

Many people simply like to indulge themselves, for whatever reason. Remember that very few people have ever died from being told, "No." The damage to your psyche from denying yourself something will last but a few moments, but the damage to your budget, your credit history, and your family's well-being may go on for years if you don't have the courage to control your spending!

Can you remember what you charged?

If you have a balance on your credit card, right now—without looking at your statement—see if you can recall what you charged. What was so important that you had to pledge your future earnings so that you could have those items immediately? As one young woman noted, the clothes from the mall which she had charged on her credit card were items which she neither needed nor used and, in fact, had already given away. She estimated that it would take her another year to pay off the balance, and she couldn't even name a specific item that she had purchased! Such is frequently the case with impulse spending.

Tips and Tricks to Controlling Impulse Purchases

Some of the following suggestions may sound a bit cheesy or even childlike. Well, so be it. Credit is a valuable financial planning tool, but one which you dare not use unless you can control it. Be committed to doing whatever it takes until you become financially mature enough to handle your credit responsibly. *You simply WILL NOT attain financial freedom if you cannot control your spending!*

- **Pay cash.** You are much more likely to purchase only items that you need when you have to pay cash for everything. Some people are able to use debit cards or checks in lieu of cash, because they realize the money is leaving their account. However, if you have the same problem with debit cards that you do with credit cards (they're both plastic), or if you bounce checks, then you're stuck using a fist full of dollars.

- **Use envelopes.** This is probably one of the simplest and oldest cash management systems in existence, but it is still very effective for those who have difficulty apportioning their money. Create an envelope for each of your budget categories, writing both the name of the category and the dollar amount on the envelope. Cash your paycheck and immediately divide out the cash into the envelopes. As you spend money from an envelope, record what you purchased along with the date and the amount right on the envelope, and then calculate the remaining balance left in that envelope. This truly helps you see where all the money goes.

- **Remove yourself from the presence of the temptation.** Have you ever gone shopping for another vehicle and the dealer or salesperson allowed you to drive it home and keep it overnight? Don't be overwhelmed by their generosity. They want to keep you in the presence of the vehicle—they want you to "bond" with the vehicle. Not only that, they want you to show off the vehicle to your friends and family and hear all their oohs and aahs—positive reinforcement that the vehicle is cool and you look great driving it. They want to make it difficult for you to give it back the next day.

The next time you're tempted to purchase something, whether it's a new car or something else, purposely remove yourself from the presence of the object. Put the item back, leave the store and go walk around. Do something to take your mind off the object or even go home. Give yourself some cool down time to logically think it over and to re-examine your spending plan. If it's something you truly need that fits your budget, you can go back and get it. But many times you'll decide that you don't need it, and surprisingly enough, *most items seem to lose their appeal when you leave the store!*

Note that salespeople do **NOT** want you to leave the presence of the object or to have cool down time, because they know you'll be much less likely to purchase it. Salespeople also strive to create a sense of urgency (the price is only good through midnight tonight!) and uniqueness (this is the last one!) in order to get you to act now.

Stop and think about it—do you really believe there will never be another sale? Do you really believe there is not another couch anywhere that will look good in your living room? Do you really believe this is the only car in the universe for you, when there are thousands and thousands of cars for sale every day in a multitude of locations around the world?

- **Ask yourself what will happen if you DON'T buy this item?** Will your well being or that of your family be affected? If you don't purchase this item, will you or your family suffer? If you do purchase this item, how will you and your family be better off? Will this item make a positive contribution to your life, or will its cost create a burden for you and your family?

- **Do I have to have it now?** If you determine that the item will positively enhance your life and/or that of your family, then ask yourself—*do I have to have it NOW?* Can you wait for another paycheck so that you can pay cash? What is so compelling that you must have it today? Many times, just asking these questions serves as a reality check and will help you put the proposed purchase into perspective.

- **Freeze your credit card.** This trick comes from a student who was absolutely committed to gaining control of her spending habit. She washed out an empty margarine tub, filled it with water, dropped in her credit card, and placed it in the freezer. Then when she went to the mall, where she frequently overspent, and found something compelling—she had to come home first and defrost her credit card. This literally gave her some cool down time and forced her to think about her purchase—and also consider if it was worth the time and effort to go back to the mall. She rarely returned to make the purchase, and in a few months, she no longer had to resort to this self-imposed method of control.

- **Use a prepaid card.** Parents sometimes get prepaid cards for their children so that they are allowed only a set amount of spending money per week or per month. Nothing stops an adult from using a prepaid card as well. If you tend to overspend, for example, on entertainment or eating out, purchase a prepaid card to use only for these items, and when it's used up, then no more spending until next month. You can also purchase prepaid cell phone minutes and phone cards.

- **Use duplicate checks.** You may not write many checks, but having a copy of those you do write really helps with the record keeping—particularly if you happen to share the same checkbook with someone who doesn't have a clue what the checkbook register is for.

- **Use your bank's bill payment system and/or a money management program.** Two of the most useful tools for money management, these items can really help you keep a handle on your finances.

Most bank bill pay systems allow you to set up payments in advance so that you can apportion out your expenses for the month—with the added bonus that your bills get paid on time. Then record your scheduled bill payments in a money management program (such as Intuit's Quicken, Microsoft's Money or Moneydance), using the dates of the scheduled payments.

For any bills that you pay by check, go ahead and write the check as soon as the bill arrives, putting it in its envelope and writing the date that you need to mail it in the stamp area. Record all your checks in your money management program, and stack your to-be-mailed bills in a handy spot until it's time to stamp them and stick them in the mailbox.

Your money management program helps you keep your spending on track by showing you what your account balance will be as each payment comes due. This system really helps when money is tight and you have to carefully manage your cash flows. (Note: You can usually download transactions from your bank account into your money management program, which is very helpful when you first set up your system. Later, however, if you're waiting to download what you've already spent, you're not being proactive—you're managing after the fact.)

Paying Down Debt

Now that you've gotten serious about controlling your spending and gaining financial independence, how do you determine what to pay off first? The textbook school of thought is usually to pay off the debt with the highest interest rate first, because that's mathematically logical. Unfortunately, that sometimes takes too long before you start to feel like you're actually accomplishing something.

With money, feelings are often more important than logic. Many people have been successful at eliminating their debt by tackling their smallest debt first. So stop and think, what would be the appropriate order for you? And then put a pencil to it.

Make your debt game plan!

1. Make a list of all your debts along with the required minimum payments, how many payments are left, the interest rates and the balances remaining.

2. Rearrange your debts by the order in which you'll pay them off, using the worksheet provided at the end of this chapter.

3. Target your primary or No. 1 debt with gusto (it's going to be a special little fella!), and try to pay extra every time. Where will the extra come from? You may have money sitting in the budget that can be used, or maybe you can *make* room by cutting out a discretionary item. If you are paying extra on other debts, consider paying only the minimum required on those debts and apply the extra to your No. 1 debt.

If your budget is super tight and all you're paying now are the minimums, then be watchful for any extra money that comes in and apply it to your No. 1 debt. Look for rebates you could send in or used books you could sell. One family traveled in connection with their jobs, and they always applied their mileage reimbursements to either debt repayment or retirement accounts. *So start looking for money*, and you'll be surprised what you find! Remember, small amounts make a big difference over time.

4. When your No. 1 debt is paid off, take all the money in your budget that had been going there and combine it with the minimum you had been paying on your No. 2 debt. Now you've got a super payment with which to tackle that second debt, which now becomes your new primary or No. 1 debt!

5. Continue on down the line, and every time you pay off a debt, take everything you had been paying on all your previous debts and combine that with the minimum for your current target debt.

Don't be surprised or discouraged if the hardest debt to pay off is your No 1 debt. That's because your budget is at its tightest when you first begin. Getting rid of that first debt represents a *major milestone*, because now you've given your budget some breathing room. Not only will No. 2 will be easier, but with each debt you eliminate, you'll gain more and more momentum. You will be able to see your progress which will in turn help propel you forward even more rapidly.

Getting your debt under control can seem like an impossible task, but it's not. You'll be encouraged by each small success, and *not incurring new debt is half the battle!* Other debt considerations are covered in Chapter 7, including credit cards, student loans, home mortgages, the tax deductibility of certain debt, and establishing and maintaining credit.

Paying Down Your Debt

Seeing all your debt listed together can be a powerful motivator to help you control your spending and further steel your resolve to eliminate debt. Use this form to list out all your debt along with the terms of each debt. Examples of debt to be listed:

- Credit cards
- Personal (unsecured) loans to institutions
- Personal loans to individuals
- Auto loans
- Student loans
- Home mortgage(s)
- Other loans, secured or unsecured
- Other debt obligations, such as outstanding traffic tickets or money owed the IRS

List each debt according to your priority in paying it off. Be sure to consider your own personal situation, such as the tax effect or any pressing issues, such as legal judgments against you. As you pay off a debt, be sure to cross it off the list with a red pen or colored marker and pat yourself on the back!

Debt Worksheet

Date of balances: _____

Debt	Outstanding Balance	Number of Remaining Payments	Effective Interest Rate	Minimum Monthly Payment
1.				
2.				
3.				
4.				
5.				
6.				
7.				
8.				
9.				
10.				
11.				
12.				

(You may reproduce this form as needed.)

30 Minute LIVING

Suggested Action Plan

- *Carefully examine your use of debt.* After reading through this chapter, what do you need to improve in handling your debt? What are you doing well?

- *Review your budget.* Where do you have variances? If you are consistently going over your budget in a certain area, you probably need to adjust your budget.

- *What are the terms of your debt?* The young man referenced at the beginning of this chapter had no idea that he was effectively paying over 33% on his credit card. With the new laws in place, it's easier to see what your debt is actually costing you. Examine all your statements to see what rates you're paying and the actual dollars lost to interest.

- *How are you tracking your expenses?* If you don't have a money management program on your computer, consider installing one. Or check out what's available online, such as www.mint.com. Not only will it help you see where your money's going, but it makes tax time easier as well.

- *Consider an accountability partner.* If you are struggling to control your spending or simply want to improve your resolve, find a trusted friend who will hold you accountable each week. Just knowing that someone is going to ask about your spending will give you an added incentive to stay on budget. The questions can be determined ahead of time, such as—
  - Where were you successful in staying on budget?
  - Where did you overspend in your budget?
  - What caused this overspending?
  - Were you able to make up this expense in another area of your budget?
  - What can you do differently in the future, or does your budget need adjusting?

Chapter 7
Understanding Your Debt

Like ice cream, debt comes in various flavors. It's definitely not as tasty, and underneath all the possible added-on features, it's still debt. You owe somebody money, and you have to pay it back.

The previous chapter addressed how to manage and control your debt. In this chapter we will examine some of the most commonly held forms of debt, the various features of debt and issues you need to consider in dealing with your debt. You need to know what you're getting into, because, like ice cream, there are some flavors you'd just rather not try!

Secured versus Unsecured Debt

Debt can be categorized as either secured debt or unsecured debt.

- With *secured debt*, an asset of value is pledged against the loan. This asset serves as "collateral" for the loan, and often it's a big-ticket item with a recorded title. Frequently, the asset that's being financed, such as a car or home, secures the loan. If you don't make your payments, then the asset can be seized to satisfy the loan (i.e., Repo Man hauls your car off in the middle of the night and the bank resells it). Financial assets, such as CDs or savings accounts, can also be used to secure debt.

- With *unsecured debt*, you still have the legal obligation to repay the debt, but no specific asset is pledged against it. This type debt is often called a "signature" or "character" loan, because it's issued based upon your reputation and creditworthiness. Therefore, if you fail to repay unsecured debt, it's your good name and credit score, along with your ability to obtain credit in the future, that take the hit.

Interest Rates

The *interest rate* charged on debt usually depends on the level of risk to the lender. Secured debt presents a lower risk because there is an asset that can be repossessed if you don't repay your loan according to the terms. On the other hand, unsecured debt is a higher risk because there's nothing the lender can seize in the event of default. In general, the interest on unsecured debt is usually substantially higher than for secured debt, even for a lender's best customers.

Creditworthiness also plays a big part in the interest rate that lenders offer. Borrowers with lower credit scores will likely pay a higher rate across the board than will those with better credit scores. In fact, traditional lending institutions often refuse to make loans to those whose credit scores are deemed too low.

Credit Cards

Credit cards can be issued as either secured or unsecured debt.

- With *secured* credit cards you typically have to make a cash deposit with the banking institution that issues the card. The limit of the amount you can borrow using this type of card is usually a percentage of your deposit. Because lenders typically consider the borrowers on these cards to be at higher risk of default, the interest rates are usually fairly high as well.

  So who would want this type of credit card? After all, you're essentially paying the bank for the privilege of borrowing your own money. For people who don't have a credit history, secured cards offer a way to build one. For those who have had past credit problems, they can serve as a means to rebuild your credit.

- Most credit cards are *unsecured*. As with the unsecured loans mentioned previously, unsecured credit cards are issued on your good name and credit history. The lender sets the limit as to the total you can charge. As long as you don't go over your limit and pay at least the required minimum on time, then you are free to charge and pay off at will.

Credit Card Laws

Numerous federal laws regulate credit card lenders, with one of the more recent being the Credit CARD Act of 2009.[38] What follows are various highlights of this quite lengthy law. Bear in mind this law also allows numerous exceptions to the overview presented here.

1. In general, interest rates cannot be increased during the first year after an account is opened. If rates are raised after that time, the increase will apply only to new charges from that point forward. The old rate will apply to the previously existing balance.

2. A notice of 45 days is required before rates or fees can be increased.

3. If your interest rate (Annual Percentage Rate or APR) is increased, the lender must tell you why. And if the company does increase your rate, it must re-evaluate the increase every six months. If appropriate, the creditor is to reduce your rate within 45 days of completing the evaluation.

4. Caps will apply on certain fees charged, and companies can no longer charge you an inactivity fee for not using your card.

5. You must opt-in to be allowed to make transactions that will take you over your credit limit. If you don't opt-in and your lender does allow you to go over the limit, you cannot be charged an over-the-limit fee.

6. Creditors cannot issue a credit card to someone younger than 21 unless that person either has the ability to make the required payments or obtains a cosigner who does have the ability to pay.

---

[38] The Federal Reserve Board now offers a Web site to keep consumers informed of the credit protections and features now in effect. Also at the site, find an interactive tool to help you figure out how long it will take to pay off a certain balance. www.federalreserve.gov/creditcard (Articles are available in both English and Spanish.)

7. Creditors can no longer use the "two-cycle" method of calculating interest charges.(For people who carried a balance from one period to the next, the two-cycle method often greatly increased the APR they were effectively paying. Frequently, they were unaware how high this rate actually was.) Interest charges can now be calculated over only the last period so that you're not still being charged for items you paid off the time before.

8. Payments are to be due on the same date (like the 12th of every month), and the credit card company should send out the bill at least 21 days before the payment is due.

9. The monthly credit card bill is to include information on how long it will take you to pay off your existing balance if you make only the minimum payment each month (assuming you make no additional charges). It should also tell you how much you would have to pay each month in order to pay off the existing balance in three years.

10. You may have several interest rates that apply to your account, such as a rate for new purchases and a higher rate for cash advances. If you pay more than the required minimum, the excess should go to the balance with the highest interest rate. (In the past, the excess would frequently go to the balance with the lowest interest rate first, leaving the one with the higher interest rate to keep on soaking you for more.)

Terms on **Your** *Card*

How do you find out about your card's terms? When you first sign up, you are supposed to have made available to you (whether you read it or not) the terms and conditions of the credit agreement. If you get the offer in the mail, there should be a disclosure box somewhere in the literature.

If you sign up online, the same disclosure information should be made available, possibly in a clickable link.[39] For credit cards that you already have, some of the information may be in the fine print on the back of your statements, or you can likely find it online at the company's Web site.

Note that it never hurts to call customer service and ask that certain fees be removed or the interest rate lowered. If the person with whom you speak states that he or she does not have that authority, politely ask to speak to someone who does. Be courteous! While this person may be low on the ladder, he or she is a *gatekeeper* to the higher ups.

The worst that can happen to you is that you might be told "No," and you've probably been told that before. It's not like someone can reach through the phone line and slap you, so it doesn't hurt to try.

---

[39] The Federal Reserve Board provides a wealth of personal finance and consumer information. Scroll through the listings to find the publication, "5 Tips for Getting the Most from Your Credit Card." www.federalreserve.gov/pubs/brochure.htm

Student Loans

Student loans are both a blessing and a curse. While they enable students to receive an education that they might not otherwise be able to attain, they create a heavy financial burden for students and often their parents as well. Unfortunately, the amount of outstanding debt per student has been increasing in recent years.

It's one thing to incur student loans that can easily be paid off in five to ten years. But it's quite another to choose a low-paying profession and rack up a high amount of debt. While it's possible to spread the repayment over 30 years, consider the fact that in 30 years most people will be close to retirement age. And during that time period, they also will need to provide for their family, set aside money for retirement and pay for a myriad of other financial obligations.

Quite simply, having to pay on student loans over such a long time period reduces the funds available for other necessities of life. So as a practical matter—

Don't rack up more in student loan debt than the earning potential of your degree can support!

Remember, too, that there is no shame in living very frugally during one's college years and taking out as few loans as possible. In fact, living the life of a starving student has long been a rite of passage into adulthood. College only lasts for a few years, but student loan debt can last seemingly forever.

As an added benefit of living on the lean side, you quickly learn how to prioritize your finances. People who have never had to economize often experience greater difficulty when faced with a financial crisis later on in life than do those who have had to live frugally in their younger years. If you can manage to get through college with low or even no student loan debt, you'll be miles ahead later.

The topic of student loans is a study in itself, the extent of which is beyond what can be covered in this chapter. For more information, a good place to start would be Student Aid on the Web. This site is offered by the Federal Student Aid Office of the U.S. Department of Education and provides free information on preparing for and funding education beyond high school.[40]

Home Mortgages

Home mortgages are secured loans, with the home itself pledged as security until the loan is paid in full. You stand to lose your home if you don't make the payments as agreed upon in the terms of the loan. That being said, some states provide a *homestead exemption* which protects some or all of the value of your primary residence from creditors, depending on the state in which you live.[41]

[40] Visit Student Aid on the Web at: studentaid.ed.gov/PORTALSWebApp/students/english/index.jsp
[41] Research the homestead exemption available in your state at:
www.lawchek.net/resources/forms/que/homestead.htm

What are the costs of borrowing, and how are those costs calculated?

With any debt, it is important that you understand the answers to both of these questions, but doubly so with long term debt such as a home mortgage. That's because —

> The *longer* the time period over which you pay borrowing costs, the *greater* the difference even a *small change* in those costs can make!

The costs of borrowing typically consist of interest (an ongoing cost) and any other fees or charges made in connection with the debt (usually an up-front cost). Fees and changes vary widely, and obviously the more you can hold down these costs, the better off you'll be. However, the interest rates on home mortgages tend to be relatively low in comparison to other debt.

Calculating Interest on a Home Mortgage

Generally, interest is calculated for each period only on the balance outstanding at that point in time. The loan payments are *amortized* over a given time period, which means that equal payments are to be made each time period in an amount sufficient to exactly satisfy the loan at the maturity date. The payments are calculated using a given interest rate, and part of each payment goes toward interest, while the remainder is applied toward the principal.

The chart which follows shows the first six months of a $100,000 loan calculated at an annual rate of 6% (divided by 12 to get the monthly rate), with monthly payments to be made over a 30-year period.

Month	Beginning Balance	Payment	Interest	Principal	Ending Balance
1	$100,000.00	$599.55	$500.00	$99.55	$ 99,900.45
2	$ 99,900.45	$599.55	$499.50	$100.05	$ 99,800.40
3	$ 99,800.40	$599.55	$499.00	$100.55	$ 99,699.85
4	$ 99,699.85	$599.55	$498.50	$101.05	$ 99,598.80
5	$ 99,598.80	$599.55	$497.99	$101.56	$ 99,497.24
6	$ 99,497.24	$599.55	$497.49	$102.06	$ 99,395.18

The monthly payment of $599.55 will remain the same for the life of the loan (assuming the interest rate is a fixed rate). However, the portion that goes toward interest will *decrease* each month, while the portion that goes toward principal will *increase*. So before you make your first payment, you owe the entire $100,000. The interest due for month one would be calculated thus: $100,000 x (0.06/12) = $100,000 x 0.005 = $500. *The interest is paid first* (in this case $500), and whatever is left goes toward principal.

After you make this payment, then your new outstanding balance will be $100,000 minus the principal repaid of $99.55, or $99,900.45. That balance will then become your beginning balance for month two, and you repeat the whole process. But note that in month two you'll owe interest only on $99,900.45, not on $100,000. The interest charges go down slightly to $499.50, and the remaining amount of $100.05 is applied toward the principal.

If you want to pay extra on your loan, first find out how it works with your lender. You may need to specifically state each time how you want the extra applied. If you want the extra to go toward reducing principal, the lender will take out the interest due that period and apply the rest toward principal. Next month, your payment will be the same, but the extra paid will have reduced the time you'll have left to pay on your loan. It will also reduce the total dollars you'll pay in interest over the life of the loan.

> To save the most dollars in interest, the sooner you reduce principal in the life of your loan, the better.

On the other hand, you may want the extra to go toward paying next month's payment. This is particularly helpful if you know funds will be tight next month, but it won't change how long you'll have left to pay on your loan. You lender may limit how many months you can pay ahead.

It's such a Great Day when you get to the end of a loan! Here's what the last six months of this same loan look like:

Month	Beginning Balance	Payment	Interest	Principal	Ending Balance
355	$3,535.18	$599.55	$17.68	$581.87	$2,953.31
356	$2,953.31	$599.55	$14.77	$584.78	$2,368.52
357	$2,368.52	$599.55	$11.84	$587.71	$1,780.81
358	$1,780.81	$599.55	$ 8.90	$590.65	$1,190.17
359	$1,190.17	$599.55	$ 5.95	$593.60	$ 596.57
360	$ 596.57	$599.55	$ 2.98	$596.57	$ 0.00

Notice that while your payment and interest rate are the same, fewer dollars now go toward interest. Your payment is still calculated in the same manner, but on a much lower balance. For example, the interest in month 355 would be $3,535.18 x (0.06/12) = $3,535.18 x 0.005 = $17.68.

When you get to month 360, that last payment is just enough to completely satisfy the debt. (If you have an actual loan, your last payment may be a different amount than the rest of your payments, depending on how your lender handles your loan.)

Graph 7-A, which follows, illustrates the repayment of this same $100,000 debt over the 30-year time period, again with the monthly payments calculated using an annual interest rate of 6%. (Note for simplicity that the monthly payments of $599.55 were rounded to $600.)

Graph 7-A

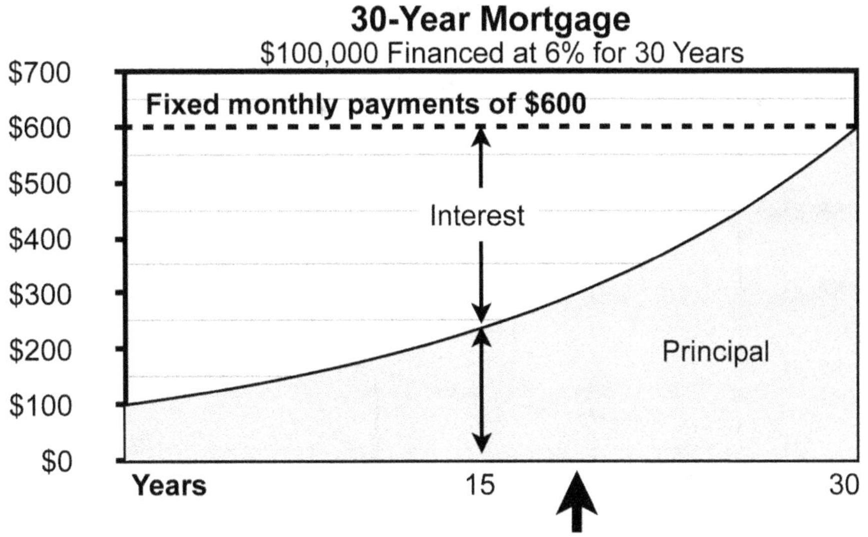

30-Year Mortgage
$100,000 Financed at 6% for 30 Years

Fixed monthly payments of $600

Interest

Principal

$700
$600
$500
$400
$300
$200
$100
$0

Years 15 30

(The large arrow marks how long it takes before half of your monthly payment of $600 goes toward paying off principal. In the example above, it takes about 18.5 years.)

In this particular example, it takes about 18.5 years (large arrow) before half of the monthly payment goes toward principal (or $300 out of the $600 payment). As the graph shows, before you reach the large arrow, *more than half of your monthly payment is absorbed by interest!* Only *after* the large arrow will more of your monthly payment go toward principal than goes toward interest.

The higher the interest rate and the longer the time period over which a loan is repaid, the longer it takes for a significant portion of the monthly payment to go toward principal.

Graph 7-B shows the difference a higher interest rate (10% in this case) makes in the repayment of principal. Notice how even *less* goes toward principal at the beginning of the 10% loan as compared to the 6% loan, and how it takes *longer* for the curve to climb higher. By looking at the large arrow you can see that it takes almost 5 years longer, or a little over 23 years, before half of the monthly payment goes toward principal.

Graph 7-B

30-Year Mortgage
$100,000 Financed at 10% for 30 Years

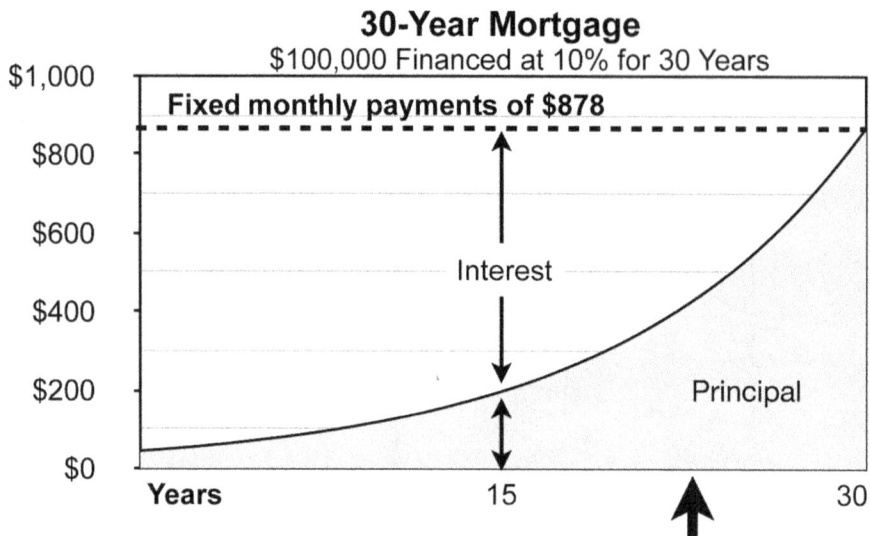

(In this example, it takes over 23 years before half of your monthly payment of $878 goes toward paying off principal.)

What both of these graphs illustrate is that for years most of the monthly payments made on a long-term loan are eaten up in interest. To lessen the amount lost forever to interest, the borrower can: 1) seek a lower interest rate if available, 2) pay off the loan more rapidly than is required, or 3) possibly both.[42] Many times, however, the borrower may have little control over the interest rate charged, which means that paying off debt rapidly is often the best way to minimize interest costs.

Graph 7-C, which follows, compares paying off the 10% interest rate loan in 15 years versus 30 years. In order to pay off this $100,000 loan in 15 years, the monthly payments must be increased to $1,075, or $197 more than is required for the 30-year loan. In both cases, the principal amount repaid is $100,000. However, the interest on the 30-year loan amounts to $215,925, while that of the 15-year loan totals $93,430, a difference of $122,495!

---

[42] Note that the tax deductibility of home mortgage interest will be discussed later in this chapter.

Graph 7-C

$100,000 Mortgage
Financed at 10% for 15 & 30 Years

Pmts of $1,075 for 15 yrs.

Diff. of $197/mo.

Pmts of $878 for 30 yrs.

$1,250

$750

$500

$250

$0

Total interest paid $93,430

Total interest paid $215,925

Principal paid $100,000

Principal paid $100,000

Years   15   30

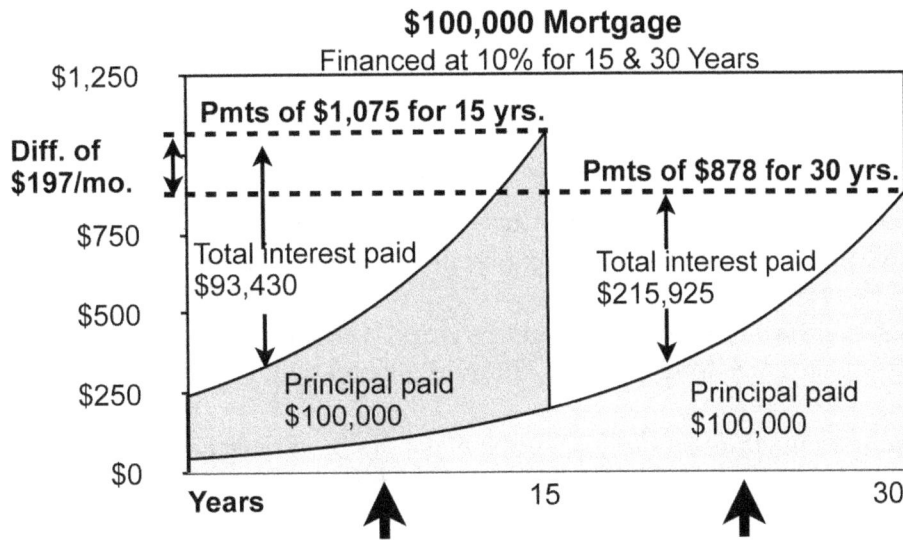

(The first large arrow marks the point at which half of the monthly payment on the 15-year loan goes toward principal, a little over 8 years. The second large arrow marks the point at which half of the monthly payment on the 30-year loan goes toward principal, just over 23 years.)

These graphs all illustrate the basic shape of the debt curve — low on repaying principal at the beginning of the loan and climbing higher as time passes. The faster you can climb the debt curve, the fewer dollars you lose in interest. As stated earlier, that's accomplished by either getting a lower interest rate so that more of your payment goes toward principal from the start, or by shortening the time your loan is outstanding by paying off your debt more rapidly than is required, or both.

Now, stop and think what happens when you buy a home, sell it after five to seven years, and buy a more expensive home with a heftier mortgage. You've traveled only a short distance up the debt curve, paying mostly interest during those first few years. Then you start over at the beginning with a new debt curve, again paying mostly interest.

The same thing happens with people who take out home equity loans. They have built up equity and climbed up the debt curve by paying on their loan. Then they take their equity out and slide back down the curve.

Perpetual Debt

While you're visualizing yourself sliding around on the debt curve, picture how the curve for credit card debt looks. If you don't pay your balance in full every month and instead carry a balance, your debt curve will be just about a flat line for a very long time. That's because the higher the interest rate, the longer it takes for the curve to start to climb. If you pay a little on your balance but then charge more stuff, that only stretches the curve out further. Remember this:

If you pay only the minimum required, you're turning whatever you've charged on your credit card into long-term debt, essentially financing it like a home. You simply cannot climb out of debt when you continually add to it.

Tax Deductibility of Debt

Ah, but you say—my home mortgage is tax deductible! Few things are as frequently misunderstood as tax deductions. But if taxes were easy to understand, would legions of people be able to make their living off tax preparation and consulting?

Here's a brief overview of how tax deductions work. [Disclaimer: This material is not meant to be taken as specific tax advice for your individual situation.]

First, if something is tax deductible, it's not a wash. It doesn't just cancel out your spending the money in the first place. Here's the way a tax deduction works:

- You earn money during the year.

- You spend some of that money on certain things deemed worthy of tax deductibility, such as interest on a home mortgage, gifts to qualified charities, property taxes, and state income taxes.

- The government forgives you the federal income taxes that you otherwise would have to pay on that portion of your income spent on these tax-deductible items.

So here's an example of a tax deduction. Let's say you spent $10,000 of your income on interest on your home mortgage during the year and that you're in the 25% marginal federal income tax bracket. Normally you would have had to pay $2,500 in taxes on that amount of your income. But because you spent your money on a tax-deductible item, you are forgiven the taxes that otherwise would have been due. So you spent $10,000, but you're relieved of $2,500 in taxes that you otherwise would have had to pay. This means that after you net things together, you're still out $7,500 of the $10,000.

Second, only the interest on a home mortgage and the property taxes on the home itself are eligible to be tax deductions. The amounts paid on the mortgage principal and the homeowner's insurance are not.

Third, just because an item is eligible to be a tax deduction doesn't mean that you will actually be able to deduct it on your return. You must itemize your deductions on a Schedule A in order to claim these deductions.

---

[43] Tax laws are not particularly straight forward, and there are many exceptions to the rules! You may indeed need to consult a professional. For help understanding tax terms, search on a word or term at Investopedia. www.investopedia.com.
[44] What's your marginal tax bracket? It's the highest federal income tax rate at which any of your money is taxed. It's the rate that your last dollar of "taxable income" is taxed at. What's taxable income? It's not necessarily every cent you make. Instead, it's the number on line 43 of the 2011 regular Form 1040. It's the amount remaining after the income section is totaled up, the adjustments are subtracted, and the deductions and exemptions are taken. View a Form 1040 at the IRS Web site to see the parts of the form and where things go. www.irs.gov/pub/irs-pdf/f1040.pdf

Many people will not have enough of Schedule A-type deductions to make it beneficial to itemize and will simply take the standard deduction instead. (You either itemize deductions on a Schedule A or you take the government's standard deduction allotment, but not both. Therefore, your Schedule A-type deductions must be *more* than the standard deduction in order for you to be better off itemizing.)

For example, if you're married and filing jointly, your standard deduction allowance is $11,600 (for 2011). So you wouldn't bother filing a Schedule A unless you have spent over $11,600 in total during the year on things like gifts to charity, taxes and mortgage interest on your home, or high medical expenses.[45]

So in summing up this whole protracted explanation of tax deductions, remember this: *Don't spend money on something just because it's tax deductible.* Spend money on items because you need them and they fit your spending plan. A tax deduction, if it even applies to your situation, merely takes out a little of the sting—you're still out the lion's share of the expense.

Establishing and Maintaining Credit

Three main credit bureaus currently exist, TransUnion, Experian, and Equifax. These companies collect information from various sources and provide credit reports as well as numerical credit scores to lenders. Lenders use this information to help them decide whether to grant someone a loan or not. You can get a free copy of your credit report every year, but if you want to know your score, you'll have to pay.[46]

With so many people having overdosed on debt, it seems incredible that others have trouble establishing credit in the first place. Here are a few suggestions for establishing credit:

- **Open a bank account**—usually you'll need to show that you have one or more bank accounts when applying for credit.

- **Have other accounts that leave a trail**—accounts that you have established with the phone and utility companies can often be used to show potential creditors that you are trustworthy and have the ability to manage your finances. You may have to request that these companies report your account information to the credit bureaus.

- **Apply for a credit card**—make sure it's one you're likely to be approved for because you don't want a denial to show up on your credit report. Such cards could include department store and gasoline cards which usually have fairly low charging limits. Also, ask if your bank offers a credit card.

- **A secured card may be an option**—as mentioned earlier, these cards require that you leave on deposit with the banking institution a certain amount, say $500. Your credit limit will likely be no more than that amount, so you're effectively borrowing your own money. Only people who have difficulty obtaining credit by other means would want to apply for this type card.

---

[45] View a Schedule A at the IRS Web site to get a better idea of the types of deductions you can list. www.irs.gov/pub/irs-pdf/f1040sa.pdf   For further information, pull up the accompanying instructions for a Schedule A. www.irs.gov/pub/irs-pdf/i1040sca.pdf Also refer to the Form 1040 Instructions Booklet. www.irs.gov/pub/irs-pdf/i1040gi.pdf
[46] You may obtain your free credit report at www.annualcreditreport.com.

- **Get a small loan from the bank where you have an account**—deposit the loan proceeds in a savings account at that bank and use it to pay back your loan month by month. Of course, you'll have to pay a little extra for the interest, but this will give you a track record. If you've exhausted your other options, this one may work.

Maintain your credit by always paying at least the minimum amount required on your accounts by the due date. *Late payments can really damage your credit score, particularly late mortgage payments.* Your credit score should improve after six months with no late payments, and will usually improve even more after 12 months. If denied credit, find out why. You are entitled to a free copy of your credit report within 30 days of being denied credit, so be sure to ask for it.[47, 48]

Other Considerations in Paying Down Debt

As you are formulating a plan for paying down your debt, here are a few more things to consider:

- **Taxes and consumer debt**—under current tax laws, the interest on consumer debt, such as on a personal loan, auto loan or credit card, is not deductible.[49] For most people, the only interest they may be able to deduct would be that paid on student loans and home mortgages. So if you, for example, happen to have a car loan financed at about the same interest rate and for the same time period as a student loan, you would want to pay off your car loan first. In such a case, the student loan would be less costly if you're able to deduct the interest. (Note that student loan interest can be deducted whether you itemize your other deductions or not.)

- **Preserving your borrowing capacity**—although student loans usually have low interest rates and the interest paid is tax deductible, having this debt and/or other consumer debt outstanding hinders your overall borrowing capacity. Particularly when you are ready to purchase a home, it may be advisable to try to pay off some of your other debt first. If the lender sees that a certain amount of your paycheck is already spoken for, it means less will be available for paying on the mortgage. You may not be able to qualify for as high a mortgage amount as you would like.

- **Paying an extra amount early in a loan**—paying an extra amount early in a loan has a greater impact than paying extra later in the loan. When you pay extra, you're removing principal forever from the outstanding balance, meaning you no longer have to pay compound interest on that portion.

---

[47] The Consumer's Guide offered by The Federal Reserve Board presents numerous topics and tools on using credit and understanding credit card offers and the credit laws. www.federalreserve.gov/creditcard The Federal Trade Commission also provides consumer information on "Credit & Loans." ftc.gov/bcp/menus/consumer/credit.shtm

[48] Find more information in the Federal Reserve Bank of San Francisco's booklet, "How to Establish, Use and Protect Your Credit." www.frbsf.org/publications/consumer/credit.html

[49] People who own their own businesses may be able to deduct certain of these items. Tax laws are complex, and this information is meant to be general in nature. It may not apply in your situation.

Referring back to the loan illustrated in Graph 7-A of $100,000 financed at 6% over 30 years, assume you paid $1,000 per month for the first 12 months of that loan and then the required $600 per month for the remainder of the loan. You would knock about 42 months (or 3.5 years) off the end of the loan and save over $20,000 in interest over the life of the loan. However, if you waited until the end of the loan and paid $1,000 per month for the last 12 payments, you would only shorten the loan by about nine months and save about $247 in interest.

- **How to pay extra on a loan**—few loans these days have a prepayment penalty for paying off your debt early, but you still want to check and make sure. Before you pay extra on your loan and include it with your monthly payment, find out how that extra will be applied—toward the principal, the interest or toward next month's payment. If you mail in a coupon or pay online, you may have a place to choose which one you want. (If you don't stipulate, the lender's default choice may not be what you want.) If your income is erratic or you're concerned about your budget, you may want to apply the extra toward next month's payment. If not, then you would want to apply the extra toward the principal. (Applying it toward interest is probably not a good idea barring some extenuating circumstance.)

Note: Paying extra on the principal doesn't affect your monthly payment. Next month you will still owe the same payment as always. Rather, it will *shorten the life of your loan.* How much shorter will depend on how far along you are in your loan repayment schedule. (Refer to the example given in the bullet point above this one.)

- **Margin of Safety**—if you don't borrow the maximum amount allowed by the lender, you leave yourself a margin of safety. You'll have a little bit extra left in your budget, so when financial difficulties arise, you'll be more likely to still be able to fulfill your debt obligations. On the other hand, if you borrow as much as you possibly can, you won't have much wiggle room in your budget for unexpected expenses and are more likely to go under very quickly when difficulties arise.

  Also, if you give yourself a margin of safety, then you are able to pay extra on your debt and thereby reduce the amount of interest you pay over the life of the loan. To illustrate the impact that a margin of safety can have, let's again consider the $100,000 mortgage referenced above. If you were able to pay $1,000 per month every month for the life of the loan, rather than the required $600, you could pay the loan off in 139 months, or in about 11.6 years rather than in 30, and save almost $77,000 in interest over the life of the loan! Because you're not required to pay $1,000 per month, only the $600, when you do have a financial emergency, you've got $400 per month that you can use if you need to.

It's hard to build wealth when your debt load has become a heavy burden. Systematically paying down debt faster than is required and not incurring new debt are key elements to lightening that load. With the understanding you've gained in this chapter of how debt works and the debt repayment plan you prepared in Chapter 6, hopefully you now have a handle on your debt and are on the road to building wealth and creating financial independence!

30 Minute LIVING

Suggested Action Plan

- *Find the going rates.* Pull up www.bankrate.com to find the current rates on credit cards and home mortgages as well as on savings accounts and CDs.

- *How much will the payment be?* Use one of Bankrate's many calculators to find payments on loans or to see how your savings stack up through time. www.bankrate.com/calculators.aspx

- *What other fees and charges will there be?* With home mortgages currently being offered at very low interest rates, you may want to consider refinancing your home. Remember that you will have to pay closing costs, which may total several thousand dollars. You'll want to shop various lenders and compare costs. Then calculate how long it will take you to recover the costs in order to be better off refinancing.

- *Examine your tax return.* Pull out last year's tax return and examine it carefully. If you filed a Schedule A, which items made the most difference? Which made the least difference, or none at all? If your tax return has many pages, spread them out on the table so you can see how everything connects back to the 1040 form. The more you understand about your own taxes, the more money you'll be able to keep in your pocket, because you'll learn what makes the most difference for you.

- *Learn more about credit and debt.* Pull up the Consumer Information page offered by the Board of Governors of the Federal Reserve Board to find topics such as "5 Tips for Improving Your Credit Score" and "5 Tips for Shopping for a Mortgage." www.federalreserve.gov/pubs/brochure.htm

Chapter 8

Insuring Your Life

Out of the fire, an industry is born!

In September of 1666, fire broke out in a baker's shop on Pudding Lane in London, England. What later became known as the Great Fire of London raged across the city for four days and destroyed over 13,000 structures. From this devastation, a new industry was born when the first fire insurance company was established the following year in London. Interestingly enough, the Great Fire was also credited with preventing the plague from recurring![50]

When the English colonists came to the New World, they brought this concept of insurance with them. They soon put it to good use, as many of their homes and buildings were constructed of wood and frequently were in close proximity to one another. Because they used fire for cooking and heating and oil lamps and candles for lighting, fires inevitably occurred. Without electricity to pump water or motor vehicles to transport water, fires in colonial days were difficult to extinguish and did a great deal of damage. Ben Franklin, who later discovered electricity, founded the Union Fire Company in Philadelphia in 1736. This was the country's first program for fire protection and later evolved to become a fire insurance company.[51]

Today, insurance continues to play an important part in providing protection and preserving wealth. This chapter discusses the underlying concepts of insurance in general[52] and then examines the features of various types of life insurance. Additional information on insurance is presented in Chapter 9: Insuring Your Health and in Chapter 10: Insuring Your Property.

How Insurance Works—The Concept

The underlying principle of insurance deals with pooling, and what the early settlers did was to contribute money to the pool. Those who owned structures that were at a greater risk of burning, such as apothecary shops and breweries, were either not allowed to join the pool or else had to pay more. When an insured structure burned, the money in the pool was then used to repair or replace the building.

---

[50] Pull up this site to read an account of the Great Fire of London. www.fire-extinguisher101.com/great-london-fire.html This site explains more about how the first insurance company was established. www.irmi.com/expert/articles/2001/klein07.aspx

[51] The Franklin Institute presents a timeline of Ben Franklin's life—"The Life and Times of Benjamin Franklin." www.fi.edu/franklin/timeline/timeline.html A more detailed account entitled, "Insurance: Philadelphia Contributionship," is presented at the U.S. History web site. www.ushistory.org/franklin/philadelphia/insurance.htm

[52] The information presented on insurance is general in nature. Different companies may use different terminology, and the coverage provided may vary from one company to the next. You must consult the individual company concerning the specifics of the policies offered by that company.

You can think of insurance as sharing the pain with others. Today, everyone with an insurance policy is contributing money to their particular pool when they pay their premiums. When you pay, you're bearing a little bit of the pain—you're giving up your money. But it's not a huge pain; it's more like a sting.

When tragedy strikes, the insurance company takes money from the pool to help pay for restoring the property of those who suffered the loss. In a manner of speaking, the pain is spread around over everyone who participates in the pool. Everyone is willing to suffer a little pain so that no one person has an unbearable pain. Without the insurance, the loss would be financially overwhelming for one person to bear alone.

Where does all MY money go?

This question frequently comes up. Some people will pay in for years and never have a claim or only a few small claims on their insurance. Their money seemingly goes into a big black hole.

The simplistic answer is that your premiums have been used to pay for the losses of the other people in your pool. If you have selected a good insurance company and you do have a loss someday, the money will be there when you need it. If you *never* have a claim, your reward is that you have not had to suffer through such a tragedy. Just ask someone whose home has burned down if it's not a reward to never have to go through such a loss!

How Insurance Works—The Premiums

Your insurance premiums can be thought of as consisting of several basic components. The company needs to set premiums high enough to cover:
1. Expected losses
2. Adjustments
3. Extraordinary losses
4. Overhead expenses

The following is a brief overview of each of these components.

1. Expected Losses

The insurance companies must determine how much each policyholder's premiums should be. Going back to the illustration of insurance in colonial days, if on average one home in the village burned each year, then the amount for each person to contribute to the pool should be approximately the cost to replace one structure divided by the number of participants in the pool. That's the basis today as well—the expected losses for a given time period divided among the number of policyholders.

How do insurance companies know what losses to expect?

They look at the past to see what has occurred in various instances and at various times. Then they ask—what is expected in the future? How will things change, or to what extent will things stay the same? They take all this data and employ the law of large numbers to help them calculate the odds that a certain loss will occur during a given time period.

What is the law of large numbers?

Consider what happens when you flip a coin. If you flip it only a few times, you might end up half the time with heads and half the time with tails. Or you might just as easily end up with all heads or all tails. The outcome could vary widely with only a few flips.

However, assuming the coin is evenly weighted, if you flipped it a million times, it's quite likely that the outcome would be very, very close to half heads and half tails. If you repeated several more sets of a million flips, it's likely that the outcomes would vary only slightly from one set of flips to the next. With many, many flips, the outcome becomes much more predictable — it will be very close to the average, or mean, time after time after time.

Insurance companies employ actuaries, and it's their job to calculate the odds that a certain loss will occur during a given time period. They examine the historical data for the items specifically being covered, such as homes, and use statistical calculations to help determine what the appropriate premiums should be.

2. Adjustments

Next come any adjustments for extra risk. As mentioned in early days, if someone's home or structure was more of a fire hazard, that person had to pay extra because he or she was more likely to have a loss. It's the same today. Wooden structures still cost more to insure than do masonry structures because they burn more easily, particularly those with wooden shingle roofs.

However, today there are many insurance pools, each with a different set of exposures (exposures consist of whatever is being insured, such as autos, homes, or lives). Your home, for example, may be a better fit in one company's pool than in another, and the premiums could be substantially lower for the same coverage.

When you apply for an insurance policy, the company tries to determine:

- The *odds* that a covered event will occur; for example, death if it's a life insurance policy, or damage or loss if it's an auto or home policy. The greater the odds that the given event will occur, the higher the premiums will be.

- The *level of risk* that whatever is being insured brings to the rest of the pool as a whole. A home close to the coast might add very little extra risk to a big company with many homes insured all around the country. However, it might add significant risk to a small company that already has quite a few coastal homes insured. The greater the risk, the higher the premium will be adjusted, or if the risk is too high, the company may deny coverage.

3. Extraordinary Losses

What if more houses burned in one year than the village expected? Unless extra money had been contributed to the pool, the people whose homes burned last were out of luck! The pool would have already been used up paying for those homes that burned first.

Today, insurance companies need to collect extra so that unexpected losses as well as the expected losses will all be covered. Even though on average one home per year burns in a given area, this year may be an exceptionally dry year and three homes burn. Next year may be a rainy year and no homes burn.

What happens during any given year may or may not be the average number, so insurance companies need reserves in case an extraordinary number of losses occur. If you're the last one to suffer a loss during a given time period, you need to be compensated as well. No one wants to hear that the company is out of money at the time of his or her greatest need!

4. Overhead Expenses

Like most other businesses, insurance companies have overhead expenses that must be paid regularly. Not only do they have the expense of their buildings, computers, personnel, etc., but without insurance agents, adjustors and appraisers, the company's policy holders would have a difficult time filing claims and getting paid when losses occur. Insurance companies must make sure their budgets allow for a sufficient amount of overhead so that their businesses operate smoothly.

All of the above mentioned expenses go into determining what your premiums should be for coverage during a given time period. Also factored in would be the dollar amount and type of coverage desired. For example, the premiums on a million dollar whole life insurance policy would be much higher than those on a $100,000 whole life policy. Those premiums, in turn, would be higher than those on a $100,000 term life policy.

The three basic types of insurance that most people need are:

- **Life insurance**—money for your loved ones in the event of your death (the remainder of this chapter covers various aspects of life insurance).

- **Insurance for your physical body**—health insurance, disability insurance and long-term care insurance (covered in Chapter 9).

- **Insurance for your property**—auto, home, and other property insurance (covered in Chapter 10).

LIFE INSURANCE

You insure your life in order to benefit someone else. In the event of your premature death, your life insurance pays your beneficiaries the amount stipulated by the policy.

Who needs life insurance? Primarily, it's for:

- Those who have others depending on their income.
- Those who wish to pay off debts.
- Those who wish to leave a gift.

Policy Premiums

The premiums on life insurance are determined in the same manner as are those of other types of insurance policies — on the probability of loss during a given time period. However, life insurance differs fundamentally from other types of insurance. On your homeowner's or auto policy, for example, a loss may or may not occur, and the amount of the loss can vary widely. It's quite possible that you may suffer a large loss, a small loss or have no loss at all. Life insurance, however, is on human life, and humans are mortal. Death is a given and not a maybe. The only question is *when*, and there are no degrees of loss. It will be all or none.

Law of Large Numbers

Life insurance can be used to illustrate the law of large numbers that we referred to previously. Data from death reports, such as gender, age, smoker or non-smoker and other information are routinely collected, and the statistics are compiled into mortality tables. Actuaries use this historical data to calculate your odds of dying during any given year of your life. For example, if you are a 35-year old female, on average you would be expected to live another 46.7 years.[53] The statistics also show on average how many females die each year between the ages of 35 and 36.

The larger the group of 35-year-old females the company has insured, the more predictable the number of deaths become. You will recall from our earlier example of the coins — the more times you flip a coin, the more likely your average will be very close to 50% heads and 50% tails. In the same manner, the larger the number of insured 35-year-old females, the closer the number of deaths in any given year will be to the overall average for 35-year-old females.

So, for example, if the insurance company knows that on average 1 out of every 100 of the 35-year-old females that it has insured dies each year, then it knows to arrange its investments so that it will have enough money available to pay the beneficiaries for that number of expected deaths. Note that insurance companies can and do affect their own averages by accepting or denying coverage to people of lower or higher risk of death.

Health Information

If you apply for a life insurance policy, you will almost always be asked to provide some amount of health information. Depending on your age and the type policy, the information required can range from answering a few questions to having to undergo medical tests and a physical exam. The higher the health risk you present to the company, the higher your premiums will be. If the risk is deemed too high, you will be denied coverage.

Risk Factors

Insurance companies collect money from the premiums and invest what's not currently needed. The longer the time period before they expect to pay off your claim, the longer they

---

[53] This data was taken from the National Vital Statistics Report, Vol. 59, No. 9, United States Life Tables 2007, Table A. www.cdc.gov/nchs/data/nvsr/nvsr59/nvsr59_09.pdf Data will vary, depending on the time period for which the data was collected. The Centers for Disease Control and Prevention provides extensive mortality information and tables along with causes of death and various demographic information. www.cdc.gov/nchs/deaths.htm

can leave that money invested. The longer they can invest the money, the less you have to provide out of pocket. Companies will require higher premiums for those who are deemed to be at a greater risk of dying sooner rather than later.

So who usually dies sooner?

- Males, even from birth, tend to die at a higher rate than do females.

- People who smoke. Be aware that if your blood test reveals a certain level of nicotine, you may be considered a smoker. This can occur with cigars or nicotine patches as well as with cigarettes.

- People who carry excess weight in relation to their height.

- People with certain medical conditions, diseases or infections, particularly those with heart disease or cancer.

- People who are older. Each year down the timeline obviously puts you closer to death. However, in your favor, the older and healthier your parents and siblings, the longer your timeline is likely to be.

- People whose occupations or activities put them at a greater risk. For example, you may be asked if you are a pilot, skydive, ride a motorcycle or travel to certain areas.

Term Life Insurance

The main distinguishing feature among various types of life insurance is *cash value*—either a policy builds cash value or it doesn't. The simplest type of life insurance is term life insurance, and it does not build cash value. It provides death protection during the given period of time, and if you die during that time period, the policy pays out to your beneficiary. If you don't die, you either renew your policy for another term or you simply let it expire. With term life insurance, your policy does not build up any savings or investment value. If you live past the given term, your reward is that you're thankfully still alive, but you don't get any money back.

Yearly Renewable Term Insurance

As its name implies, this most basic form of insurance requires that you renew it each year. While the premiums will usually be lower than those for level-premium term, you may have to show proof of insurability each year. The older you are and the greater your other risk factors, the more scrutiny you will be subject to. Your premiums are likely to increase each year, because with every year that passes, your likelihood of dying during the next year increases somewhat.

Level-premium Term Insurance

Most people choose to buy level-premium term rather than yearly renewable term. While the premiums may be somewhat higher, they are averaged over the given time period and will remain the same throughout the life of the policy.

Most people prefer knowing what their premiums will be and that their coverage is secured over the given time period rather than having to renew it each year. You never know what accidents or illnesses will occur down the road. Also with level-premium, the death benefit remains the same each year. Here's an example: Jim, age 30, purchases a 20-year level-premium term life insurance policy. For $100,000 in coverage, he will pay $120 every year for the next 20 years. His total cost over the next 20 years will be $120 x 20 = $2,400.

Decreasing Term Insurance

This type of term insurance is typically sold to cover debts. Examples of decreasing term insurance include mortgage life and credit life insurance. The premiums remain the same for the life of the loan, but the death benefit is designed to cover the outstanding loan balance which goes down, or decreases, as the loan is paid off. Generally these types of policies are designed to *pay the lender* in the event of your death and not your family, so your loved ones do not have flexibility in how to use the payout.

If you want the debt paid off in the event of your death, it's usually much more cost effective, particularly for young people, to buy regular level-premium term insurance for the duration of the loan or longer.[54] For the same premium, most people can usually buy several times more coverage, which stays level over time and doesn't decrease, and the payout goes to their loved ones rather than the banker. You are *not* required to purchase insurance from your lender to cover your debt, although the lender may urge you to do so. The lender may actually profit from selling you this insurance.[55]

Group Life Insurance

Group life is usually obtained through your employer or through an association and will almost always be term insurance. Applying for group life usually does not require a medical exam. This can be a great blessing for people with health conditions that make it difficult or impossible to get an individual policy. In fact, the only way that some people will ever be able to get life insurance is through group coverage from their employer, their spouse's employer or a trade or professional association.

Group insurance may be cheaper than an individual policy purchased on your own, particularly for younger people. As you get older, however, it may become more cost effective to purchase an individual policy. Also, if you ever leave your company, you may have to give up the group coverage, while an individual policy is yours and goes wherever you go.

---

[54] Because the rates are based on life expectancy, the younger you are, the less likely you are to die during the time period of the loan and usually the cheaper regular term insurance will be in relation to credit life insurance. As you get older, there may come a point where credit life premiums will be cheaper.

[55] The Insurance Information Institute provides general information on all types of insurance. This article discusses individual policies, group policies and credit life insurance. www.iii.org/individuals/life/basics/howsold

Here's an example: Jim, age 30, purchases group term life insurance through his employer. His rates go up every five years. So for each $1,000 of coverage, his rates and premiums for $100,000 of coverage are as follows:

Age	Monthly rate per $1,000 coverage	Monthly premium for $100,000 coverage	Annual premium for $100,000 coverage
30-34	$0.05	$5	$60
35-39	0.06	6	72
40-44	0.07	7	84
45-49	0.13	13	156

Note that even though these are the quoted rates now, as time passes the insurance company may increase its rates. So by the time Jim gets to be 40, the monthly rate may have gone up to maybe $0.10 per $1,000 coverage for those aged 40-44.

With group insurance, there is usually a limit as to how much coverage can be purchased. Also, to obtain the higher amounts that may be offered by the plan, a physical exam or tests may be required, even for group insurance.

Cash Value Life Insurance

Several types of life insurance build cash value, with the main categories being whole life, variable life, universal life and variable universal life. These policies feature death protection plus a saving component. The basic differences among policies which build cash value are how the savings component is invested and the flexibility (or lack thereof) in the payment of the premiums. The table which follows outlines the features of the various types of policies that build cash value.

Note that in order for a policy to build cash value, the premiums must be high enough to cover both the cost of the death protection as well as have some left over to put into the cash account. The cash account builds up through time and is part of the amount paid out in the event of death. While the policyholder is still alive, the cash account is a form of savings which the policyholder can take a loan against, withdraw, or allow to build up.

[56] This information is general in nature. Companies may call their products by different names and may offer many variations of features.

Table 8-A: Comparison of various types of life insurance policies

Type of Life Insurance	Cash Value Account	Payment of Premiums
Whole life	Account builds up at a rate guaranteed by the insurance company, which is usually a low rate compared to other investments at the time. However, many companies will pay higher than their guaranteed rates if possible, depending on the investment returns of the company itself.	Premiums are a fixed amount.
Variable life	Cash account is invested in market-based investments, usually mutual funds. While variable policies offer the possibility of higher returns, the account can lose money as well, and your beneficiaries could receive a lower payout than what you expected (depending on the terms of the policy).	Premiums are a fixed amount.
Universal life	Cash account generally earns a money market rate of interest. This rate may be higher than what a whole life policy would pay.	It's possible to alter the amount paid in premiums. However, paying lower premiums may deplete the cash account.
Variable universal life	Combines the features of both variable and universal. Like variable life, the cash account is invested in market based investments, usually mutual funds, and is subject to the above-mentioned risks of variable life.	Like universal life, it is possible to alter the amount paid in premiums.

Loans on Cash Value Policies

Even though it may be possible to take a loan from the cash value which has accumulated in a policy, there are consequences for doing so.[57]

- If you die with a loan outstanding on your policy, the loan amount will be subtracted, with interest, from the amount your beneficiaries would otherwise have received.

- When you repay a loan against your policy, you must also pay the interest. That's because when you took the money out of your policy, it stopped earning a return. When you pay the interest on your loan, you're replacing the earnings that would otherwise have accrued if you'd left the money alone.

- If you surrender your policy (turn the policy back in to the company before you die) or let the policy lapse (stop paying premiums) and you have a loan outstanding, the loan is then considered taxable income by the IRS (the portion that is due to gains in the policy is taxable, but generally not your return of premiums paid).

  This feature can be a real kick in the pants. Say you have a financial need, such as having lost your job. You take a loan from the cash value of your policy, spend the money, and then have to let your policy lapse because you can't pay your premiums. It's a good bet that some of the loan amount may have to be listed as income on your tax return, and it may be difficult for you to pay the extra taxes due. Cash value is allowed to grow tax free

---

[57] Bankrate discusses taking a loan against a life insurance policy in its article, "Are Life Insurance Loans a Bad Idea?" www.bankrate.com/finance/insurance/are-life-insurance-loans-a-bad-idea-1.aspx

while it's in the policy, but when it's removed permanently from the policy, the growth portion is then taxable. (Ask your agent about your policy's features.)

Letting a Policy Lapse

If you don't pay your insurance premium on time,[58] you have a short grace period, usually around 30 days, during which time you still have coverage. Once the grace period is over, then it depends on the policy. With term insurance, your coverage will likely be terminated once the grace period is over and you still haven't paid the premium due. With policies that build cash value, the insurance company typically uses the built up cash value until it's all gone to pay the premiums for you. How long you continue to have coverage depends on how much cash value you have built up.

What should you do if you wish to quit your policy? If your policy has built up any cash value, you probably want to get that money back out of the policy. To do so, you need to write the company. State that you wish to cancel your coverage effective immediately and ask that the cash value be sent to you. Otherwise, as stated previously, the company will drain the cash value dry using it to pay your premiums for you. Granted, that extends your death protection, but if you already have other coverage in place, then you should try to get your money back. Remember that any gain on the cash value refunded to you will be income taxable.

Which Type of Life Insurance is Right for You?

Financial planners tend to argue that if you purchase term insurance and invest the extra amount that would otherwise go into building cash value, you will end up with more money, and you will have easier access to it and greater control.

Insurance salespeople will counter with the argument that term insurance is *temporary* and akin to renting a house, while whole life (or other insurance that builds cash value) is *permanent* and like *buying* a house because you are building a store of value. Like the name implies, whole life insurance is designed to provide coverage for your whole life (or from the date of purchase forward), while term is good for only the given period.

Each type of insurance has its merits, but unfortunately any given type of insurance may be sold to someone for whom it's not the optimal choice. One size does not fit all, and different products are more appropriate for some people than for others. Rarely is the general condemnation of an entire category a fair assessment. But before we discuss the appropriateness of the various products, let's first examine the vested interests of the parties giving advice.

As a consumer, always ask yourself who profits by your decisions.
If you are purchasing insurance, insurance agents have a monetary incentive to try to sell you the product that makes them the most money. Term insurance usually offers the agent

[58] The Insurance Information Institute discusses the topic, "If I can't pay my premium, what should I do?" www.iii.org/articles/if-cant-pay-premium-what-should-i-do.html

96

a much lower commission than do other types of life insurance. With permanent insurance, however, agents frequently receive both upfront commissions at the time of the sale and trailing commissions for a number of years afterward. But bear in mind that a commission structure does not make an agent unethical—people make themselves ethical or unethical, and almost no one is immune from having to deal with conflicts of interest, as we shall soon see.

Now think about how financial planners stand to profit by your decisions. If planners make commissions off the products they sell to you, whether its investments or insurance, they, too, have a monetary incentive to try to sell you the product that makes them the most money. Fee-only financial planners, however, don't earn commissions. Instead, they typically make their money by taking a percentage of their clients' assets that they manage. For example, if you have $500,000 of assets managed by a fee-only planner who charges 1% annually, you're paying her $5,000 per year to manage your assets. Her pay goes up or down, depending on how she manages your assets.

This fee-only structure is designed to minimize conflicts of interest, but be aware that it does not eliminate them. The fee-only planner has a monetary incentive for you to buy term insurance and invest the money that would otherwise go to the cash value of a permanent policy. The term insurance premium is relatively inexpensive, which takes only a small amount out from under her management, and investing the difference with her keeps more money under her management. If instead you purchased an expensive whole life policy, a steady flow of your money would be going out from under her management every time you pay your premiums. And remember that her fees are based on the value of your assets under her management.

The topic of insurance can make for very opinionated discussions, and you will read articles that issue blanket condemnations of certain products or hear people express very polarized views. As with any financial decision, you need to gather as much accurate information as possible, examine your particular situation, find agents or advisors who are ethical and trustworthy, and then make a decision based on what is in your and your loved ones' best interests.

So let's examine for whom the various types of life insurance are appropriate, beginning with one of the most important needs, that of young families.

Term Insurance

For young families with a high need and a low budget
Term insurance can be particularly beneficial for young families. For a newborn to become grown and financially independent usually takes about 22-25 years. During the time that parents are raising their children, one of them may choose to stay home to care for the family. If the breadwinner were to pass away, the one who has stayed home may need to go back to school or be retrained for a job that pays enough for him or her to support the family alone. Even if both parents work while raising their family, one parent's salary alone may not be sufficient if the other were to pass away. For those who are raising children alone, an adequate amount of life insurance is doubly important.

Bottom line, people with young children need a lot of death protection for a number of years, and they don't usually have a lot of money. Budgets tend to be tight because of the demands of raising a family and because young people are still developing their careers. Fortunately, term insurance is usually inexpensive for fairly healthy young people, and it offers a great way for young families to afford the large amount of protection they need.

For disciplined savers

Term life insurance is also appropriate for people of various walks in life who have the self-discipline and financial savvy to regularly invest on their own. For such people, indeed, they can probably do better by buying term and investing the difference.

Cash Value Life Insurance

For those who have difficulty saving

Life insurance which builds cash value is appropriate for people who have difficulty sticking to a savings or investing plan. The cash value component offers a forced savings plan for such people, and while it may not be the optimal way to save, it's better than nothing.

For those who are risk averse

Cash value life insurance may also be an option for those who are so risk averse that they would prefer the guaranteed rate offered by whole life insurance or the money market rate offered by universal life insurance rather than invest on their own.

For those in higher tax brackets

While the rates of return offered by these type policies are low compared to other returns available at the time, cash value is allowed to build up inside a policy tax free. This makes a low return much more attractive, particularly for those in the higher marginal income tax brackets. The example which follows illustrates this point.

Say that your whole life policy offers a guaranteed 5% rate of return on your cash value and that your marginal tax rate is 25%. In order to determine if this 5% rate of return is acceptable or not, ask yourself this question — *what rate would I have to earn on a regular taxable account so that I would have 5% left after paying taxes?* In this case, it would be 6.67%. (The math is presented in the footnote.)[59]

---

[59] You would have to earn a higher rate of return, X, such that after you subtract 25% of X you are left with a 5% return. The equation would be:

$$X - 0.25X = 5\%$$

To solve the equation, you would then have 0.75X = 5%. Dividing both sides of the equation by 0.75 gives you X = 6.67%. This means you would have to earn 6.67 on a taxable investment in order to be left with a 5% return after paying income taxes at the marginal rate of 25%. If you live in a state with a state income tax which taxes your investments, or if your marginal tax rate is greater than our example, or both, then you would have to earn an even higher return to be left with a 5% return. How high? If you let T equal your cumulative tax rate (use the decimal form), you would plug it into this equation:

$$X(1 - T) = 5\%$$

The following table shows the before-tax return needed in order to be left with a given after-tax return under various tax rate scenarios.[60]

Table 8-B: Finding the before-tax returns needed in order to be left with a given after-tax return.

After-tax Return	Cumulative Tax Rate (federal + state + local):							
	15%	20%	25%	30%	35%	40%	45%	50%
3%	3.53%	3.75%	4.00%	4.29%	4.62%	5.00%	5.45%	6.00%
4%	4.71%	5.00%	5.33%	5.71%	6.15%	6.67%	7.27%	8.00%
5%	5.88%	6.25%	6.67%	7.14%	7.69%	8.33%	9.09%	10.00%
6%	7.06%	7.50%	8.00%	8.57%	9.23%	10.00%	10.91%	12.00%
7%	8.24%	8.75%	9.33%	10.00%	10.77%	11.67%	12.73%	14.00%

As the table shows, *the higher your cumulative tax rate, the increasingly more attractive a low rate of return on which you do not have to pay taxes becomes.* The U.S. federal income tax structure is progressive, which means the more you make, the progressively higher the rate at which you're taxed. And don't forget the concept of risk and return — to get a higher rate of return, you will likely have to take a greater risk. So for those who lose half (or 50%) of their investment return to taxes (federal plus state plus local), they would have to take on greater risk and earn 10% in order to be left with the same 5% return that could have been had with less risk within an insurance policy.

Of course, if you surrender your policy before death and take the money out, you will pay taxes on the gain portion. However, if your policy stays in effect until death, the tax shield means the dollars you paid in premiums have more earning power inside the policy than they would have had in an investment of similar risk outside the policy. Also, upon your death, the proceeds received by your beneficiaries are generally not income taxable for them (although estate taxes may apply). For these reasons and more, life insurance may be used as an estate planning tool.[61]

For those at greater risk of bankruptcy or litigation

Another plus for cash value life insurance is the fact that historically, the courts have left this asset alone. When people have filed bankruptcy or had legal judgments against them, life insurance policies, at least in the past, have been largely off limits. So if you're in a profession where you're more likely to get sued or have a greater chance of facing bankruptcy or litigation, life insurance which builds cash value may provide you a way to shelter more of your assets. Bear in mind, however, there are no future guarantees as to what the courts will do or what future laws may be passed.

---

[60] This table shows the point of indifference. For example, those in the 25% marginal income tax bracket would be indifferent between earning 5.33% on a taxable investment and 4% on a tax-free investment because they would end up with the same after-tax return either way. The return on a taxable investment must be greater than 5.33% in order to be more attractive than a 4% tax-free return.

[61] Refer to IRS Publication 525: Taxable and Nontaxable Income, for more information on taxes on life insurance proceeds. www.irs.gov/pub/irs-pdf/p525.pdf

For those who have existing cash value policies

If you already have an existing policy which builds cash value and wish to replace it, be extra cautious. Before you terminate any existing policy, get the new policy fully in place first so that you will have no coverage gap. Disaster seems to strike at the most inopportune times.

Also, be sure to find out how much cash value has already built up in your existing policy. If you have had your policy for several years, it could be that you are further along in the schedule of how cash value builds in your particular policy. A significant portion of each premium could now be going toward the savings component. From this point forward, your existing policy may offer a decent means of saving.

Finally, if you already have a policy which builds cash value and have since developed a medical condition, be extra cautious about canceling your existing policy. Obtaining new coverage may be difficult, expensive, or maybe impossible. Keeping what you have may be your best or only viable option. Even if you can get group term insurance at work, consider the fact that jobs come and go, and usually the insurance goes away with them. If you cancel your cash value policy and then lose your job, you could find yourself unable to get more insurance of any type.

Concluding Thoughts on Life Insurance

Particularly with life insurance, the generalities often presented may not be applicable to you or your loved ones. You need to find what will be the best fit for you and your given situation. You may wish to consult an insurance or financial planning professional whom you can trust to act in your best interest. Be aware of any conflicts of interest that could play a part in their advice. Also, their training and knowledge may be limited to their own products and experiences. *Never ever feel obligated toward a salesperson or consultant, no matter how personal the relationship. Your loyalty is to yourself and your loved ones.*

Life insurance helps protect the people you love and care about by putting money in place should you not be around to provide for them yourself. Other types of insurance may also be needed to protect your wealth and well-being. Chapter 9 addresses health, disability and long-term care insurance, while Chapter 10 discusses property insurance.

30 Minute LIVING

Suggested Action Plan

- *Examine your life insurance needs.* Who depends on your income? How many years would they need for your income to be replaced? What other things need to be considered?

  Think about a spouse who may need to go back to school for additional skills or training, children who need to be supported through college, special needs children who may need to be supported for the rest of their lives, parents or other elderly dependents. What debts would you like to pay off, or what special gifts would you like to make?

Who or what needs to be considered?	How long?	Estimated amount
Total life insurance needed		

- *Examine your existing life insurance policies.* Whose life is the policy written on? What is the face amount? What type of policy is it (term, whole life, universal, etc.)? If it's something other than term, how does it build cash value and how much has built up to date? Who are the beneficiaries? Have any loans been taken against the policy?

Whose life?	Face amount	Type policy	Cash value (if any)	Any loans?	Beneficiaries

- *Compare your needs with the policies you already have.* Considering your budget and the options you have (perhaps you have access to inexpensive group insurance at work or through your profession) or don't have (perhaps you have a medical condition that makes obtaining insurance difficult), research and implement what would be best for you and your loved ones.

- *Give your loved ones a list of all your policies and state where they're located.* After all, if they need the payout due to your death, you won't be around to tell them where the policies are.

CHAPTER 9

Insuring Your Health

Protecting your Greatest Asset

A young woman raised her hand when the class discussion turned to health insurance. Many college students have had limited experience dealing with such issues, but this woman was married and a little older than the rest of the class. The room fell into total silence as she related her story.

Her husband had changed jobs and was in the process of obtaining health insurance with his new employer. His old employer had offered him COBRA, the option for him to continue with that company's health insurance, but he had declined. He felt the premiums were too expensive, as he would have had to pay the entire amount of the premiums himself.

During this interim period, his car was hit by a train. Modern medical advances saved his life, but he was left a paraplegic. The young woman was forced to quit her job as well in order to care for him. Because of the astronomical medical bills and no income, the young couple lost their home along with almost everything else.

Fortunately, they had been able to move in with his parents, but the situation was less than ideal. The parents were already caring for his sister who had been permanently injured in an accident and had no insurance. The hospital had written off their bills, but in return the couple had signed an agreement that if they came into money in the future, a certain amount would go to the hospital.

As she finished her story, I asked her—in looking back, now how expensive did the COBRA payments seem? She said they would be nothing, just a drop in the bucket, in comparison to what it had cost them to be without health insurance.

Your health and your ability to work are truly your greatest assets. Having adequate insurance helps you to pay for the cost of maintaining, restoring, rehabilitating and caring for your physical body and mental health during your working years as well as beyond when you're no longer able to work.

This chapter will discuss the three main forms:

- Health Insurance
- Disability Insurance
- Long-term Care Insurance

Health Insurance

Health insurance helps pay for medical expenses. The portion of your expenses and the various types of expenses covered will depend upon the terms of the policy offered by your insurance company. Many people do not have adequate coverage due to the high cost of premiums. Recent legislation has sought to provide health insurance for more Americans, but the actual impact of this new law is still uncertain.[62]

Health Insurance Terminology

In any field of study, it's important to understand the terminology. Insurance in particular seems to have a language all its own. So before addressing the various features of health insurance, let's take a look at what the words mean.[63]

Deductible—the amount you must first pay out of pocket before the insurance company will pay anything. If your policy has a $100 annual deductible, then you must pay the first $100 of qualified expenses which occur that year before the insurance company will pay anything.

Co-insurance or Participation—after you've met your deductible, the insurance company will probably not pay 100% of the rest of your allowable expenses for the year. You may have to pay a portion, or "participate." (Hint: The "co" in co-insurance or co-payment means you have to pay something.)

As an example, say that your insurance company requires you to pay 20% while it pays 80%, and you have a $500 eligible expense with a $100 annual deductible. If this is your first expense of the year, then you must pay the first $100. The remaining $400 is split—80% or $320 for the insurance company, and 20% or $80 for you. Your total out of pocket in this example would be your deductible plus your co-insurance portion, or $100 + $80 = $180. On the other hand, if you had already met your deductible from a previous qualified medical expense this year, then you would have to pay only 20% of the $500 expense, or $100 ($500 x 0.20).

Co-payment—when you go see the doctor or purchase a prescription medication, you may have a co-payment, or more simply stated, a co-pay. A yearly deductible may or may not apply for doctor visits, depending on your company. You may have, for example, a $25 co-pay every time you see your family physician, while the co-pay may be $50 or $100 every time you see a specialist. Prescriptions frequently have two or three levels of co-payments, with generic drugs usually having the lowest co-pay and brand names being higher.

Waiver of Co-insurance—in certain instances, the insurance company will waive or not require you to pay the part you would normally have to pay. For example, your company may waive your co-pay on a physical exam once a year. In such cases, the insurance company

---

[62] America's Health Insurance Plans, or AHIP, is a national trade association for health insurers which also provides useful consumer information at its Web site. www.ahip.org.
[63] This information is general in nature. Different companies may state things differently or use other terminology. Be sure to consult your own company for the specifics of your policy.

is willing to pay 100%. That's because discovering problems early can prevent or lessen the severity of illnesses or conditions that would otherwise cost the company much more if not discovered and treated until later.

Stop-loss Provision or Out-of-pocket Maximum—perhaps you need surgery that costs $50,000. If you have to pay co-insurance of 20%, that's $10,000 out of pocket—a hefty chunk of change. Some health insurance policies have a stop-loss provision to put a limit on your annual out of pocket expenses. So if your policy has a $5,000 stop-loss provision, then your out-of-pocket is capped for the year, and the insurance company pays 100% of the amount that's over $5,000. Unfortunately, not all policies have this provision.

Lifetime Maximum— the Affordable Care Act now prohibits health plans from placing a lifetime dollar limit on many of the benefits you receive. However, limits can still be imposed on services that are not considered "essential." Once your company has paid out the lifetime maximum amount, it will no longer pay on these non-essential services.[64]

Types of Health Insurance

Health insurance is of two basic types: traditional indemnity, also called fee-for-service, and managed care plans.[65]

Traditional Indemnity Health Insurance

This type health insurance typically offers the most freedom of choice to the insured, but it usually costs more than managed care plans. With this type insurance, you generally can use any doctor and hospital which accepts your insurance, and you do not have to get a referral to see a specialist. In some instances, however, you may have to pay out of pocket first and then apply for reimbursement.

This is the way it typically works with traditional indemnity health insurance: you pay the first amount of expenses each year (the deductible) out of pocket. Then if you incur further expenses, the insurance company splits those costs with you. Typical splits include 80–20, 75–25, and 70–30, with the company paying the higher percentage and you paying the lower. Also, if you choose to go to a doctor not on the network list, many companies pay less, say a split of 60–40 or even 50–50. Better plans also feature an out-of-pocket yearly maximum or stop-loss limit.

The table which follows illustrates the cost structure for a policy which features a yearly $500 deductible, pays 80% of eligible expenses beyond the deductible, and caps the yearly out-of-pocket maximum at $5,000. In this example, you rack up $25,000 in medical expenses for the year.

---

[64] Refer to www.healthcare.gov for information on the Affordable Care Act. Pull up this page to learn about Lifetime & Annual Limits. www.healthcare.gov/law/features/costs/limits/index.html

[65] Companies may use different terminology and provide many variations of features. It's important to learn the specifics of your policy.

Table 9-A: Example of the cost structure in a traditional indemnity plan

Deductible $500—you pay this entire amount.	
Insurance Company—80% [For the next $22,500 in expenses, the insurance company pays 80% and you pay 20%.] $22,500 x 0.80 = $18,000	You—20% $22,500 x 0.20 = $4,500
The insurance company pays 100% of the last $2,000 in expenses.	
Totals paid during the year: Insurance Company: $18,000 + $2,000 = $20,000	You: $500 + $4,500 = $5,000

Of course, not all policies have a yearly out-of-pocket maximum. And even though the insurance companies pay a great deal of the cost, they may not be paying as much as it would appear. That's because big insurance companies have bargaining power while individuals typically do not. It's likely the insurance company may have received a fairly substantial discount on the portion it paid—the cut-rate warehouse price, if you will—while you paid the manufacturer's suggested retail price.

Managed Care Plans

There are quite a few variants of these type plans, all of which are usually more restrictive than traditional indemnity plans in your choice of doctors and hospitals. Here are some of the more widely known plans.[66]

Health Maintenance Organizations (HMOs)—these plans are typically the least expensive but also the most restrictive. If you don't use the doctors and hospitals on the approved list, you'll pay for the entire cost yourself. Your primary care physician must give you a referral to a specialist, and you must get approval to go to the hospital. These plans are usually available only as group medical plans through your employer.

Point-of-Service (POSs)—these plans are not quite as restrictive in that you usually have more doctors and hospitals to choose among. But you must still have a primary care physician who acts as the gatekeeper and through whom you must obtain a referral before you can see a specialist.

Preferred Provider Organization (PPOs)—these plans feature a network of doctors and hospitals for you to choose among. And while you can see someone outside the network, the PPO will not pay as much of the cost as it would if you chose a doctor or hospital within the network. Of all the managed care plans, these plans typically offer the greatest number of choices in doctors and hospitals and also the greatest amount of freedom in seeing specialists within the network.

---

[66] MedHealthInsurance provides more information on various types of health insurance plans. www.medhealthinsurance.com/plans.htm

Disability Insurance

Depending on your gender and the risk involved in performing your occupation, you are much more likely to be disabled for a period of time during your working career than you are to die.[67]

Disability insurance kicks in and pays a portion of your income when you are unable to work due to an injury or illness.[68] While most people understand the importance of life insurance, many simply have not considered what they or their families would do in the event that the main breadwinner could no longer work. Many workers have either inadequate disability insurance or none at all. Important features of disability insurance include the following:

Type of Coverage — one of the most important distinctions to understand about disability insurance policies is that of *own occupation versus any occupation.*[69]

- With *own occupation* coverage, you are considered disabled if, because of illness or injury, you are unable to perform the material duties of your occupation. (Your occupation is the one you are engaged in at the time of your disability.)

- With *any occupation* coverage, you must be unable to work in any occupation for which you are reasonably suited by your education, training or experience. Some policies combine these coverages, with own occupation applying for the first few years and any occupation coverage thereafter.

The higher your income, the more advantageous own occupation coverage becomes!

Let's say you're a surgeon who happened to cut your hand badly while doing a wood working project in your free time. Even though your fingers were all reattached, you never regained the dexterity needed to do surgery. You can still do many things with your hand, however, such as pecking at a computer keyboard to enter data while performing an administrative job that pays only a fraction of what you earned as a surgeon. It's likely that own occupation coverage would begin paying disability payments in this instance, while any occupation coverage probably would not.

Many policies provide for both types of coverage in what may be called split definition coverage. For a time period immediately following the disabling accident or illness, perhaps for two years, you receive payments under the own occupation definition. After the stipulated time period, you will then have to qualify under the any occupation definition to continue receiving payments.

---

[67] For statistics and information on worker injuries, illnesses and fatalities, visit the Web site of the Bureau of Labor Statistics. www.bls.gov/iif/home.htm#tables

[68] Find the "Guide to Disability Income Insurance" and "An Employer's Guide to Disability Income Insurance" on this AHIP page. www.ahipcoverage.com/2012/05/07/disability-income-insurance-what-you-need-to-know/

[69] AXA Equitable provides this helpful article, "How Disability Income Insurance Policies Define Disability." www.axa-equitable.com/insurance/disability-income/how-policies-define-disability.html

Length of Coverage — concerning the length of time that benefits are paid, there are two basic types — short-term and long-term. Short-term disability starts shortly after your disability, but the benefits last for only about two to five years at most. Long-term disability may not start until you are many months into your disability, and the benefits may last until you reach age 65, or possibly for the remainder of your life.

Renewability of Coverage — another important feature of a disability income policy is whether it's cancelable, non-cancelable, or guaranteed renewable.

- A *cancelable* policy is not desirable, because it can be canceled at the insurance company's discretion.

- A ***non-cancelable*** policy is the best, because not only can the company not cancel your policy (provided you pay your premiums), but also your premiums will never increase.

- Because non-cancelable tends to be expensive, ***guaranteed renewable*** is very popular. With guaranteed renewable, your premiums can be increased, but only for an entire class of policyholders and not because of your individual circumstances.

Disability Insurance Terminology

Again, understanding the language used in disability insurance is vital to knowing what your policy will cover. If you wait until you're injured to find out, it'll be too late to do anything about it!

Disability Benefits — disability insurance typically pays only 50–80% of your monthly salary. (If you were paid 100%, you might not have an incentive to ever go back to work!)

Benefit Period — this is the length of time for which you can receive payments, once you are disabled and past the elimination period.

Elimination or Waiting Period — once you are disabled, this is the length of time you must wait until your benefit payments begin. With short-term policies, the waiting period is usually from zero to 14 days. With longer-term policies, the waiting period can vary quite a bit, from 30 days to two years. Some employers may offer, or you may purchase on your own, both short- and long-term disability policies, with the long-term starting up when the short-term stops.

> The longer the waiting period, the lower your premiums will be. Longer waiting periods decrease the time period the insurance company will have to make payments, should you ever be disabled. Also, longer waiting periods make it more likely the company will not have to pay at all, because by then you may have recovered or passed away.

Future Increase Option Rider — this feature can usually be added onto a disability policy and allows the participant to purchase additional amounts of coverage at various intervals in the future. This rider is especially important for younger workers who would hope to earn substantially more as they progress through their careers. It wouldn't be desirable to have disability benefits based on your "starter" pay for the rest of your working career.

Cost of Living Adjustment (COLA) Rider— once you are disabled, a COLA rider allows for your benefits to increase periodically in order to better keep pace with inflation. Without this rider, your benefits would remain the same for as long as you receive them. Again, the younger the participant, the more important this rider becomes.

Rider— by now you've probably deduced that a rider is a feature added to the basic policy. They're like when you buy a new car — you have to pay extra for anything that's not standard. Other riders available on disability policies include benefits for a partial disability, allowing you to still collect some amount of benefits if you are only partially disabled, as well as residual benefits if you go back to work but are unable to perform all of your normal responsibilities.

Other Disability Insurance

Social Security— even though Social Security provides for some amount of disability income to covered workers, don't count on qualifying for it. Social Security's definition of disability is probably the most restrictive there is. It's meant to be for long-term, total disability, not for short-term or partial disabilities.

> To be eligible, you must have a medically determinable physical or mental impairment that results in your inability to engage in any substantial gainful activity AND is expected to result in your death OR to last at least 12 months.[70]

In the unfortunate event that you are deemed eligible, your benefits won't start until the sixth month after the Social Security Administration determines that you're disabled, and then you won't receive a payment until the following month. So, for example, if Social Security determines that you were disabled in June, you won't receive a payment until the sixth month (December) has ended, or sometime in January.[71]

Worker's Compensation— many states require employers to provide worker's compensation. This coverage usually applies only to injuries or illnesses occurring while the worker is on the job. Unfortunately (or fortunately if you're the employer), only about 4% of all long-term disabilities are caused while on the job, meaning that about 96% of the illnesses and injuries which result in long-term disabilities occur off the job.[72]

To add further insult to injury, so to speak, is the issue of taxation of benefits. As a general guideline, if the premiums were paid with before-tax dollars, the benefits received will be taxable as income. This will be the case with employer sponsored benefits when the employer pays the premiums and receives a tax deduction for doing so. It will also be the case if you're paying your own premiums with before-tax dollars. So not only will you receive only a percentage of your salary, perhaps 50%–80%, but this amount will also be subject to income taxes. (Ditto for Social Security disability income benefits and even unemployment benefits — that is if your income is even high enough at this point to incur federal income taxes.)

---

[70] For more information on Social Security disability insurance, pull up the Disability Planner. www.ssa.gov/dibplan/dqualify4.htm

[71] To learn more about the payment of SS benefits, refer to: www.ssa.gov/dibplan/dapproval.htm

[72] These statistics and further information on disabilities and disability insurance are available in the AHIP consumer guide, "Guide to Disability Income Insurance," referenced earlier.

Add to this unsavory mix the fact that injuries and illnesses often mean high medical and health care costs that may not be covered entirely by health insurance. Your spouse, if you have one, may have to quit working or work fewer hours in order to help care for you. And even though medical expenses can be tax deductible, only the portion that's greater than 7.5% of your adjusted gross income counts, and that's only if you have enough total qualified deductions to file a Schedule A on your federal tax return.[73] It's no wonder that a serious injury or illness can ruin your finances in short order.

Long-Term Care Insurance

Long-term care insurance is typically associated with covering the cost of nursing home care. Better policies, however, also cover the cost of home health care, adult day care, assisted living and other services to help when those who are insured can no longer fully care for themselves.

As insurance goes, long-term care insurance is relatively new, and policy features along with the services covered are still evolving. Many companies that once sold long-term care policies no longer offer them. That's because many of the earlier policies were seriously underpriced, and the premiums the companies collected on them were inadequate to cover the costs of the care that the policies promised.

The cost of providing care can be quite high, depending on where you live and the type of care needed. These costs can quickly eat through a person's life savings. Health insurance typically does not pay for this type of ongoing long-term care, and Medicare pays only a very limited amount. Medicaid, which provides help to those with low incomes, currently pays for almost half of nursing home costs. However, in recent years, it has become much more difficult to qualify for Medicaid. [74, 75]

Long-Term Care Terminology

Yes, there's more! Terminology is key to understanding what your insurance policy covers and how to qualify for receiving benefits. It's also important that your loved ones know about the provisions of your policies, because they're likely to be the ones dealing with the insurance company. If you decline mentally or physically, you may not be able to handle your own matters. [76, 77]

Activities of Daily Living (ADLs)—these activities include bathing or showering, dressing, transferring (such as from the bed to a chair), eating, walking, and toileting. If you can no longer perform these activities alone, then some form of care is needed. Long-

---

[73] Refer to the section, Tax Deductibility of Debt, presented in Chapter 7: Understanding Your Debt, for a more in-depth discussion on how tax deductions work. Unfortunately, only a small percentage of taxpayers are ever able to deduct any of their medical expenses.

[74] For various options in paying for nursing home care, pull up this Medicare page: www.medicare.gov/nursing/payment.asp

[75] Medicaid is funded by both the federal and state governments, but is administered at the state level. To learn more about the general provisions, pull up this site and click on "ElderLaw101." Also at this site, select your state to find more state-specific information. www.elderlawanswers.com

term care insurance policies will typically start paying for care when the policyholder needs assistance with two or more of these activities, or if they have cognitive impairment due to senile dementia or Alzheimer's disease.

Types of Care—facilities can provide several levels of care.

- Someone who needs *custodial care* needs help with the activities of daily living, such as bathing, but doesn't need specialized services or nursing care.

- Someone who needs *skilled care* requires nursing and/or rehabilitative care. They need to be cared for either directly by skilled personnel, such as nurses and therapists, or their care givers may need to be under the supervision of skilled personnel.

- Those who need *intermediate care* occasionally need skilled care, but not on a daily basis.

Elimination or Deductible Period—this is how long you must pay out of pocket for your care, once you enter the nursing home or otherwise become qualified to receive benefits under your long-term care policy. The elimination period usually ranges from zero to 180 days. The longer the elimination period, the lower your premiums will be.

Currently, Medicare benefits include some amount of payment for 100 days of nursing home care following a three-day qualified hospitalization.[78] Many people choose a long-term care policy with an elimination period of about the same length (90-100 days) so that the policy takes up where Medicare leaves off. However, there are no assurances that Medicare regulations will remain unchanged through the years.

Duration of Benefits—some policies will pay benefits until a certain dollar amount is reached, while others will pay for a maximum number of days or for lifetime coverage. The same policy may also pay different amounts, depending on whether the care is given at home, in an assisted living facility or in a nursing home. Some will even have a reset feature. This is particularly helpful when, for example, someone breaks a bone and rehabilitates in the nursing home but is able to go home later. The benefits time clock resets back to the beginning if they no longer need policy benefits for at least a certain period of time.

Pre-existing Conditions and Exclusions—pre-existing conditions are health problems you already have when you purchase the policy. Some policies may not cover your long-term care needs due to your pre-existing condition for a period of time, maybe up to six months, after you obtain the policy. Many policies do not cover long-term care needs that are due to certain mental or nervous disorders, alcoholism, drug abuse, or intentionally self-inflicted injuries, nor are they likely to cover what is paid for by government services. (Note that cognitive impairment due to senile dementia or Alzheimer's disease *is* covered.)

---

[76] Find AHIP's consumer guide, "Guide to Long-Term Care Insurance" along with other long-term care topics on this page. www.ahip.org/Issues/Long-Term-Care-Insurance.aspx

[77] The U.S. Department of Health and Human Services provides an extensive glossary of terms associated with aging, disability, and long-term care. aspe.hhs.gov/daltcp/diction.shtml

[78] For more about Medicare's coverage of long-term care, pull up the handbook, "Medicare & You." www.medicare.gov/Publications/Pubs/pdf/10050.pdf

Inflation Rider—costs typically increase through time. If you purchase a policy that provides a fixed dollar amount of coverage, that coverage may be largely inadequate by the time you actually need care. For example, a policy purchased 15 years ago that provides $40-per-day coverage won't go far towards covering costs today that may average about $120-180 per day. And in another 15 years, it'll cover even less.

Policies which have an inflation rider allow for the coverage to increase through time, but they vary in how you pay for these increases. With some, the original premiums are priced to allow for inflation (making them more expensive to start with), but with other policies you are given the option to purchase additional coverage at certain times in the future.

Considerations in Purchasing Long-Term Care Insurance

Numerous issues need to be considered before purchasing long-term care insurance.

Who should purchase long-term care insurance?

If you have assets you want to preserve for your loved ones and you can afford the premiums, then you would probably want to consider long-term care insurance. Otherwise, you will have to use up most of your money before you would be eligible for Medicaid.

On the other hand, people with fewer assets and who live on a more restricted budget, particularly those on assistance programs, would probably become eligible for Medicaid rather quickly. A policy is not likely to be advisable in such cases.

People of limited means who want to be responsible for themselves and not depend on their family may purchase a policy they can afford to pay for as long as they are working. However, after retirement, not only does their income go down, but the premiums get more expensive if they purchase inflation riders periodically. If they don't purchase the riders, the dollar amount of coverage becomes less significant.

For example, an elderly friend purchased a $40-per-day policy when she was in her 60s and still working. Once she quit working, she felt like she couldn't afford the additional premium needed to increase her coverage, so she left it at $40 per day. Now that she's in her 80s and nursing home care is at least $140 per day and rising, the amount her policy will cover becomes less and less significant. However, she doesn't want to drop her policy because now she's more likely to need the coverage with each passing day.

You need to purchase long-term care insurance while the premiums are still affordable for you.

Like other forms of insurance, the premiums are based on how likely the company thinks it will be that they'll have to pay the benefits. The older you are when you purchase a policy, the more likely you will need long-term care and the higher the premiums. Most companies will not write a policy on those who are 80 or older.

Tax considerations

Premiums on long-term care insurance are eligible to be tax deductible as medical expenses on your tax return. However, as referenced earlier in this chapter, few taxpayers ever benefit from this deduction. Only the portion of your medical expenses that is greater than 7.5% of your adjusted gross income counts, and that's only if you have enough total qualified deductions to file a Schedule A on your federal tax return.[79]

So, for example, if you have $50,000 in adjusted gross income, your qualified medical expenses would have to be greater than $3,750. Only what's over that would go toward your itemized deductions on your Schedule A. Further, the IRS limits the dollar amount, depending on your age, of your long-term care premiums that can even be included in this deduction.[80]

But there's more to the tax story. The good thing is, benefits that you may receive from your long-term care policy are not taxable as income.[81] Also, employers and the self-employed may be able to deduct the premiums paid on long-term care insurance as a business expense.[82] Definitely you would need to consult with your tax professional concerning your particular situation.

Consumer protection considerations

With long-term care insurance, there is a 30-day "free look" period in which you can change your mind in purchasing the policy. This is designed to protect the elderly from high pressure sales. Also, if you fail to pay your premiums, the policy can be reinstated for up to five months later. This is particularly helpful when, for example, paying the bill gets lost in the shuffle due to illness or hospitalization, or due to cognitive impairment.

Finally, you would want to buy a policy from a large, reputable, well-funded company. It may be many years in the future before you need to use your policy, and you want the company to still be around when you need them. Chapter 10: Insuring Your Property, addresses, among other things, the topic of Choosing an Insurance Company.

Understanding insurance in general and the provisions of specific policies sometimes takes a great deal of effort. Insurance that deals with your physical bodies deserves special consideration, as it can directly impact your quality of life as well as help protect your ability to work and earn a living. It can be financially devastating to discover — after the fact — that your coverage was inadequate, and you may not be able to obtain the quality of care and rehabilitation needed to restore your body to the fullest extent possible.[83]

---

[79] Refer to the section, Tax Deductibility of Debt, presented in Chapter 7: Understanding Your Debt, for a more in-depth discussion on how tax deductions work.

[80] Refer to the IRS Publication 502: Medical and Dental Expenses, for more information on the tax deductibility of long-term care premiums. www.irs.gov/pub/irs-pdf/p502.pdf

[81] Refer to IRS Publication 525: Taxable and Nontaxable Income. www.irs.gov/pub/irs-pdf/p525.pdf

[82] Refer to IRS Publication 535: Business Expenses. www.irs.gov/pub/irs-pdf/p535.pdf

[83] As referenced earlier, www.elderlawanswers.com and www.ahip.org provide a great deal of information as well as numerous links to other helpful sites.

30 Minute LIVING

Suggested Action Plan

- *Inventory your medical, disability and long-term care policies.* Make a master list of your policies, using the table below if desired. Others in your family need to be able to find this information in the event you are incapacitated and they need to handle dealings with insurance companies. Also, if you lose your insurance card, you have the contact info handy to call for a replacement card. If you have individual policies, be sure and note where the policies are located.

Type policy	Who is covered?	Group Number, Policy Number, etc.	Company	Company contact info	Other info

- *Inventory your parents' or other loved ones' insurance policies.* If you help others with their personal business, you need access to the same information mentioned above. Because of privacy issues, if you wait until your loved one is incapacitated and then try to find out information from the insurance company, the company may not speak with you or may first require you to present a power of attorney.

- *Find local programs available for elders.* Pull up the Administration on Aging site at www.aoa.gov and search under "Elders and Families" for Local Programs.

- *Plan ahead.* If you haven't considered which doctor to call or which hospital to request in the event of an accident or illness, check your health plan's provisions now. You may need to ask friends and coworkers for references in order to make an informed choice. People who are generally healthy and rarely use medical services can be caught unaware as to what to do if they have an unexpected need.

CHAPTER 10

Insuring Your Property

Insurance Lesson from the Neighborhood

It was mid-December, and Texans in our part of the country still had their air conditioners going. The young couple across the street were both graduate students, and as soon as exams were over, they left to go visit family in California for three weeks. Shortly thereafter, a cold front arrived, bringing snow (a rarity in our part of the country) followed by several days of very wet, freezing weather. When things thawed out and started to dry up, another neighbor happened to notice water coming out around the foundation of the young couple's home. He shut off the water at the meter in their yard, and there the house sat.

When the couple returned, the damage to their home and furnishings totaled half of what they had paid for the home originally. Water pipes ran through the attic space of their home. When they froze and burst, the water, which had run for days, ruined all the ceilings and ran down through the walls. Almost every piece of drywall in the home had to be replaced. Many of the boards on their beautiful wood floors warped. Much of their furniture and other possessions had to be tossed. Workers were in their home daily for over three months.

How much did all this cost the young couple? The $100 deductible on their homeowner's insurance was it! Being clueless about insurance, when they bought the home, they simply decided to continue with the type coverage the previous owner had. That elderly gentleman, a retired banker, happened to be very financially savvy. His choice of replacement cost coverage proved invaluable to the young couple. The entire neighborhood witnessed its value as well. Personally, it's a term we had never heard before, and it's the coverage we've never been without since!

Property Insurance

While life, health, disability and long-term care insurance all deal with your physical body and well-being, property insurance covers your possessions. Types of property frequently covered by insurance policies include:[84]

- Automobiles
- Homes and possessions inside homes
- Motorcycles, boats, and other specialty items
- Commercial property

---

[84] Learn more about the basics of property insurance policies in this National Association of Insurance Commissioners' report, "Understanding Your Insurance Policy."
www.naic.org/documents/consumer_alert_understanding_your_ins_policy.htm

Liability

Not only can property be lost, stolen, damaged or destroyed, but also with property of all types comes the issue of *liability*—something that's not a factor in life and health insurance policies. Liability is a big issue with property, because people who come onto property that doesn't move (for example, your home) can get hurt, and property that does move (cars, boats, motorcycles, etc.) can cause damage and destruction to both the body and the property of other people. No wonder property insurance can be so expensive!

Regulation

This chapter covers various aspects of auto and homeowner's insurance, the two types most frequently held by consumers, as well as the topic of choosing an insurance company. Because insurance is *regulated at the state level*, information presented here will be general in nature. Your state's department of insurance will be the best source for information on specific policy requirements and on companies and agents who are licensed to do business in your state. Complaints are also filed with the state office. [85, 86]

Auto Insurance

For many of us, our introduction to the complexities of insurance began with an auto policy when we first got our driver's license. Due to the fact that teenage drivers are among the most expensive to insure, a new driver in the family causes more than a fair amount of concern in most households! A few tickets and fender benders later, family harmony becomes a thing of the past, with the household budget stretched to the breaking point from skyrocketing auto premiums. More than one teenager has been known to work in a fast food joint just to pay for auto insurance.

Liability Coverage

Most states have laws that require at least a minimum amount of liability coverage on vehicles, but these amounts will vary from state to state.[87] The limits are usually written as a series of three numbers.

To explain how this required coverage works, take as an example the Texas minimums of 30/60/25, and assume that this is the coverage your policy provides.

- The first number is the amount of liability coverage your policy would provide to any *one person* to whom you cause *bodily injury* with your auto—in this case, that would be $30,000. Note that this is the limit *per accident*, so if you have another accident, the same limits apply in the next accident as well.

- The second number is the *total amount* of liability coverage for bodily injury your policy would provide *per accident*. No matter how many people you injure in one accident, the total for all of them together that your insurance company would pay out for bodily injury would be $60,000.

---

[85] To find your state's insurance Web site, pull up this map made available by the National Association of Insurance Commissioners. www.naic.org/state_web_map.htm
[86] Search for complaint and financial information of companies at NAIC's Consumer Information Source. (Note the "s" on the https.) https://eapps.naic.org/cis
[87] For more information on auto insurance and to find the required minimum limits for your state, pull up info.insure.com/auto/minimum.html.

- The third number is the amount of coverage your policy would provide for *damage you cause to someone else's property*. In this example, that would be $25,000. Again, this is the limit *per accident*.

So let's say that as you were pulling into the Tiny Mart for gum and a soda, you got distracted. You put your foot on the accelerator instead of the brake, and your car crashed through the front window of the store. The injuries to the three people standing in line at the counter that you hit amounted to $12,000, $15,000 and $35,000, while the damage to the store totaled $30,000.

If you only have the Texas required minimum liability insurance of 30/60/25, the most these people could individually collect would be $12,000, $15,000, and $30,000. The person with $35,000 in injuries will not be fully covered. To make matters worse, all the bodily injuries together amounted to $62,000, but the insurance company will not pay out more than a total of $60,000 for bodily injuries in any one accident. One or more of these people will not be fully compensated. The most the store could collect for property damage would be $25,000, leaving $5,000 not covered. So this illustrations brings us to a very pertinent question—

What happens when the amount of damage caused is greater than the policy limits? *You are liable* for the damage you cause, regardless of whether you have purchased the required minimum level of insurance required by your state or not. It's likely the injured people and the owner of the store will try to collect the amount of damages not paid by your insurance company from you personally, possibly with a lawsuit. Frequently, the state required minimums are not nearly enough to cover all the damage caused by an accident.

Property Coverage on Your Vehicle

You are required to have liability coverage, which deals with the damage you cause other people—their bodily injuries and their property. To cover your own vehicle, you will need *comprehensive and collision coverage* on your auto policy as well. If you have a loan on the vehicle, your lender is likely to require you to carry this additional coverage in order to protect its investment. If you own your car outright, then it's up to you whether to carry this coverage or not.

- Typically, you'll have *deductibles*—maybe $50-100 on the comprehensive part, and $500-1,000 on the collision part. On each accident or claim that you make on your policy, you will have to pay this much out of pocket. When your company determines how much you should be reimbursed, this amount will be subtracted from what you would otherwise receive. If the amount of damage is equal to your deductible or less, then you pay out of pocket.

  Many people choose not to file an insurance claim on damages they can afford to pay for themselves for fear the insurance company will increase their future premiums or drop their coverage entirely. While different companies handle things differently, the more frequent your claims and the more extensive the damage, the more likely your premiums are to increase, particularly if you received a traffic citation for the accident or were arrested.

117

- *Collision* covers the damage to YOUR car when it collides with something, regardless of who is at fault. This is helpful when you're shuffling cars around in your driveway and back into another of your own vehicles, or you take a corner too fast and smash your fender on the guardrail.

  If the collision is another party's fault, their insurance is supposed to pay for the damage to your vehicle.[88] However, you may decide to file instead on your own policy if the other company doesn't respond as you feel they should. Then, after the claim is settled, it's likely your company will attempt to collect damages from the other insurance company or from that person in a process called *subrogation*.

- *Comprehensive* covers damages to your car from things other than collision. For example, your car is parked in your driveway and the neighbor's tree falls over, crushing the roof of your car. Because this type of damage is not nearly as likely to occur or to be as extensive as that resulting from a collision, the deductible for comprehensive is usually lower than that for collision.

"No-fault" Laws

In an effort to keep down insurance fraud and lawsuits, some states have enacted no-fault laws. Basically, this means that you are responsible for insuring your own body and property. So when there's an accident, your insurance pays to take care of you, your passengers and your property, while the other people's insurance takes care of them. This has worked better in some states than in others.

Uninsured/Underinsured Protection

This is coverage you can add to your own insurance policy in the event someone without insurance hits you, or if their policy's coverage is not enough for all the damage they do to you or your vehicle. Across the country, the odds are about one in seven that the driver who caused the accident will be uninsured,[89] with those odds being much higher in certain states.

If the person who hits you cannot afford insurance, they're not likely to have the money to pay for the damage they've caused, either. If they carry only the required minimum coverage, that amount may be insufficient. This coverage is usually quite affordable and typically includes damages from a hit-and-run driver or injuries you may sustain as a pedestrian.[90]

Personal Injury Protection (PIP)

Some states require personal injury protection. This covers medical expenses, lost wages and funeral expenses for you and your passengers who are injured in an accident. If you have adequate health insurance and disability insurance, you may want to purchase only the minimum amount, if it's required in your state.

---

[88] State laws vary quite a bit. If you're traveling and have an accident in another state, your insurance company will hopefully make allowances for differences in the laws of that state. In "no-fault" states you may be responsible for your own vehicle, regardless of whose fault it is.

[89] Find the percentage of uninsured drivers in your state. Scroll to the second page of this News Release from the Insurance Research Council entitled, "Recession Marked by Bump in Uninsured Motorists." www.insurance-research.org/sites/default/files/downloads/IRCUM2011_042111.pdf

[90] Refer to the article, "The benefits of uninsured/underinsured motorist coverage." www.insure.com/car-insurance/uninsured.html

Premiums on Auto Insurance

People often wonder where all their money goes if they don't have an accident. Chapter 8: Insuring Your Life, discusses one of the basic concepts of insurance, that of pooling. When you pay your auto premiums, you are essentially pooling your money together with the other people who have policies with your insurance company. The policyholders who have claims during a given time period get the money. The money doesn't accumulate on your behalf if you don't have a claim, because it's been used up by those who did have a claim. Next time period, you pay another premium and the cycle starts over.

How much you pay in premiums has to do with the participants in your pool and the level of risk you bring to the mix. Inexperienced or young drivers are typically riskier, as are people who clock a lot of miles on the road, just because they're out there so much. If you're in a pool with safer drivers who have few claims, your rates should be less than if you're in a high risk pool. Whatever pool you're in, the more claims you have and/or tickets you receive, the greater the risk you add to your pool. When you add more risk, your rates are likely to increase, or you may be moved into a higher risk pool where everybody has higher rates.

Of course, that's an oversimplification. How your company manages and invests the money it takes in and how much the company has in reserves to meet extraordinary claims, along with other factors, such as how expensive your car is to repair and the amount of damage your vehicle can cause to others, also affect your premiums. It doesn't hurt to shop around, because you may fit into one company's pool better than that of another company.

Remember that companies which advertise low rates may not really have low rates, at least not for you. Some companies are also more likely than others to cancel your insurance when you have a claim. When that happens, you're likely to be thrown into the dreaded high risk pool and may have to stay there for several years. Other companies often won't accept someone who's been canceled by another company within a given number of years.

What happens if you don't pay your premiums on time?

Insurance laws vary from state to state, but you will have a grace period, perhaps 10-30 days. You may want to have your payment automatically drafted from your bank account to avoid paying late, because you certainly don't want to risk having your insurance canceled.[91]

Homeowner's Insurance

Your home is typically one of your largest assets. Homeowner's insurance is designed to provide coverage for:[92]
- The home itself
- The contents of the home
- Other structures on the property
- Liability for protection from lawsuits
- Medical payments to others who may get injured on your property
- Loss of use when you're not able to stay in your home because of damage

---

[91] Visit the Car Insurance Learning Center for a wealth of information, including a Car Insurance Calculator and Car Insurance Definitions. www.carinsurance.com/LearningCenter.aspx

Not only do you want to protect your investment in your home, but if you have a mortgage, your *lender* also wants to make sure you have adequate insurance because that company's money is at stake as well. In fact, you'll likely be *required* to have homeowner's insurance as a condition for obtaining a mortgage in the first place.

Coverage on Homeowner's Insurance

Typically, the amount of coverage provided by the various parts of the homeowner's policy all hinge on the amount of coverage on the structure. As an example, let's assume your home is insured for $100,000.

1. The home itself is covered against damage from fire, hail, wind, lightning, and other disasters or perils. (Which perils are covered is very important, and we will discuss that in the types of policies that you can purchase.) Note that if your home costs more to replace than the amount of your policy ($100,000 in this example), your policy will *not* pay more than the amount you have insured. It's important to have a policy that increases over time as building costs go up, so that you will ideally have *replacement cost coverage*, or coverage sufficient to replace what you have lost with a like structure.[93]

Note that the ground on which your home is built is considered indestructible (sinkholes notwithstanding!) and therefore is not insured against loss. So the cost of your lot is not a factor in determining how much it would cost to replace your structure. Your insurance policy may need to be for more or less than what you paid for your home due to the fact that the land value is subtracted out. Also, you paid *market value* at the time you purchased your home, which may be significantly different than its *replacement cost*.

The amount for which you should insure your home becomes a real issue when the market value of the home is far less than its replacement cost. Someone who buys a large older home needs to check on insurance costs first, because the cost to adequately insure the property may be much higher than what he or she had budgeted. Some insurance companies have special policies for these type homes.

2. The contents of the home are typically insured for 40%-70% of the structure and include things like your furniture, clothes and other personal items. So if your home is insured for $100,000, then the most you could receive on the contents would be $40,000-70,000, depending on the terms of your policy.

If your home's contents are worth more than what your policy provides, then you might want to consider adding a *personal property endorsement, rider or floater* to cover the extra, particularly on things like jewelry, furs, silver, antiques or collectibles (stamps, baseball cards, etc.). In fact, most policies specifically limit coverage on these and a number of other items, including *electronics, firearms* and *cash*, so it's important to know *how much* and *which items* your policy will and will not cover.

[92] For more information on homeowner's and renter's insurance, visit the Web site of the Insurance Information Institute at: www.iii.org/individuals/HomeownersandRentersInsurance
The National Association of Insurance Commissioners presents a comprehensive "Consumer's Guide to Home Insurance." www.naic.org/documents/consumer_guide_home.pdf
[93] Replacement cost coverage and other features of homeowner's insurance are discussed in this Insure.com article, "Home insurance basics." www.insure.com/articles/homeinsurance/basics.html

Note that certain things typically are *not* covered in the contents. If you have a business at home, things associated with your business, like your computer or product inventory, are not covered under your homeowner's insurance. You're expected to have a business policy to cover your business items. Also, if you have renters, whether you rent out the whole house or just a room, your policy will not cover your renters' property. They are expected to have their own policy.

You definitely want to get *replacement cost coverage* on your contents as well as your structure, because as noted earlier, that is an amount sufficient to replace the item with another of like value (remember that your deductible will probably apply regardless of the type coverage you have).

Otherwise, you'll receive a depreciated value in the event you have a claim. Usually called *"actual cash value,"* this lesser-type coverage means you'll receive replacement cost *minus* depreciation since the time of purchase. Let's say your five-year old television was stolen. A new one of comparable value costs $1,000, but five years' worth of depreciation would be subtracted from that amount first, and then you'd get the difference. Considering that most policies have a deductible of $250, $500 or even higher, you'd probably get zero on your claim.

Documenting the contents of your home is a great idea. Take a video camera and slowly walk through the house, circling around in each room to capture the entire contents as well as architectural features. Speak while recording, making note of special items, for example—t*his Mega brand 42" plasma flat-panel HDTV was purchased in 2012 from Big Box Store for $800*—to create a "home documentary." Taking numerous still shots with a digital camera is also very helpful.

You can download the photos and video to your computer and save them in various ways, such as on a flash drive or CD which you can place in your bank safe deposit box or give to a good friend or relative. That way if your home burns down or your computer is stolen, you can still send photos to the insurance company as proof of what was lost. (By the way, saving treasured family photos in this way is also a good idea. When people are forced to evacuate their homes, they tend to grab pictures and photo albums because memories are so special.) It's also a good idea to scan important home ownership documents as well as the floor plans and pictures of the exterior of your home.

3. Other detached structures on your property are usually covered at 10% of your policy amount. So continuing with our example of a home insured for $100,000, detached structures such as a garage, gazebo or tool shed would be covered for a maximum of $10,000. Other structures on your property can also include fences, a swimming pool, maybe even trees and shrubbery. You would definitely have to read your policy to understand the specific things covered.

4. Liability protection of usually $100,000 or more is also provided by the standard homeowner's policy. This part covers other people, either their bodily injury or damage to their property, while they are on your property. It also covers the damage that you, your family or your pets cause to other people while on their property. Should there be a lawsuit, it covers the cost of defending you in court and damages awarded against you, up to the limits of your policy. In order to obtain greater liability coverage, you would also need to purchase an *umbrella* or *excess liability policy*.

5. Medical coverage for others — although individuals are expected to have their own health coverage, your homeowner's policy provides a small amount of medical coverage should someone be injured while on your property. The amount may be as low as $1,000 per claim, but it will help with minor accidents and injuries. Be aware that your policy will not cover medical bills for you, your family or your pets.

6. Loss of use — this portion of your homeowner's policy provides for your additional living expenses, such as hotel bills and restaurant meals, should you be unable to live in your home due to damage from fire or some other covered disaster. The amount of this coverage varies, depending on the policy and the insurance company. If your home is extensively damaged or destroyed, you may exhaust this portion of your policy's coverage long before you can live in your home again.

What's NOT Covered

Perils are bad things that can happen to cause a loss on your home. Depending on the type of homeowner's coverage you have (discussed in the following section), some policies will cover loss from more kinds of perils than will others. However, almost all homeowner's policies will *specifically exclude* covering damages that occur as a result of the following:[94]

- *Flooding* — insurance policies may cover water damage when the water comes from within the home (for example, the toilet overflows or a pipe bursts).[95] Rarely will your homeowner's insurance policy cover damage from water which comes into your home from the outside, which could occur from a natural disaster or something like a broken sprinkler head.

  Flood insurance must be purchased separately from the National Flood Insurance Program (NFIP).[96] The policy will not go into effect for 30 days, so you can't wait until a monster storm shows up on the weather channel to go buy coverage.

  Be aware that a small amount of water can do extensive damage and that approximately 30% of flood insurance claims occur in areas that are NOT deemed high risk. Also consider that new construction and development in an area can alter natural runoff patterns, particularly when large areas are paved. This prevents water absorption in the areas where the ground is now covered. Be sure to check out your address.[97]

---

[94] For more information, pull up, "A Homeowner's Guide to Natural Disasters." homeownersinsuranceguide.flash.org/knowyourchoices.htm

[95] Be sure to understand how water damage is covered on your policy. You may need an endorsement to cover water damage caused from sources within the home. The Insurance Education Group provides information on what's included in the different policy forms. www.insurance-education-group.com/home-policy-forms.html

[96] Although this program is offered through the Federal Emergency Management Agency (FEMA), your insurance agent may be able to help you obtain coverage. Learn more about the National Flood Insurance Program at: www.floodsmart.gov Check the risk of a specific address flooding by using the tool: One-Step Flood Risk Profile.

[97] Pull up FEMA's site to learn how to plan and prepare for disasters and flooding. www.fema.gov

- *War* — should your property be destroyed as the result of war in your area, it's likely that your homeowner's policy will not cover it. (As an aside, your other insurance policies, such as your life insurance or your auto insurance, are not likely to pay, either.) Although personal property that you take with you while traveling may norm ally be covered under your homeowner's or renter's policy, it will typically be excluded if you travel to a war zone. Military personnel may need to purchase special insurance.[98]

- *Other perils and property* — most homeowner's policies will exclude damages that result from earthquakes and nuclear radiation. For earthquakes, you may be able to add an earthquake endorsement to your existing policy or purchase a separate earthquake policy.[99] For radiation damage, the nuclear power plants are supposed to handle these claims.

  Also excluded will be coverage on your auto (maybe it's in the garage when the house burns down, but your auto policy should cover it), business property, your pets, and certain other specific items. Be sure and ask your agent about any exclusions or items that may have limited coverage (such as jewelry, coins and collectibles). As mentioned in #2 above, you may need to get a rider or floater in order to have adequate coverage on certain things.[100]

Types of Coverage

"All-risk" or "special form" policies provide greater coverage than do those with "named peril" or "broad form" coverage. With named peril coverage, or HO-1 policies, only damages that are the result of the specific events named in the policy are covered. These perils typically include fire, theft, and hail, among others. The broad form, or HO-2, covers more perils than does the named peril form, but again, the perils that are covered are specifically stated. Special form or open perils policies, HO-3 and HO-5, define what's covered a little differently. Realizing that it's almost impossible to name every contingency that could happen, these policies state what will NOT be covered. Their coverage, then, includes everything else.

Of the forms HO-3 and HO-5, the HO-5 provides more extensive coverage. While both forms cover your dwelling, or the structure, for all perils except those specifically named, they handle the contents differently. The HO-3 form covers the contents of your home only against certain named perils. The HO-5 is a full open perils policy and covers the contents of your home in the same manner as your dwelling.[101]

---

[98] For more information, pull up the Web page, "Insurance Issues for Military Personnel," presented by the National Association of Insurance Commissioners at: www.naic.org/consumer_military_insurance.htm
[99] Find out about "Earthquake Insurance Basics" at: www.insure.com/articles/homeinsurance/quake.html
The NAIC provides this comprehensive guide: www.naic.org/documents/consumer_guide_earthquake.pdf
[100] Read "Home Insurance Exclusions: What Your Policy Won't Cover" at:
www.insure.com/articles/homeinsurance/exclusions.html
[101] The Insurance Education Group, referenced earlier, provides an explanation of what the different policy forms cover. To learn more about various aspects of homeowner's, renter's and condo owner's coverage, click through the topics offered. www.insurance-education-group.com/standard-home-package.html

Water Damage—be aware that water damage is a special and important issue in homeowner's policies. There is a distinction between water that comes from within the home, such as a burst pipe, and water that comes from outside the home, such as flooding. You can pretty much assume that your policy will not include the latter. For that, you'll need flood insurance, as discussed previously.

To make sure your policy covers damage as a result of water that comes from within the home, you need to specifically address this issue with your insurance agent or company representative. A little water goes a long way, particularly if your home sits in it for a while. It's not just the flooring and furniture, but also the baseboards and drywall, and the ensuing mold and rot that can occur as well as possible damage to the foundation. Because of variances in state laws, you may need an endorsement added to your policy.

Renter's Insurance

Policies for renters, or HO-4 policies, are somewhat different from homeowner's insurance policies in that they do not cover the structure, only your property inside. While the landlord is responsible for insuring the building, his or her insurance will exclude the property inside that belongs to the renters.

These policies are usually very affordable and typically provide some amount of liability and medical coverage for people who may get hurt while visiting you. They will probably NOT, however, provide coverage for loss of use should the property be damaged and you have to temporarily move out.

Condo Owner's Insurance

Policies for condo owners, or HO-6 policies, are different from both homeowner's and renter's policies. Because of the shared ownership of the condo, the exterior and the interior are insured separately. Usually the condo owner pays association fees or dues which go toward caring for the shared aspects of the condo. The insurance on the exterior is typically one of the things the association pays for with these fees.

Coverage for the entire interior of a condo unit is the individual owner's responsibility. A condo owner's policy will include some amount of coverage on the dwelling, because the owner is responsible for certain parts of the structure, namely the interior walls, floors and ceilings. The policy will also cover the contents and provide for loss of use should the owner have to temporarily move out because of damage.[102]

Choosing an Insurance Company

Yes, you need to be able to afford your premiums, but selecting the insurance company which offers the lowest quote on a policy could be a major mistake! Unfortunately, you may not find that out until you have a loss, and then it's too late.

---

[102] This article, "The Basics of Renter's Insurance," provides helpful information for both renters and condo owners. www.insure.com/articles/homeinsurance/renters.html

Companies are not the same in:
- their *financial ability* to pay claims,
- their *willingness* to pay claims,
- the *amount* they are willing to pay on a claim, and
- the *timeliness* in which they act.

In short, you need a company that will come through for you in your time of need. The following are important factors to consider when choosing an insurance company.

Size of the Company

With any type of insurance, large companies have a distinct advantage due to the law of large numbers discussed in Chapter 8. The more houses (or cars or lives or whatever you're seeking insurance for) they have insured with a certain set of characteristics, the more likely the losses will be very close to the average or mean during any given time period. Less deviation from the average means greater predictability for the company.

Why is predictability important? The better a company can predict its losses, the more likely it is to have the money available for you or your beneficiaries when you have a loss. The less predictable a company's losses, it will either have to build up much more in reserves than it otherwise would need (by charging you higher premiums), or it will stand a greater likelihood of being financially devastated when unexpectedly large losses occur. You don't want an insurance company that runs out of money to pay its claims.[103]

Large companies are also more likely to have *diversity in their exposures*. That means they have insured people from different walks of life or property from all around the country rather than localized in one region. This lessens the likelihood that a significant percentage of whatever the company has insured will be affected at any one time if a disaster strikes in a certain area or affects a specific group of people.

Some would argue that because an insurance company of whatever size can purchase *reinsurance*,[104] the size of a company is irrelevant. Reinsurance means the insurance company buys an insurance policy on themselves, which helps reduce the risk of the insured insurance company. When extraordinary losses occur, their own insurance policy kicks in so they have a financial backup.

Reinsurance is a complex business that is evolving, with much of the reinsurance being provided by international companies. It is difficult to evaluate whether your company has sufficient reinsurance, on a continuing basis, and whether the reinsurance company they have chosen will have the financial ability to pay its claims. If you choose to go with a smaller insurance company, these are things you would probably want to research first.

---

[103] A.M. Best provides helpful information on understanding both the financial strength ratings (FSR) and the financial size categories (FSC) of insurance companies in this guide. www.ambest.com/ratings/guide.asp
[104] For more information on reinsurance:
www.iii.org/media/hottopics/insurance/reinsurance www.reinsurance.org

Financial Strength and Ability to Pay Claims

The financial strength of the insurance company should also be a primary consideration when choosing a policy. After all, an insurance policy amounts to a *promise* by the issuing company to pay you money should the events covered by the policy occur. If the company doesn't have the financial ability to make good on its promises and pay its claims, then you've simply wasted your money in paying the premiums. You may as well have thrown your money in the garbage.

Insurance companies are rated on their financial strength, and just like in school, the more A's, the better.[105] Several companies provide ratings, with A. M. Best being the oldest and probably the most frequently quoted.[106] The top rating that A. M. Best awards is A++. Standard and Poor's (S & P) is another frequently quoted source of insurance company ratings, with its top rating being AAA.[107]

When comparison shopping, the insurance companies you're considering should be able to provide you with their ratings. Generally, you would not want to choose an insurance company rated lower than a single A.

Your life, your health, your ability to work, and your property deserve careful consideration. They comprise your greatest assets. Make sure you are protected with the appropriate insurance in an adequate amount without being over-insured. You want just enough insurance so that you're not using up money that could better be invested and earn a return. Investments of various types will be discussed in the next four chapters.

---

[105] Find contact information for all five agencies which currently rate insurance companies at: www.insbuyer.com/insurancenrating.htm

[106] For an explanation of A. M. Best's ratings and the significance of each, pull up: www.ambest.com/ratings/about.asp Ratings on insurance companies are provided free at their Web site, but you must sign in.

[107] Learn more about S&P ratings: www.standardandpoors.com/ratings/insurance/en/us/

30 Minute LIVING

Suggested Action Plan

- *Examine your auto policy.* What are your coverage limits? Read through your policy, and if there are items you do not understand or need more information, contact your company or your agent.

- *Examine your homeowner's or renter's insurance policy.* Read through your policy to see the coverage and limits on your policy. If there are items you do not understand or need more information, contact your company or your agent.

- *Learn more.* Insure.com provides numerous articles on insurance, including, "15 things you didn't know your car and home insurance policies cover." The list of items that may possibly be covered include flat tires, your student's possessions in a dorm room and family grave markers. www.insure.com/car-insurance/you-did-not-know.html

- *Save money.* Find suggestions in this Insure.com article, "12 ways to save money on car insurance." www.insure.com/car-insurance/policy-save.html

- *Research your insurance companies.* Use the Interactive Tools presented by Insure.com to see how your insurance companies are rated, compare car insurance, find state-specific information and look up car safety ratings. www.insure.com/articles/interactivetools

Chapter 11

Understanding Your Retirement Accounts

Where Do You Want to Be?

While eating lunch one day in my husband's home town, we noticed a group of older people there in the restaurant. My mother-in-law walked over and started visiting, and as she introduced them to me, she pointed out that two of them had been my husband's grade school teachers. These ladies, retired for a number of years, had just returned from an extended tour of China. Come to find out, they regularly took trips of this nature.

In stark contrast to these ladies were several highly paid professionals who were also family friends from the same town. When we happened to run into them a short time later, my father-in-law commented that "Bill" would never be able to retire. Although he easily earned ten to twenty times more per year than what these teachers' salaries had ever been, he managed to keep himself heavily in debt. No matter how much he made, he and his family spent more. And because it was up to him to set money aside for his own retirement, there was never anything left.

Financial planners often observe this same phenomenon: people of fairly modest means who manage to live comfortably, both during their working years and in retirement, while people who earn and/or inherit many times more live mired in debt with little hope for financial stability in the future. Financial misery is more often the result of a mindset, rather than circumstances.

> Truly, *it's what you do* with however much is at your disposal that makes the difference. No matter how much money you make, you can always spend more.

One of the greatest reasons to save and invest is to be able to provide for your future, which seems to arrive faster than anticipated! By putting some thought now into what you want your future to look like and where you want to be, you'll be in the position later to call your own shots in life. Whether you desire to retire, start your own business, explore your interests, devote your time to a worthy cause, spend more time with family — whatever you aspire to, it will be your choice.

It's a sure bet that future retirees will need more personal savings, both in the form of tax-sheltered retirement accounts and in investments held in regular taxable accounts. A little planning now can make a lot of difference later on in life. This chapter examines some of the changes future retirees can expect and the various types of retirement accounts that are currently available, their features and how to utilize these accounts.

Why Retirement in America is Changing: Social Security & Medicare

Previous generations have depended heavily on Social Security and Medicare[108] to meet their retirement needs. In the very near future, it's likely these entitlement programs will have to change. The numbers simply won't work for the programs to remain as they are today. How these programs will change depends upon the actions taken by our elected government officials. However, because of the massive predicted costs, if these programs survive at all, some combination of the following is likely to occur:

- Limiting access to the programs by disallowing certain groups to participate, such as the "wealthy," or by reducing the benefits or by increasing the age at which participants become eligible for benefits.
- Raising taxes on younger generations.
- Increasing the costs for those who participate in the programs.
- Increasing the national deficit, saddling future generations with even more debt.
- Taking money away from other existing programs.

What all this means for those who are still working is that all the money you are paying in today in Social Security and Medicare taxes (on your paycheck, FICA means Federal Insurance Contributions Act, referring to the law which created Social Security) may provide only very limited future benefits for you. These programs will likely be insufficient to meet your needs.

Social Security

It's important to understand that Social Security was never designed to be a savings system; rather, it's a system which redistributes wealth. What you pay in today is NOT set aside in some account waiting for you with your name on it. The system was designed such that current workers pay the benefits of retired workers, so that what you pay in today may be going to your great-uncle Charlie.

This arrangement worked when the system was signed into effect by President Roosevelt in 1935. Back then there were about 20 workers for every one retired worker. Workers typically retired at age 65 and then generally lived only about 5–10 years in retirement before passing away.

America's demographics have changed dramatically since then. Now there are only about 3 workers per retired person, with that ratio projected to shrink to 2 workers per retiree by the time those who are now our youngest workers are ready to retire.[109] Couple these population changes with our increased life expectancies, and you can understand why the original design of the Social Security system does not fit our current circumstances. Americans today may live 30 years or more in retirement!

---

[108] To learn more about Social Security and Medicare, visit their sites: www.ssa.gov and www.medicare.gov.
[109] To learn more about how Social Security works, visit The Concise Encyclopedia of Economics. www.econlib.org/library/Enc/SocialSecurity.html

Medicare

Having access to quality medical care has played a big part in Americans being able to live longer lives. However, the cost of that care has risen dramatically in recent years. Medicare, the health insurance system for Americans age 65 and older, picks up much of the medical tab for retirees. Short of simply increasing the nation's spending on health care, several options exist for containing these costs:

- Reducing the prices on Medicare's reimbursements to health care providers.
- Limiting or rationing Medicare participants' use of health services.

Either of these options will erode the quality of health care to retirees. If they are not paid sufficiently, doctors, hospitals and other health care providers may choose to limit or possibly eliminate the services they offer to those on Medicare. If health care services are limited or rationed, the quality of life of Medicare participants will suffer and mortality rates will rise.

Retirees will likely have to bear more of the cost of quality health care out of pocket, either by purchasing private insurance, paying a greater portion of the cost or paying directly for services. Combine these increased health care costs with the uncertainties of Social Security, and it's easy to see that it will take proportionately more to retire comfortably in the future than it has in the past.

Why Retirement in America is Changing: Retirement Programs

Many companies have reduced or eliminated traditional pension plans in favor of savings-type programs. These savings programs, such as a 401k or 403b, *shift the burden of providing the needed funds for retirement to the participant*, rather than the company.[110]

- With a *pension plan*, an outcome is promised. How much the employee ends up with in retirement is determined by a formula, and the burden is on the employer to make sure the plan is funded sufficiently so that the promised outcome can be fulfilled. These plans tend to be more costly for employers.

- With a *savings plan*, there is no promised outcome. Depending on how the program is set up, the employer may or may not be required to contribute. Whatever you end up with in your account is what you will have to work with in retirement. Outcomes can vary widely, depending on how much money is contributed, how long the money has to grow after it's contributed and what investment choices are made during the time the money is in the account.

---

[110] Because money in retirement plans is tax-sheltered, the IRS determines how the various plans are to be set up and maintained. For more comprehensive information, refer to "Types of Retirement Plans" at www.irs.gov/retirement/sponsor/article/0,,id=155347,00.html and to "Help with Choosing a Retirement Plan" at www.irs.gov/Retirement-Plans/Help-with-Choosing-a-Retirement-Plan

Employer-Sponsored Retirement Programs

There are two basic types of employer-sponsored retirement programs: *defined benefit plans* and *defined contribution plans*. The table which follows highlights their features.

Table 11-A: Comparing the Features of Defined Benefit and Defined Contribution Plans

Plan Type	Defined Benefit (DB)	Defined Contribution (DC)
Examples of plans	Traditional pension-type plans where the retirement benefit is determined by a formula. There are no individual accounts.	401(k), 403(b), 457, Profit Sharing, Money Purchase, Payroll Deduction IRA, SEP, SIMPLE and others with individual accounts.
Who contributes?	Generally the employer, although some plans may allow or even require employee contributions.	Employer and/or employee, depending on the plan. In some plans, employers match employee contributions up to a certain limit and contribute only if the employee contributes. In others, employers contribute regardless of employee contributions, or they may not be required to contribute at all.
Who makes investment decisions?	Employer or plan administrator chosen by employer.	Employee. Investment choices are limited to those available within the specific plan.
Are loans allowed?	Possibly, depending upon how the plan is set up.	Possibly, depending upon how the plan is set up.
Benefits received upon retirement	Defined by a formula that could incorporate the participant's age at retirement, years of service, average pay during the final years of service or other specified factors. Participant may or may not receive the benefits until death.	Unknown. During employment, individual accounts are established for plan participants, and whatever the account balance grows to become at retirement is how much the participant has to work with in retirement.
Are benefits subject to taxes?	Yes. The exception would be on any contributions made with after-tax dollars.	Yes. The exception would be on any contributions made with after-tax dollars.
What happens when you change employers?	Depending on how the plan is set up, employees who leave before retirement may or may not be allowed to take anything with them and may or may not be entitled to any retirement benefits later.	DC accounts are much more portable. EmployEE contributions always belong to the employee. Any vested portions of employER contributions can also be taken when the employee leaves.
What if the employer goes bankrupt?	The Pension Benefit Guaranty Corporation (PBGC) helps insure the benefits of DB plans from companies which go bankrupt. However, the maximum pension benefit allowed under PBGC is capped.	DC plans are not insured by PBGC, but the employee account belongs to the employee and should not be affected. However, any unvested or unfunded portions of the employer account may be lost.

Bear in mind that even though the plans must follow certain regulations, they will vary from company to company. Also note that some employers provide both a defined benefit plan and a defined contribution plan for their employees, so examine the information you receive on your retirement accounts to determine what you have. For specific questions on your plan(s), contact your personnel or human resources department, or the plan administrator.

Defined Benefit Plans

These are the traditional types of retirement plans that most people associate with retirement. The *benefit* you are to receive in retirement is *defined*; for example, work 25 years for XYZ Corp., and at retirement receive $2,000 a month until you die.

Unfortunately, these plans are going the way of the dinosaur. Fulfilling this promise at the end of your working career has become too difficult and costly for corporate and governmental institutions alike. While 79% of state and local government workers are covered by defined benefit plans, that is true for only about 20% of America's workers in private industry (as of 2009).[111]

Of the defined benefit programs that do exist, underfunding is a problem for some, both in the private and government sectors. In order to cut costs, various jobs have been privatized or outsourced, or even eliminated. Additionally, some employers have frozen their defined benefits plans. That means these plans may be closed to employees not previously participating, or limits may have been placed on future benefits, or both.[112]

The *cash balance* type of retirement program has become popular in the past few years, with some companies converting their traditional pension plans into cash balance plans in order to save costs. While these are still a form of defined benefit plan, they *define the account balance at retirement* versus the benefit to be received in retirement.[113] These plans tend to be less advantageous for workers 40 and over.[114]

One of the seeming advantages of defined benefit plans over defined contribution plans is that qualified defined benefit plans are protected by the Pension Benefit Guarantee Corporation (PBGC),[115] while defined contribution plans are not. A company that is unable to fulfill its obligations toward its pension plan may be able to turn it over to the PBGC.

However, there is a maximum yearly benefit that can be paid by PBGC, so if your company's program is taken over, you may not receive all that you were originally promised.[116] Another concern is that the PBGC itself is underfunded due to the financial woes of various corporations who have turned their plans over to PBGC, a problem that is likely to get worse.[117]

---

[111] Refer to this U.S. Bureau of Labor Statistics news release: www.bls.gov/news.release/pdf/ebs2.pdf Their Program Perspectives Publications also provide useful information. www.bls.gov/opub/perspectives
The U.S. Bureau of Labor Statistics provides data on specific industries at this site: www.bls.gov/iag
[112] Refer to this BLS Publication: www.bls.gov/opub/perspectives/program_perspectives_vol2_issue3.pdf
[113] Find more information on cash balance plans at the Department of Labor's Web site.
www.dol.gov/ebsa/faqs/faq_consumer_cashbalanceplans.html MarketWatch presents this informative article entitled, "Cash-balance pension plans are growing fast."
www.marketwatch.com/story/cash-balance-pension-plans-growing-fast-2010-04-15
[114] The AARP Public Policy Institute presents an overview of cash balance plans in its brochure entitled, "Cash Balance Pension Plans and the Older Worker." assets.aarp.org/rgcenter/econ/ib78_pension.pdf
[115] Learn more about the Pension Benefit Guarantee Corporation. www.pbgc.gov
Also refer to their Fact Sheet: www.pbgc.gov/res/factsheets/page/guar-facts.html
[116] For information on the current benefits available, refer to the article, "PBGC Maximum Insurance Benefit Increases for 2012." www.pbgc.gov/news/press/releases/pr12-07.html
[117] Read Wikipedia's overview: en.wikipedia.org/wiki/Pension_Benefit_Guaranty_Corporation

Defined Contribution Plans

Today, defined contribution plans are much more prevalent among businesses that offer retirement programs. The most widely used tend to be 401(k) and 403(b) plans, depending on the type of business sponsoring the plan.

Instead of companies making a promise at the end of your working career, as with the defined benefit plans, they *define* or make a promise as to the *contribution* they will make today to an account on your behalf. How much you end up with in that account is what you'll have to work with in retirement, and there are no promises as to what that amount will be.

Although variances exist in these programs, many are set up with the company matching employee contributions up to a certain limit. Note that the match does NOT have to be dollar for dollar—it can be more or less. While some companies will contribute a certain amount whether the worker contributes or not, many companies will contribute only if the worker contributes. Some plans are set up such that the employer is not even required to make contributions.

Unfortunately, while workers may recognize the advantage of contributing to these plans, their contributions usually come out of their current salary, thus reducing their take-home pay. Many simply feel like they cannot afford to contribute much, if anything, to their plans. Even more unfortunately, the most advantageous time to contribute is at the beginning of one's working career in order for the power of compounding to work over time, but this is often a time when money is tight. Further inhibiting the effectiveness of these programs is the fact that when people change jobs, they may cash out their benefits and never redeposit them in another retirement account, or they may lose their job and be forced to spend the benefits.

While defined benefit plans must have their contributions actuarially determined[118] in order for the business to have set aside enough to fund the projected benefits, there is no such safeguard for defined contribution plans. *It's up to the worker* to make sure enough funds are available. Essentially, defined benefit plans place the monkey on the company's back, while defined contribution plans place it on the worker's back. And most workers simply have no idea of how much it will take for them to support the lifestyle they desire in retirement, particularly for the number of years they may live in retirement.

What should current workers do?

Employer-sponsored programs offer workers a desirable way to save for retirement because of their attractive features:

- ***Employer Contributions***—if your employer offers matching contributions of some type, this equates to FREE MONEY being placed in your account for you. Say, for example, that your employer matches your contributions on a dollar-for-dollar basis,

---

[118] Find a brief explanation of actuarial science by Wikipedia. en.wikipedia.org/wiki/Actuarial

such that for every $1 you put in, your employer puts in $1. Your $1 contribution turns into $2, giving you an immediate return of 100%. That's hard to beat!

- **Tax-deferred Contributions**—what you contribute from your own paycheck into a tax-qualified salary reduction plan (most employer-sponsored plans qualify) is not currently taxable. This reduces the amount of your pay subject to taxation, which lowers your federal income taxes due. The net effect of this is that you're able to contribute at a discount.

- **Tax-free Growth**—once your money is inside a tax-sheltered account, it is allowed to grow tax free. Depending on how your account is invested, your money has the potential to grow to a much greater amount than it could with yearly taxes being siphoned off.

Workers need to utilize these features and, depending on their individual situations, create their own personal strategies for accumulating the funds they need.

Suggested Planning Strategies:

1. Make it a point to **understand the features** of your current retirement program. Know whether it's a defined benefit or defined contribution plan, if you can take the money in your account with you should you leave the company and, if so, when your account vests.[119]

2. If your plan allows you to contribute, try to **max out your contributions.** For sure, try to max out the portion on which you can receive an employer match. As mentioned previously, this is free money. If you don't take advantage of the match, this is an opportunity lost forever.

3. Explore any **other savings options that may be offered through your employer**. You may be allowed to make tax-deferred contributions into separate accounts.

4. If you are self-employed or have a side business or do consulting such that you file a Schedule C with your federal income tax return, consider **setting up your own retirement plan**, which you can do in addition to an employer-sponsored plan (up to certain limits).[120]

5. Whether you have an employer-sponsored plan or not, you may be eligible to **contribute to a Roth IRA** or **traditional IRA** as long as you or your spouse has "earned income." [121, 122]

6. In addition to retirement accounts, you need **savings in regular taxable accounts** as well. You'll use these accounts for handling emergencies during your working career. Later, you may need to tap these accounts in order to supplement your retirement funds.

---

[119] Remember, what you have contributed out of your paycheck should always be yours. Vesting applies to what your employer has contributed. When you have been with your employer long enough, depending on how the plan is set up, the employer's contributions vest to you as well. That means you can take them with you when you leave the company. Refer to the section, "What happens when you change employers?" in the table previously presented on the types of retirement plans.

[120] Self-directed retirement plans are addressed later in this chapter. There are various types of these plans, and you will probably wish to consult a tax professional in order to set up a plan appropriate for your given situation.

Other Retirement Planning Considerations

As you accumulate funds, remember that the balance you see in your account is not likely to be what you actually have to live on. That's because your retirement funds have two big enemies: taxes and inflation! Here are some things to consider include:

- **Taxes** – your retirement accounts allow you to tax shelter a portion of your income, but only for a while and not forever! Eventually the money must be withdrawn. Withdrawals are fully taxable at the regular income tax rates in effect when the funds are withdrawn. The lower capital gains rates do not apply.

- **Social Security** – it's important to know how money withdrawn from your retirement accounts (remember, it's treated as income) will impact your Social Security benefits. For current retirees, a portion of their Social Security benefits may be taxable if their income (including tax-exempt interest) plus one-half of their Social Security benefits totals $25,000 for a single person or $32,000 for married filing jointly (as of 2011).[123] So you may not be able to keep as much of your Social Security benefit as you had planned on.

- **RMDs** – after you reach a certain age (usually 70 ½, but the timing depends on when your birthday falls during the year), you must start making withdrawals, if you have not already done so, in order for the government to start collecting taxes. These withdrawals are called Required Minimum Distributions, or RMDs.[124] Part of your financial planning needs to address both the timing of when you should start taking your RMDs and how you will use that money. Note that Roth IRAs are the exception to this rule. Because contributions were made with after-tax money, you are not required to make withdrawals from Roths.

- **Inflation** – in addition to taxes, inflation will take another bite out of the money you've set aside in your retirement accounts. To illustrate, let's say that you plan on withdrawing $50,000 per year in retirement, and for the sake of simplicity, we'll ignore taxes, which are unpredictable at best. The graph which follows shows what happens to the purchasing power of your money, given various rates of inflation. Note that at an even modest rate of 2% inflation, after 30 years your purchasing power will be cut almost in half!

---

[121] Individual Retirement Arrangements, or IRAs, are discussed later in this chapter.

[122] "Earned income" means income which you earn by working, as opposed to "investment income" (also called "unearned income" by the IRS) or "passive income" from items such as real estate investments. This IRS page briefly describes earned income. www.irs.gov/individuals/article/0,,id=176508,00.html
IRS publication 925 deals with passive activities. www.irs.gov/pub/irs-pdf/p925.pdf

[123] Refer to IRS Publication 915: Social Security and Equivalent Railroad Retirement Benefits www.irs.gov/pub/irs-pdf/p915.pdfU and to the Form 1040 Instructions www.irs.gov/pub/irs-pdf/i1040.pdf.

[124] Here's a brief explanation of RMDs by Investopedia:
www.investopedia.com/terms/r/requiredminimumdistribution.asp
Find more in-depth information in the IRS article entitled, "Retirement Plan FAQs Regarding Required Minimum Distributions." www.irs.gov/retirement/article/0,,id=96989,00.html This table of RMDs is provided by Bankrate. com. www.bankrate.com/finance/money-guides/ira-minimum-distributions-table.aspx

Graph 11-A: The Effects of Inflation Over Time on Your Money's Purchasing Power

How Inflation Erodes the Purchasing Power of Your Money
Here's what happens to a fixed income of $50,000 per year:

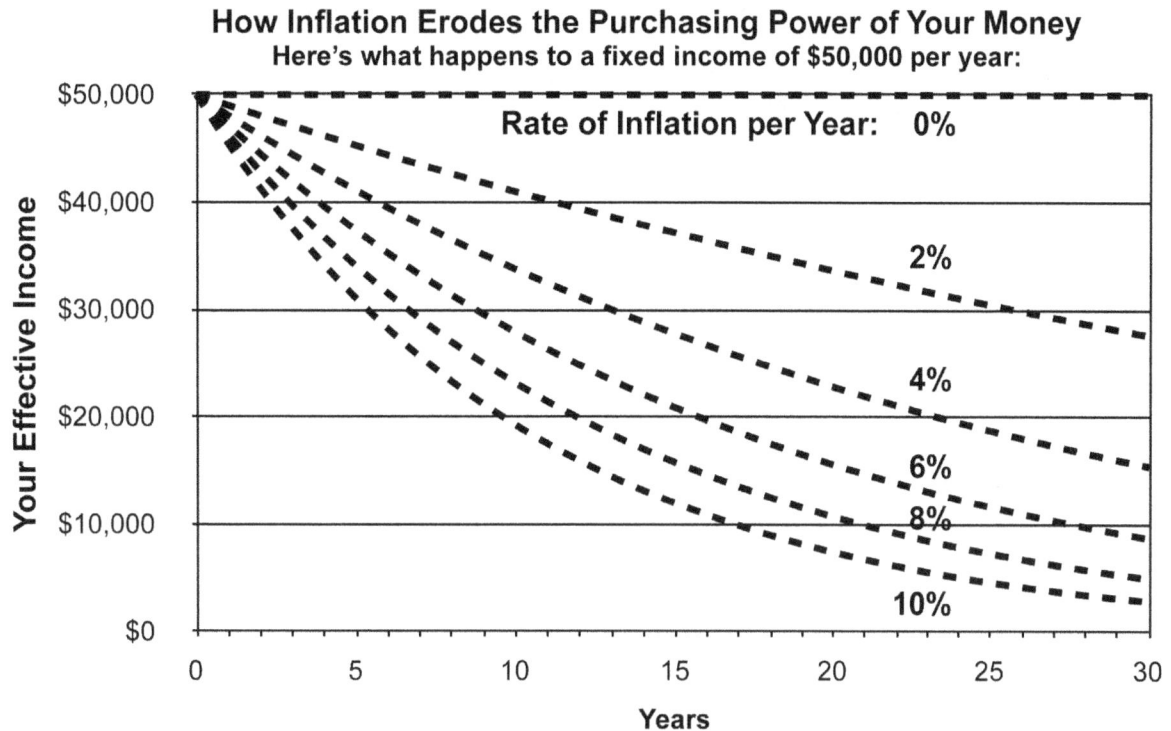

Remember, this graph shows only the effects of *inflation* over time. Whatever taxes are imposed on your income will only accelerate further the erosion of its purchasing power!

What can you do on an individual basis?

In addition to any of your employer-sponsored plans, you may also be eligible to participate in one or more individual retirement programs.

Individual Retirement Arrangements (IRAs)

IRAs provide a means for people to save retirement money on their own. Like other retirement accounts, once the money is inside an IRA, it is allowed to grow tax-free. However, whether you can deduct your contributions that go into the account or must pay taxes on the withdrawals that you take out of the account depends on the type of IRA that you have. The table which follows shows the contribution limits (as of 2012) for the various types of IRAs.

Table 11-B: Contribution Limits for Individual Retirement Arrangements (IRAs)

Tax Filing Status	Traditional Deductible IRA	Traditional Non-deductible IRA	Roth IRA
Single or head of household	To contribute maximum, modified AGI must be less than $58,000; phaseout between $58,000 & $68,000; higher than $68,000 cannot contribute.	This IRA is for people who are not eligible to deduct their contributions but still wish to make a non-deductible contribution. However, if you still qualify for the Roth IRA, which has higher limits, that would be preferable to the traditional non-deductible IRA because no taxes are due on qualified withdrawals from a Roth, nor do you have to take required minimum distributions. On traditional non-deductible IRAs, taxes will be due on the growth portion of your withdrawals, and you must take required minimum distributions.	To contribute maximum, modified AGI must be less than $110,000; phaseout between $110,000 & $125,000; higher than $125,000 cannot contribute.
Married filing jointly or qualifying widow or widower	To contribute maximum, modified AGI must be less than $92,000; phaseout between $92,000 & $112,000; higher than $112,000 cannot contribute. If your spouse is covered by a retirement plan at work but you are not, your AGI must be less than $173,000 to contribute the maximum, and if it's above $183,000 you cannot contribute.		To contribute maximum, modified AGI must be less than $173,000; phaseout between $173,000 & $183,000; higher than $183,000 cannot contribute
Reference in IRS Publication 590: www.irs.gov/pub/irs-pdf/p590.pdf	Refer to Chapter 1 concerning who can contribute and how to determine modified adjusted gross income.		Refer to Chapter 2 concerning who can contribute and how to determine modified adjusted gross income.
Note: These limits are for tax year 2012 and usually change every year. AGI stands for adjusted gross income, and you find it on your tax return. Pull up a Form 1040 to see how it's determined. It's your income after adjustments have been made, such as adding in everything which must be included as income and subtracting items which can be excluded. On the 2011 tax form 1040, AGI is the number on line 37. www.irs.gov/pub/irs-pdf/f1040.pdf			

Note that regardless of the type of IRA, you (or your spouse if you file a joint return) must show on your tax return "earned income" (or "taxable compensation") of at least as much as you contribute to your IRA.[125] The maximum you can contribute in any one year is $5,000 (as of 2012), with people 50 and older being allowed to contribute $6,000 (as of 2012). If you have more than one type of IRA or more than one IRA account, you can split your yearly contribution, but the combined total of your contributions to all your IRA accounts cannot be more than $5,000 (or $6,000 for those 50 and over, as of 2012).

Also note that the maximum yearly contribution amounts do not apply to rollover IRAs. Rollovers are designed to hold money from other qualified retirement accounts and can receive any amount. For example, you changed jobs and had to move your 401(k) money of $100,000 from your previous employer. You can establish a rollover IRA account and have all your 401(k) money transferred over.

---

[125] Refer to the earlier footnote dealing with earned, unearned and passive income classifications by the IRS.

Remember, if you or your spouse has an employer-sponsored retirement program at work, you can still contribute to an IRA—up to a point. That point depends on the type of IRA and your level of compensation. Refer to the table above for the limits.[126]

Features Unique to the Roth IRA

If you qualify to contribute to either the traditional deductible IRA or the Roth IRA, which should you do? If you contribute to the traditional deductible IRA, you can deduct your contribution from your income on which you must pay taxes, thereby lowering your taxes for the current year. On the other hand, with the Roth you don't get the current tax break. But your reward is on the other end—zero income taxes on qualified withdrawals!

The tax break you forego today in contributing to a Roth IRA is usually quite small compared with the potential future benefit. The larger your account grows through the years, the greater the benefit of a Roth IRA.

Additionally, a Roth offers a great deal of *flexibility during your working years*. If you must make an early withdrawal after your money has been in your Roth for at least five years, then the first dollars out are considered return of your contributions. Since you have already paid taxes on your contributions, no income taxes are due unless you withdraw more than you contributed. In that case, taxes would be due on the growth portion. If your money has not been in at least five years, then early withdrawals (those made before age 59 ½) could be subject to a 10% penalty.

If you earn income beyond age 70 ½, you are no longer eligible to contribute to a traditional IRA. However, with a Roth, *there are no age restrictions*. That's because you're paying taxes upfront on the money you contribute and no further taxes are due.

Roth IRAs are superior for passing wealth on to your heirs. If you don't need the money from your Roth, you can leave it invested because you are *not required to take minimum distributions from a Roth IRA*. Then, when your loved ones receive the Roth at your death, they do not have to pay income taxes on the money either,[127] unlike other inherited retirement plan money. This allows your loved ones to potentially keep more from your Roth than they would if they inherited the same amount from your 401k, for example. The Roth is an excellent estate planning tool, something which will be discussed in the chapters that deal with planning your estate.

---

[126] Few things regarding taxes are simple and straightforward. There are many exceptions and caveats. For more information on IRAs, refer to IRS Publication 590: Individual Retirement Arrangements (IRAs). www.irs.gov/pub/irs-pdf/p590.pdf If you prepare your own tax return, a tax-preparation program is quite helpful because it asks you a series of questions to help determine if certain exceptions, limits or situations apply to you.

[127] Depending on the size of your estate, estate or inheritance taxes may apply. These are separate from income taxes.

Frequently Asked Questions Concerning IRAs

What happens to my existing IRA if I make too much money this year to contribute or am unable to contribute?

You leave the money previously invested alone and don't contribute this year. Your eligibility to contribute is determined year by year, so you contribute in the years in which you can and don't in the others.

What kind of return can I get on an IRA?

Many people go to a banking institution to open an IRA. While that is one choice, there are various others. You can open an IRA with any qualified institution that agrees to act as custodian to an IRA account, such as a mutual fund company or a brokerage firm, in addition to banking institutions. So the returns that are possible on an IRA can vary widely, depending on what securities you choose for your investment.

Can you have more than one IRA?

Of course. You can have multiple IRAs of various types, and you can contribute to several in any given year if you are eligible. However, the total of all your IRA contributions together cannot be greater than the yearly maximum ($5,000 for 2012; $6,000 if you're 50 or older).

Can you combine your IRA accounts?

Yes, if they are of the same type. Roths must be separate from traditional IRAs. And even though it's possible to combine traditional deductible and traditional non-deductible IRA account money, don't do it. Your life will be so much easier when you start to take withdrawals if you keep the two types in separate accounts. That's because on the traditional deductible, all money withdrawn is subject to income taxes, while on the traditional non-deductible, only the growth portion is subject to income taxes. The record keeping is up to you, and so is the burden of proof, should the IRS ask. If you have a traditional non-deductible IRA, you paid taxes on the money you contributed in the first place. The last thing you want to do is pay taxes a second time on your contribution portion when you withdraw it.

Can I convert my traditional IRA to a Roth IRA?

Yes. Beginning in 2010, anyone, regardless of income, may convert their traditional IRA to a Roth IRA. However, you must include the entire amount converted as income for the year in which you convert it and pay the taxes owed. In 2010 only, you also had the option of including half of the converted amount as income in 2011 and half in 2012. But unless the tax laws change, the half-and-half option was good for 2010 conversions only and will not be available in subsequent years.[128]

---

[128] Market Watch offers the article, "Rethink that Roth: 12 traps to avoid when converting to a Roth IRA." www.marketwatch.com/story/12-traps-to-avoid-when-converting-to-a-roth-2010-01-21?pagenumber=1

Tax Features of IRAs

The table which follows outlines the general federal income tax features of the various types of IRAs.[129] Any state or local income taxes would depend on where you live.

Table 11-C: Comparing the Features of Various Types of IRAs

Type of IRA	Traditional Deductible IRA	Traditional Non-deductible IRA	Roth IRA
Are contributions tax deductible?	Yes	No	No
Taxes on withdrawals made before age 59 ½ *	10% penalty plus regular income taxes on entire amount withdrawn.	10% penalty plus regular income taxes only on the growth portion withdrawn. Each withdrawal is considered part growth and part return of principal.	10% penalty plus regular income taxes only on the growth portion withdrawn. The first dollars withdrawn are considered return of principal, on which no taxes are owed. In general, contributions need to have been in the account at least 5 years before being withdrawn.
Taxes on withdrawals made after age 59 ½ *	Entire amount withdrawn taxable as regular income.	Each withdrawal consists partly of growth which is taxable as regular income, and partly return of principal which is not taxable.	No taxes. In general, contributions need to have been in the account at least 5 years before being withdrawn.
Are distributions (RMDs) required after age 70 ½?	Yes	Yes	No
Can workers older than 70 ½ contribute?	No	No	Yes
Is inherited IRA subject to income taxes?	Yes	Yes	No **

* Early withdrawals made for certain reasons may not be subject to penalty. Consult your tax professional for specific information concerning taxes on any of your withdrawals.
** Estate and inheritance taxes, which are separate from income taxes, could apply.

---

[129] Refer to IRS Publication 590 for more information on IRAs. www.irs.gov/pub/irs-pdf/p590.pdf

What can the self-employed or contract worker do?

If you work for yourself or earn Schedule C-type income, you can establish your own self-directed retirement plan. In fact, you can work for an employer, participate in an employer-sponsored plan, and still be eligible to contribute to your own self-directed plan (of course, certain limits apply). An example of such an instance would be a professor who participates in an employer-sponsored plan at the university and does consulting work on his own outside of the university.

Employee Versus Contract Worker

At this point, the distinction between employee and contract worker needs to be made.

- *As an employee*, you work for someone else. Your employer pays a portion of your Social Security and Medicare taxes, and you pay the other portion. As an employee, you should receive a W-2 statement at the end of the year, which shows your earnings for the year as well as the taxes that were withheld from your pay. Because your employer is withholding money from each paycheck and submitting these amounts to the IRS on your behalf, you are paying your taxes as you go through the year. You will list your earnings as income on a 1040 tax form.

- *As a contract worker*, you work for yourself, and you are responsible for paying all of your Social Security and Medicare taxes. It is up to you to submit money for your taxes during the year, in the form of estimated payments if needed.[130] At the end of the year, you may receive a form 1099 from a person or business that hired you which shows what you were paid during the year. You will list all your contract income on a Schedule C, which you will file with your 1040, and you may be able to deduct certain expenses against your contract income.

- *If you receive both W-2 and 1099 forms*, generally you cannot combine the two types of income on your tax return because of the differences in the way Social Security and Medicare taxes have been taken out. It's likely you'll have to list your W-2 income in the income section of your 1040 and file a Schedule C for your 1099 income.[131]

- *Differences in Social Security and Medicare withholdings* — self-employed and contract workers who file a Schedule C will also file a Schedule SE (for Self-Employment Tax) if they end up with taxable income after taking deductions.

Self-employment tax simply means that, as your own employer, you get the privilege of paying both portions of your Social Security and Medicare taxes. Traditionally, these taxes totaled 15.3% of your earned income. However, recent legislation reduced the employee's portion of Social Security taxes by 2%, making the total 13.3%, at least temporarily (as of 2012). Note that there is an income limit of $110,100 (as of 2012) on which Social Security taxes are due, but there is no income limit for Medicare taxes.

---

[130] For more information, refer to this IRS article, "Estimated Taxes."
www.irs.gov/businesses/small/article/0,,id=110413,00.html
[131] This explanation is only a brief overview. As in all things related to tax, exceptions and complicating issues abound, and you may need to consult a tax professional for your particular situation.

Here's what the breakdown looks like (as of 2012) when you have an employer and earn the Social Security limit or less during the year:

Table 11-D: Breakdown of Employer & Employee Portions of Social Security & Medicare Taxes

	EmployER pays:		EmployEE pays:		Total paid:
Social Security	6.2%	+	4.2%	=	10.4%
Medicare	1.45%	+	1.45%	=	2.9%
Total	7.65%	+	5.65%	=	13.3%

If you earn more than the Social Security limit, then on the amount that's over you will not pay the Social Security tax, but you will pay the Medicare tax.[132]

Taxes for the self-employed have proven to be a classic trap for those who first begin to earn a significant amount of taxable income. It's imperative that from the beginning you set aside a portion of everything you make, perhaps 25% to start with, into a separate account. Not only will you owe income taxes, but also you'll owe the entire portions of Social Security and Medicare taxes as explained above. And you owe it *during the year as you earn it*, not on April 15 of the following year. In fact, if you don't get in enough during the year with your estimated tax payments, *you may owe a penalty* as well, even though you settle up by April 15.[133]

Self-Directed Retirement Plans

Various types of self-directed plans are available for the self-employed or contract worker. Your choice of plans will depend on your particular needs and how many employees, if any, that you have.[134] The reason you might like to establish a self-directed retirement plan rather than just contribute to an IRA is that the maximum contribution limits are higher. Not only can you potentially shovel in a lot more money (depending on your earned income), but you can also deduct your contributions, thereby lowering your taxable income. Professional help is highly recommended in order to pick a plan that's suitable for you to establish and maintain.[135]

---

[132] As mentioned previously, the IRS has three income categories: earned, unearned, and passive. In general, unearned (like investment income) and passive (like rent collected on real estate) are not subject to these taxes. To find more info, search the Social Security Web site. www.ssa.gov The Social Security Handbook www.ssa.gov/OP_Home/handbook/handbook.html as well as the IRS instructions to form 1040 www.irs.gov/pub/irs-pdf/i1040.pdf should prove useful. Also, the IRS article, "Self-Employment Tax," explains more about how these taxes work. www.irs.gov/businesses/small/article/0,,id=98846,00.html

[133] Find a good accountant and treat her kindly! When you're self-employed, you need professional help.

[134] The IRS Publication 560: Retirement Plans for Small Business, www.irs.gov/pub/irs-pdf/p560.pdf lists the basic features of the various plans and provides a table outlining the key retirement plan rules (located in the Introduction).

Bankrate provides this helpful article entitled, "Retirement plans for self-employed workers." www.bankrate.com/finance/financial-literacy/retirement-plans-for-self-employed-workers.aspx

Kiplinger also presents the article, "Retirement plans for the self-employed." www.kiplinger.com/columns/kiptips/archives/retirement-plans-for-the-selfemployed.html

[135] The IRS also provides a very helpful site, IRS Retirement Plans Navigators, for small employers. www.retirementplans.irs.gov You can view a handy table of the various plans in a side-by-side comparison here: www.retirementplans.irs.gov/plan-comparison-table

What about transfers and withdrawals?

If you need to *transfer* your retirement money from one company to another, it's usually easier for you if it's done directly from one trustee or custodian to the other. If your company sends you a check instead, then the IRS gives you 60 days to get the money deposited with another trustee into an appropriate tax-qualified account.

> If you do not redeposit the money, it's considered *a distribution*, and generally you will owe a 10% penalty if you are younger than 59 ½ as well as income taxes on this amount. If you wait *longer than 60 days* to redeposit the money, then it will count toward this year's contribution and will be subject to whatever limits apply to the amount you can contribute for the year.[136]

So if, for example, you took out $10,000 from your traditional IRA last year for some reason, you can't just go stick the money back in. The most you can contribute this year is $5,000 ($6,000 if you're 50 or older, as of 2011).

Early withdrawals from any retirement account are not usually desirable, as this destroys the growth potential of these funds, and should be done only in an extreme emergency. For most retirement plans, "early" means you're younger than 59 ½ when you take the money out. This will trigger the 10% penalty mentioned above, plus you will owe income taxes on the amount withdrawn. (Remember that the Roth IRA is different from other retirement accounts in many of these respects.)

Retirement plans are a very important part of building wealth. They offer a way to accumulate money without taxes being drained off each year, and the penalty for early withdrawals offers an incentive to leave the money alone!

Chapters 12, 13 and 14 cover other investment topics, while chapters 15 and 16 address various estate planning issues.

---

[136] Of course, there are exceptions. Refer to IRS Publication 590 for more info on rollover IRAs and waivers of the 60-day rule as well as the 59 ½ rule. www.irs.gov/pub/irs-pdf/p590.pdf

30 Minute LIVING

Suggested Action Plan

- *Review your latest Social Security summary.* These are usually sent out a few months before your birthday. Note what your benefits are expected to be and the age at which you can begin collecting your regular benefits. Compare your projected benefit amount with Graph 11-A to see what will happen to the purchasing power of that money over time. The government may not be able to increase your benefit's cost-of-living adjustments enough to offset inflation.

- *Learn the features of your employer-sponsored retirement plan.* If you have an employer-sponsored plan, pull out your plan documents or go online to learn all the features of your plan. Someone in personnel or human resources may be able to tell you how to better utilize your plan.

- *Does your employer offer additional retirement account options?* If so, you may wish to consider participating in those as well.

- *Consider setting up your own retirement plan.* If you file a Schedule C on your tax return, you may be eligible to set up a self-directed retirement plan. You may need to consult a tax professional to determine what is best for your given situation.

- *Consider contributing to an IRA.* These accounts allow you to tax shelter additional income. The type of IRA you're eligible for depends on your personal situation.

CHAPTER 12

Understanding the Risks and Returns of Investing

Risky Business!

The topic of investments had just been introduced in class when "Jennifer" raised her hand and started telling the class about her family's experience. Awhile back, her mother had heard about a company that was destined to become the next Big Thing. It was a very small company that was fairly young and was trying to introduce a new, unproven technology. The mother had invested almost all of her savings in this company's stock, and its stock price tended to fluctuate wildly. This had caused a great deal of tension in the family, because her mother's mood fluctuated right along with the price of the stock. Jennifer said now they almost had to check the company's stock price first before venturing into the same room with her mother.

Unfortunately, what Jennifer's mother had done was more akin to going to Vegas and betting everything on one roll of the dice. Instead of taking an informed and measured approach to investing, she had risked much more than she should have and went the "get rich quick" route. The semester ended soon after Jennifer told her story, so the class never heard how things turned out. The odds, however, were definitely not good.

Investing, when done in accordance to a well thought out plan, can help you not only build real wealth, but also allow you to sleep at night. Your approach to investing should be more like you're building a structure:

- You first need a *good foundation*, which you establish by working through the steps in the financial planning process that were discussed in preceding chapters (a brief review of these steps follows in the section, Investing on Your Own, Outside of a Retirement Program).

- The *cornerstone* of your foundation is your savings, which you must leave in place to maintain the stability of your structure. If you are forced to tap into your savings, your highest priority is to replenish your savings before continuing the building process.

- Your investment *building blocks* are the individual items that you place inside your portfolio, or collection of investments. But investments are not uniform like bricks. Instead, they come in different forms with varying characteristics and levels of risk, and you can purchase them in various amounts. The items in your collection need to complement one another. Most importantly, the manner in which you build should be done according to your needs and financial goals, AND your personal tolerance for risk.

Saving and Investing

Your savings serve as a financial cushion, and the more comfortable your cushion, the better you can weather the financial storms, and they WILL occur! During your working years, having adequate savings keeps you from being pushed against the wall should you have unexpected expenses, lose your job or need to change course in life. Then in retirement, if your retirement accounts and Social Security are not sufficient to meet your retirement needs, it's your personal savings that must fill the gap. And of course, personal savings can help you achieve and maintain *financial independence* no matter what stage of life you're in!

After you've adequately funded your cash-type accounts, which were discussed in Chapters 4 and 5, you'll want to consider other investments that offer higher returns. But remember, every investment involves risk of some type. *Before* you plunk your hard-earned money into anything, you need to understand the risks involved. The purpose of this chapter is to examine the various risks associated with different types of investments and the types of returns that can be expected from your investments.

How can you save more?
So how can you accumulate more for saving and investing? Here are some suggestions:

1. Pay yourself first. This is probably the single most important guideline to increasing your savings level, creating personal wealth and ultimately becoming financially independent.

If you will immediately *skim a portion off the top* of what comes in the door and squirrel it away in a separate account, more than likely you'll never miss it. You'll be amazed at how it adds up through time. On the other hand, if you think you'll save something *after* you've taken care of everything else, you'll be equally amazed that *nothing* ever seems to be left over!

Put your savings on auto pilot and make it as easy and effortless as possible to pay yourself first. Have your bank automatically transfer a certain amount from checking to savings each month right after your paycheck is deposited. Or set up an automatic investment program so that a certain amount is withdrawn from your account each month and invested. You can do this with many mutual fund companies and also with the purchase of Treasury securities.

Put expense reimbursements and "found" money in a savings account, not in checking. If you've been living without this money already, maybe you've gotten used to not having it and will just leave it in savings. At the very least, you'll have to *think* first and then *on purpose* transfer the money into checking. Maybe you'll get the feeling you're raiding the kitty and will be stingy with reimbursing yourself. In fact, you might want your whole paycheck automatically deposited in savings and then transfer over only a portion as you need it. Money in a checking account tends to evaporate. By depositing it in savings first, you'll have to consciously think about how much you need to transfer.

2. Save your bonuses, raises and tax refunds. You'll probably never miss having this money. Some people try to justify overspending because they know that this extra money is supposed to be coming in. If that's you, try budgeting in periodic rewards for sticking to your savings plan. When you already know you're getting a reward, it may be easier for you to leave bonus money alone.

3. Analyze your past expenses and put off discretionary expenses. Honestly and thoughtfully look through your past and present monthly expenses. Analyze what must be spent now and consider what could reasonably be put off for a few days, a few weeks, or even a few months.

While it's true you do need certain things, there are lots of things you don't have to have NOW. *There are people of very modest means who are able to have both what they want and what they need because they have learned how to control their expenditures.* Besides, it just may go on sale later. And another interesting thing often occurs with the passage of time: you may come to realize you really don't want it or need it after all, and you'll be thankful you didn't spend your money on it!

Investing on Your Own, Outside of a Retirement Program

As a quick review of the financial planning process, by the time you're ready to start investing, you should have already worked through these steps:

1. *Defined your financial goals.* You know what you want to accomplish financially and how you plan to get there (covered in Chapter 1: Overview of the Financial Planning Process).
2. *Evaluated your financial position.* You understand your spending habits. You periodically review your personal balance sheet and income statements to keep track of your current financial position and measure your progress toward your goals (covered in Chapter 2: Evaluating Your Current Position).
3. *Planned your future expenditures.* You have created a budget. This provides you with a framework for allocating your expected income and a pathway for reaching your financial goals (covered in Chapter 3: Planning Your Future Expenditures).
4. *Funded your cash accounts.* You have set aside enough liquid assets to cover at least three months' worth of living expenses. Financial emergencies will not be as likely to disrupt your progress toward your financial goals (covered in Chapter 4: Understanding Your Cash Accounts and in Chapter 5: Funding Your Cash Accounts).
5. *Managed your debt.* You have your consumer debt under control and are not debt strapped (covered in Chapter 6: Managing Your Debt and in Chapter 7: Understanding Your Debt).
6. *Insured your valuables.* You carry an adequate amount of life, health, and property insurance but are not using up valuable resources by being over-insured (covered in Chapter 8: Insuring Your Life, Chapter 9: Insuring Your Health and in Chapter 10: Insuring Your Property).

Having worked through these steps in the financial planning process, you are now ready to seriously invest for your future. It's time to give your financial goals the opportunity to jump off the paper where you've written them and become reality!

Risks of Investing

Life in general is not without risk, and the same is true of investing. Even actions which are considered super safe entail risk of some type. For example, if you stick your money under the mattress, you run the risk that someone will steal it or your house will burn down. If you leave your money in bank accounts or Treasury securities, you run the risk that the low returns you're receiving won't keep pace with inflation and your money won't buy as much in the future. You also have the opportunity cost of what you could have earned if you had invested this money in something else offering a higher yield.

So when you invest, it's important that you understand the:
- *Risks that are involved in investing.*
- *Types of risk you personally can stand.*
- *Types of returns you can expect.*

One of the foremost principles of investing (which will be covered more extensively in Chapter 13: Investment Overview and Investing in Bonds and in Chapter 14: Investing in Stocks and Funds) is this:

Risk and return are positively related!
The higher the expected return, the greater the level of risk that you will likely have to take in order to achieve that return. Conversely, the less risk you are willing to take, the lower the return you can expect.

To illustrate this concept, consider two potential investments—one in short-term U.S. Treasury securities and the other in a highly speculative piece of real estate. Short-term Treasury securities are highly liquid and marketable, and are backed by the full faith and credit of the U.S. government. The real estate would not be considered liquid, it might be difficult to find another potential buyer at the time you want to sell, there could be undisclosed problems or unknown pitfalls, and there will be few, if any, guarantees.

If the expected returns were the same on these two investments, a prudent investor would go for the one with less risk. To entice someone to take the greater risk, there must be the potential for a higher return.

Individual Investment Risk and Portfolio Risk

Each individual investment presents risks of various types on its own, which will be discussed further in the sections which follow. Then, as you add new investments, you begin to build a *portfolio*. This is simply your collection of investments.

It's vitally important to consider the risk that an individual investment contributes to your mix of investments, or portfolio, as a whole. Some investments could be very risky if they were your only investment, but when held with other investments, they could actually help lessen the overall risk to your portfolio. Just as a certain building block may not appear very attractive by itself, when you insert it in your structure, in the right proportion, it may be just what you need to make the entire structure more stable.

For example, sales of luxury goods tend to do well in a strong economy but may suffer during recessions. On the other hand, sales of certain goods, such as hot dogs, tend to actually increase during a down economy. By holding a variety of investments, or diversifying your portfolio, you can have things that tend to zig when others zag. This lessens the risk to you that everything you own will go down the toilet at once.

Types of Investment Risk

The table which follows examines the various types of investment risks and ways to minimize the risk in your portfolio.

Table 12-A: Types of Investment Risk and Ways to Reduce Exposure to This Risk

Type of investment risk and the securities that are particularly susceptible to this risk:	Ways to reduce exposure to this risk:
BUSINESS RISK The risk that any one firm or company will be profitable or even stay in business due to economic or industry factors or to poor management decisions. This is risk that is specific to an individual firm. Holding the securities of only one or just a few companies exposes you to a great deal of business risk. It's like putting all your eggs in one basket.	Hold a diversified portfolio of investments from various asset classes, from companies of various sizes and from various industries and sectors. This provides a greater chance that at least some of your investments will be doing well at any given time, or at least that they won't all tank at once!
FINANCIAL RISK The risk that a company will use too much debt financing and will either be unable to fulfill its debt obligations or be so financially strapped that it realizes little or no profit. All companies potentially have this risk, and like business risk, it is specific to an individual firm.	Deal with financial risk as you would with business risk, by holding a well-diversified portfolio of investments.
MARKET RISK The first two types of risk listed above are due to *internal* factors (decisions made within the company or factors affecting just that company). Market risk deals with *external* factors over which companies have little or no control. These include changes in political, economic, or social conditions or in investor taste and preferences. Virtually all securities are subject to market risk.	It's difficult to reduce market risk. Securities are traded in the markets and as a result are going to be subject to the "climate" or conditions of the market. Depending on the country, international securities may be less correlated with U.S. markets and should be included in a well-diversified portfolio.

Table 12-A: Types of Investment Risk and Ways to Reduce Exposure to This Risk (cont.)

PURCHASING POWER RISK The risk that the return on your investment will not keep pace with inflation, meaning that you will not be able to purchase as much in the future as you can today. Investments such as bank savings accounts, certificates of deposit, money market, or short-term Treasuries are particularly subject to purchasing power risk because their returns are usually low relative to other investments.	You need a certain amount of these cash-type investments. However, in order to earn an overall return greater than the rate of inflation, at least a portion of your portfolio must include other investments on which you can expect a higher return.
INTEREST RATE RISK The risk that interest rates will change and affect the price of a security. Fixed-income securities, such as bonds, are particularly subject to this risk. Bonds are often viewed as being "safer" than stock or equity investments, but if the prevailing interest rates change, the price of fixed income investments which you already own will move in the opposite direction. The real pain comes when interest rates *rise*, because the price of fixed-income investments will *fall*. (More on this in Chapter 13: Investment Overview and Investing in Bonds.)	Hold a portfolio of various types of securities, some debt (such as bonds) and some equity (such as stock). You might also consider including floating-rate debt securities.
LIQUIDITY RISK The risk that you will not be able to sell your security in a reasonable time period without a significant loss in value. Liquidity and marketability go hand in hand—being able to turn an investment into cash and also being able to find a ready market (someone who wants to buy your investment when you're ready to sell). Tangible assets, such as real estate, collectibles and precious metals are particularly subject to liquidity and marketability risk, as are the stocks and bonds of "thinly traded" securities (those where very few investors are trading, possibly because the companies are very small or financially distressed).	Hold a portfolio that has enough liquid, cash-type securities to meet your near-term liquidity needs so that you will not be forced to sell your less liquid investments at an inopportune time.
EVENT RISK The risk that a major, unexpected event will occur that will cause a sudden decline in an investment's value. Think of the many companies that suffered because of 9-11. Virtually all companies are subject to event risk.	Such unexpected events are difficult to guard against. Holding a well-diversified portfolio which also includes some amount of international investments is probably your best defense.

Additional Risks of Investing Internationally

Well-diversified portfolios typically include international securities as well as those from U.S. companies. You can achieve international exposure in several ways: by investing in companies actually headquartered in another country, or by investing in U.S. companies that also have operations in other countries. *But be aware that when you invest in international securities you add another layer of risk — in addition to all the risks listed above!*

Table 12-B: Additional Risks of International Investments

EXCHANGE RATE RISK The risk that the value of a company's cash flows will be worth less when converted into the parent company's home currency. Even though a company is operating profitably in one country, it could show a loss when its cash flows are translated into another currency due to changes in the exchange rates.	Sometimes companies themselves can hedge against exchange rate fluctuations in the currency markets, but it may not be possible to hedge completely, especially over a long period of time.
POLITICAL RISK Potential actions by a host government, such as raising taxes, placing restrictions on operations, or even seizing property, could threaten or reduce the value of a company's assets. Companies that operate in countries with less stable governments are particularly subject to political risk.	Countries with stable and traditionally friendly governments present less political risk to foreign companies operating there. Diversify the international portion of your portfolio across various regions and countries.

Other Challenges with International Investing

- Access to information can be limited, and the investment playing fields may differ from country to country. Foreign countries and markets do not necessarily operate under all of the same rules as U.S. markets, nor do all countries and markets mandate full and fair disclosure of material or pertinent information.

- How can you know if a foreign business is a legitimate operation? While investors can and do go visit a company's headquarters, factories and showrooms in America, it's harder for an individual to go observe operations firsthand in another country. Even if you do go, companies may not allow just anybody to visit their factory floor, observe working conditions, interview the management, have access to financial information, etc.

- Different countries have different legal systems, languages and cultures. Companies which operate in foreign countries may run into difficulties which they did not anticipate. It's hard for individual investors to know about these potential problems or evaluate the impact they might have.

How can individual investors handle the challenges of investing internationally?
There are several ways investors can reduce this additional risk somewhat while holding international investments in their portfolios.

• Hold the securities of U.S. companies which also have operations in other countries. This allows you to get international exposure automatically when you buy into these companies. However, your portfolio may not be as diversified as you might desire if this is your only strategy for international investing.

• Purchase shares of mutual funds or exchange traded funds (ETFs) which include international companies. Because these funds contain the securities of many companies, investors are instantly diversified among all of a fund's holdings when they purchase a share. Diversity helps moderate not only the risks of international investing, but also reduces the impact of other investment risks as well.

Funds that are actively managed (as opposed to those which simply mirror an index) often have access to specialists with an in-depth knowledge of investing in specific countries or regions. However, narrowing down the many fund choices can be difficult for investors. Funds are discussed at length in Chapter 14: Investing in Stocks and Funds.

Returns of Investing

Having examined the risks of investing, it's now time to take a look at the types of returns to be had by investing. Generally, the returns on investments can be expressed with this equation:

Current Return + Future Return = Total Return

The discussion which follows examines these elements of return as well as the taxes that are involved.

Investments which Provide Current Returns
Current returns are the earnings you receive on an investment *during the time you own it.* In general, you will expect to pay taxes each year on these earnings. Examples of current return include:
• Rental income earned on real estate.
• Interest earned on investments such as bank accounts, certificates of deposit, or bonds.
• Dividends paid on stocks.

Investments which Provide Future Returns
Not all investments will provide current return. Some investments are purchased with *only* the expectation of price appreciation.

Future returns are the gains you expect to receive *upon the sale of the investment at some point in the future.* If the value of your investment increases while you still own it, you simply have a gain on paper, or an "unrealized" capital gain. You do not pay taxes on your gain until you actually sell your investment, or "realize" your gain.[137]

Examples of investments in which only a future return is expected include:
- Non-dividend paying stocks.
- Real estate that is not rented but is held, remodeled or developed for price appreciation purposes.

Investments which Provide both Current and Future Returns
Of course, some investments provide both elements of return. You would pay taxes on the current return year by year and also realize your gain on your tax return the year you sell. Examples could include:
- Dividend-paying stocks which also increase in value such that you are able to sell your shares for more than you paid for them.
- Interest-paying bonds that you sell on the open market before they mature at a price higher than you paid for them.
- Real estate on which you collect rent and are also able to sell for more than you paid for it.

Taxation of Returns

While the preceding sections briefly outlined how these elements of return are taxed, the table which follows gives a basic overview of *which tax rates apply* for various returns. As previously stated, however, few things are simple and straightforward when it comes to taxation. The IRS Publication 550, Investment Income and Expenses, provides more complete information.[138]

---

[137] Certain bonds appear to provide only future return because the bondholder receives no money in hand while the bond is being held. However, the bondholder is still credited with interest year by year as it accrues or builds up (this is called "imputed" interest) and may owe income taxes as if the earnings were actually received each year.

The U.S. Treasury's Savings Bonds, both EE and I, fall into this category, and with these bonds, investors have a choice of paying taxes on the interest earnings each year or deferring taxes to the end. Most people choose to defer the taxes on their interest earned, but if you choose to pay year by year, certain rules apply (for more info, research the tax considerations of savings bonds at www.treasurydirect.gov).

You may also have imputed interest with discount bonds and zero coupon bonds if they are held in a taxable account (remember, your investments held inside retirement accounts are allowed to grow tax free until you take withdrawals). Bonds are discussed more in Chapter 13: Investment Overview and Investing in Bonds.

[138] IRS publication 550: Investment Income and Expenses discusses investment income, including capital gains and losses. The glossary provided at the end explains various terminology, and Chapter 5 tells you how to get tax help. www.irs.gov/pub/irs-pdf/p550.pdf
Also refer to the 1040 instruction booklet, www.irs.gov/pub/irs-pdf/i1040.pdf, which provides information on form 1040 as well as for Schedule D and Form 8949, which are used to report capital gains and losses.

Table 12-C: Federal Income Tax Rates (as of 2011) for Various Returns:

Type of Income	Applicable Tax Rate
Interest income, ordinary dividends, and short-term capital gains	Taxed at your regular income tax rate
Qualified dividends and long-term capital gains	• Highest tax rate is generally 15%, but there are exceptions • Highest tax rate for collectibles is generally 28%

Note that our discussion on taxes is limited to federal income taxes. Depending on where you live, your earnings and investments may be subject to various state and local taxes as well. However, interest earnings on U.S. Treasury securities are exempt from state and local taxes. This would include both EE and I Savings Bonds as well as Treasury bills, notes, bonds and TIPS.[139]

Also remember that tax laws are subject to change with whatever political wind that happens to be blowing at the time. From one year to the next, certain deductions may be allowed or disallowed, or the eligibility requirements may be changed or who knows what can be changed. You may need to consult a tax professional.

Capital Gains and Losses

A *capital gain* occurs when you sell an asset for more than you paid for it. Some, or all, of the gain portion may be subject to income taxes, but not the portion that's considered your return of capital. A *capital loss* occurs when you sell an asset for less than you paid for it. Sometimes you can count the loss portion against your income for that year and reduce the taxes you owe. Of course, this is the simplified explanation, and there are other things to be considered.

Holding Period
With capital gains, it matters how long you hold the asset or property before selling. As shown in the table above, short-term capital gains are taxed at your regular income tax rate, while long-term capital gains are usually taxed at lower rates. Here's how you determine the difference:[140]

- Short-term gain or loss—occurs when you sell an asset you have owned for *one year or less.*
- Long-term gain or loss—occurs when you sell an asset you have owned for *longer than one year.*

---

[139] For more information on various Treasury securities, research the products in-depth at: www.treasurydirect.gov/indiv/research/indepth/indepth.htm TIPS are Treasury Inflation-Protected Securities whose principal is adjusted when the Consumer Price Index changes (the CPI is used as a measure of inflation). TIPS and T-bills, T-notes and T-bonds are all marketable securities, meaning you can sell them to another investor before your bond matures, if you desire. Savings bonds are registered to a particular investor. They can be redeemed, but the ownership cannot be transferred.

[140] See Publication 550 referenced above. Also see Tax Topic 409 – Capital Gains and Losses. www.irs.gov/taxtopics/tc409.html

Basis

Your basis in your asset or property also matters.[141] For tax purposes, it's the amount you have invested in a property. when you sell something, the amount over your basis is your gain. Usually your basis is the cost of the property, which includes sales tax and other costs associated with its purchase. However, as you might guess, this is not always the case. Also, the basis of your property, particularly for mutual funds, may need to be adjusted during the time you own the property, depending on certain events that occur.

Capital Losses

Some of you are probably painfully aware that the value of assets or investments can go down as well as up, in which case you would have a capital loss. If the value goes down while you are still holding the investment, then you have an unrealized loss, and there are no tax implications. When you actually sell the investment for less than your basis amount, then you have an actual or realized loss which you will report on your tax return.

With a capital loss, only one tax rate applies, which is your marginal income tax rate.[142] That's because you use a net capital loss to reduce your income for the year, which in turn lowers the amount of taxes you owe. However, while the IRS is only too happy to tax you on every bit of any gains you may have, it limits the amount of tax forgiveness you're offered on losses. The maximum amount of capital loss you can count against your income for the year is $3,000 as of 2012 ($1,500 if you're married filing separately). Losses over that amount can be carried forward and applied against future years' taxes.

Unfortunately, *not all losses are allowed to count against your income*. Several very important personal assets are excluded, most notably:

- A loss on the sale of your home cannot be deducted, even though a gain over $500,000 for married filing jointly or $250,000 if single is taxable.[143]

- Losses on investments held inside tax-sheltered retirement accounts, except in specific cases.[144] Even so, the loss would not be the more beneficial capital loss, but would be listed in the miscellaneous deduction section on Schedule A. That means if you don't have enough total deductions to itemize, your loss doesn't count, and even if you do itemize, only your loss over 2% of your adjusted gross income counts.

---

[141] See Tax Topic 703 – Basis of Assets: www.irs.gov/taxtopics/tc703.html It references other IRS publications that may apply to your situation. Also refer to Publication 551: Basis of Assets: www.irs.gov/pub/irs-pdf/p551.pdf

[142] Your marginal tax rate is the highest rate on the income tax table at which your income is taxed.

[143] Refer to Publication 523: Selling Your Home. www.irs.gov/pub/irs-pdf/p523.pdf

[144] This article from About.com explains how to claim a loss on IRAs. taxes.about.com/od/retirementtaxes/qt/IRA_loss.htm Also refer to Publication 590: Individual Retirement Arrangements (IRAs). In Chapter 1, search for the section, "Recognizing Losses on Traditional IRA Investments," and for Roth IRAs in Chapter 2, search for the section, "Recognizing Losses on Investments," or go to the index and look for "Losses." www.irs.gov/pub/irs-pdf/p590.pdf

Reporting Gains and Losses

Capital gains and losses are reported on a Schedule D and, as of tax year 2011, a Form 8949 is needed as well.[145] These forms are filed along with your Form 1040. Good record keeping is important, particularly for assets or investments whose basis may be adjusted periodically, such as mutual funds held in a regular account. Otherwise, you may end up paying more taxes than you should when you sell and realize your gain.

With this background information on investing, you're now ready to examine specific investments, which are coming up in Chapter 13: Investment Overview and Investing in Bonds, and Chapter 14: Investing in Stocks and Funds.[146]

---

[145] Pull up IRS Schedule D www.irs.gov/pub/irs-pdf/f1040sd.pdf and the IRS Instructions for Schedule D, which includes the instructions for Form 8949: www.irs.gov/pub/irs-pdf/i1040sd.pdf
View Form 8949 here: www.irs.gov/pub/irs-pdf/f8949.pdf The IRS also created an information page for this form: www.irs.gov/form8949
The 1040 instructions also include the instructions on Schedule D and Form 8949: www.irs.gov/pub/irs-pdf/i1040sd.pdf
[146] The U.S. Department of Commerce, Bureau of Economic Analysis, provides data on personal income, business and industry, the gross domestic product and various economic indicators. bea.doc.gov

30 Minute LIVING

Suggested Action Plan

- *Make a list of your savings and investments.* Find the current value for each item and then total them up. You may want to create a spreadsheet to help you keep track of their values through time. Refer back to the personal balance sheet you created in Chapter 2: Evaluating Your Current Position to make sure you have included everything.

- *Find the percentages.* Calculate the percentage of the whole that each item represents by dividing its current value by your total amount.

- *Evaluate the risks.* Think about the risk of each of the items on your list. Group items of similar risk together and add up the percentages and the dollar amount of how much you have in each of these risk levels.

- *Consider your comfort level.* Could you comfortably take on more risk in order to possibly obtain a higher return? Or do you already have more risk than you can stomach?

- *Review your goals.* Now that you have studied the risks and returns of investing, listed out your own savings and investments, evaluated their risks and determined your comfort level with those risks, it's time to revisit your financial goals. Are your goals in alignment with the overall level of risk with which you are comfortable? If not, what adjustments do you need to make? Remember that this is a personal decision, and you need to be able to sleep at night.

- *Look back through the suggestions for saving more.* What is one thing you can do now in order to save a little more?

CHAPTER 13
Investment Overview and Investing in Bonds

A Taxing Situation!

As Alex sat staring at the tax return his accountant had just handed him, he thought to himself — *How could this have happened? Why do I owe these taxes? I thought these bonds were supposed to be tax-free!*

Alex had been investing for several years, but until a few months ago, he had never sold anything out of his regular brokerage account. However, when he needed money for the down payment on a piece of property, he decided to sell his municipal bonds. He had researched these bonds carefully before purchasing them to make sure they were highly rated, and he knew that his interest earnings qualified for tax exemption. Yet, here he was, being blindsided by taxes.

Investments themselves have many and varied features. Alex had done a good job of researching the municipal bonds before purchasing them and understood their features. What he didn't understand were the tax implications of selling these bonds before maturity and that interest earnings and capital gains are taxed differently. The interest he had earned on these bonds was indeed tax exempt, but the sale of his bonds, given what he had paid for the bonds and his basis in them, had created a taxable capital gain.

Overview of Investments

At this point, an overview of investments is in order. Understanding the basic characteristics of various investments will help provide the background information needed for studying bonds, and it will also help you in building your portfolio.

What is an investment? It's an asset (something of value) that you purchase with the expectation that it will either generate income (current return) or appreciate in value (future return), or possibly both.[147] Investments in assets represent a store of wealth that you are setting aside for the future. Assets themselves can be classified in various ways.

---

[147] For more on the types of return and how they're taxed, refer to Chapter 12: Understanding the Risks and Returns of Investing.

Real Assets

"Real" assets are physical assets or identifiable assets. This would include both tangible assets as well as intangible assets.

- *Physical or tangible assets* can be seen and touched—for example, real estate property, manufacturing plants, machinery, gold, coins, stamps, baseball card collections, etc.

- *Intangible assets* would include items such as patents, copyrights, business methodologies or brand recognition (for example, the name Disney or the recipe for Coca-Cola). Although these are not assets that can be physically touched, they can be described and identified. Goodwill is also an intangible asset and is sometimes seen on corporate balance sheets when one company purchases another for more than the book value of its assets.

Real assets can be extremely valuable, but the markets for such items tend to be limited and less liquid. For example, if you wanted to sell your gold-plated DeLorean,[148] the pool of potential buyers would be extremely limited. Real assets often come in one big chunk that can't be divided into more affordable portions and still function as intended, like a manufacturing facility.

Then there are other concerns, such as the upkeep of the property, the safe storage of items that can deteriorate or the secure storage of items that can be stolen. Investor sentiment and taste may change, and an item that was once very collectible may no longer be very desirable. For these reasons and more, real assets tend to be higher-risk investments than are most financial assets.

Financial Assets

Financial assets are not physical in nature. Instead, they are paper assets that represent a *claim against other assets*. For example, if you own stock in a company, you have a claim as a part owner of that company. If you own a corporate bond, it's like you've loaned that company money and you're holding an I.O.U. that obligates the company to pay you back. These claims are usually against:

- *Companies*—in the form of stocks (ownership or equity) and bonds (debt).

- *Governments*—in the form of bills, notes, or bonds (all are forms of debt). Government debt securities include those from the U.S. as well as other countries, from the various levels of the government (federal, state and local) and from government agencies (such as Fannie Mae and Freddie Mac).

The remainder of this chapter will examine the various forms of debt and the features of each type. Chapter 14: Investing in Stocks and Funds will explore the different types of ownership or equity investments that are available.

---

[148] The home of one of these special cars used to be a bank in Texas. www.bigtexas.com/dmc Evidently it's no longer there. But in case you want to see what one looks like, here's a great shot: en.wikipedia.org/wiki/Image:Gold-D.jpg

Claims Against Companies

In Chapter 2: Evaluating Your Current Position, you created your own personal balance sheet. You found your net worth by adding up your assets and subtracting your debts. Companies also prepare their financial statements, and a company's balance sheet has the same three parts as yours: assets, liabilities (debt), and ownership (equity). Likewise, a company's balance sheet equation is the same:

$$Assets \; = \; Debt \; + \; Equity$$

Claims against a company's assets are created when the company issues *securities*. The term, *security*, is a generic term which includes most types of financial assets, such as stocks and bonds. A security is essentially a guarantee that a certain obligation will be met. To understand the various securities issued by companies, take a look at the simple corporate balance sheet which follows:

Table 13-A: Example of a Company's Balance Sheet

BALANCE SHEET

Prepared for: Big Manufacturing Corp.   As of: December 31, 20XX

ASSETS	LIABILITIES (DEBT)	
Current assets (cash, marketable securities, etc.)	**Current liabilities**—due in 1 year or less (accounts payable, accruals, etc.)	**Lower Risk**
Other assets (accounts receivable, inventory, etc.)	**Long-term liabilities:** (notes and bonds greater than 1 year)	
Investments (securities of the gov't or other companies)	• Senior or secured debt • Junior or unsecured debt (includes debentures) • Convertible bonds	
Long-term assets (property, plant, equipment, etc.)	**Total Liabilities**	
	Equity (Ownership)	
	Preferred stock	
	Common stock	
	Retained earnings (this entry is not an investment item)	
	Total Equity	**Higher Risk**
Total Assets	**Total Liabilities + Total Equity**	

Left-Hand Side: What a Company Owns

On the left-hand side of the balance sheet is a list of the company's assets. *Assets are used by the company to make money*. For example, a manufacturing company would use its property, plant and equipment to make products for sale, or a company that services air conditioners would use its fleet of vans so their service people can travel to its customers.

Right-Hand Side: How a Company is Financed

Companies finance their assets with the items that are listed on the right-hand side of their balance sheets. In other words, *their assets are secured by their debt and equity*. The mixture of how much debt and how much equity is up to the company. While it's possible to have a company financed entirely by equity, it's not possible to have an all debt company—somebody has to own it!

When you purchase a company's securities, you are essentially investing in the right-hand side of the company's balance sheet:

Securities that are in the DEBT portion are considered inherently less risky than anything in the company's equity portion, because *debt carries a legally binding obligation*. If companies do not repay their debt in accordance to the terms of that debt, legal action can be taken against them.

Securities that are in the company's EQUITY portion are considered inherently *more* risky than those in its debt portion, because companies have *no legal obligation* to declare dividends or to ensure that their stock price goes up in order for investors to reap a capital gain.

Additionally, in the event of BANKRUPTCY in which the assets of the company are sold, *equity holders, because they are owners, are last in line to receive any of the proceeds*. If the company's financial situation is so dire that its assets must be liquidated, you can bet very few crumbs will be left for the equity holders. In fact, even the debt holders may be lucky to receive a few pennies on the dollar.[149]

To understand the claims on a company's assets in the event of a bankruptcy liquidation, envision all of the investors of that company standing in line at the bank behind the velvet rope, each with his or her hand out. Investors must line up in the order of the level of risk—those holding less risky assets at the front of the line, and those holding more risky assets at the back of the line.

Not only are the equity holders at the back of the line, but there may be even more claimants in line ahead of the equity holders that you don't see on the balance sheet, such as wages due workers, taxes owed, and unfunded pension liabilities. Obviously, before you invest in a company, you first want to check it out carefully and pick a company that's not likely to go bankrupt, because this is not a line you want to stand in!

---

[149] There are several ways corporations may file bankruptcy, and their assets are not always liquidated. Corporations may file bankruptcy under **Chapter 11**, which allows them to reorganize. The company stays in business, but usually is relieved of paying some of its debt or is allowed a longer time period to repay it. If the company's financial or business situation is more serious, the company may have to file **Chapter 7**, where the company essentially goes out of business and its assets are liquidated. This article by the Securities and Exchange Commission entitled, "What Every Investor Should Know," provides more information on corporate bankruptcy. www.sec.gov/investor/pubs/bankrupt.htm

In examining the features of a company's securities, we'll start at the top of the right-hand side of the corporate balance sheet and work down, going from those with lower risk to those with higher risk. This chapter will cover items in the debt section, while the next chapter will continue going down the line with equities.

Debt Securities

Remember, the overriding concern with any debt security is the risk of *default*, that you won't get paid back what you're owed. In general, however, *the shorter the time period, the fewer the things that can go wrong*. So with similar types of debt but with different times until maturity, the shorter-term debt would usually be considered less risky.

Short-Term Debt

Companies may have various types of current liabilities or short-term debt that comes due in a year or less. Typically, however, individual investors do not invest directly in a company's short-term debt. Instead they may do it indirectly through money market mutual funds or other funds containing short-term securities. (Mutual funds are a collection of securities that are offered by investment companies and managed by professional money managers—more on them in Chapter 14: Investing in Stocks and Funds.)

Short-term debt generally ranks very low on the risk scale because the probability of default is usually minimal. Furthermore, as mentioned previously, many investors hold the short-term debt of a company through money market mutual funds,[150] and certain restrictions apply to the assets which can be held in "money market" securities.[151] The predominant risk you do run in holding any low-risk, low-return security is:[152]

> *Purchasing power risk*—the risk that the rate of inflation will be greater than the return on your investment and will eat away the investment's purchasing power through time. If the rates are about the same, then you're only staying even.

Senior, Secured or Unsubordinated Debt

Senior debt gets respect! It takes precedent over other debt in the event of liquidation because it is secured not only by the general obligation of the company (as is all debt), but also by specific company assets. Some asset or assets on the left-hand side of the company's balance sheet have been specifically pledged against this debt, and if the debt is not repaid in accordance to the debt agreement, those assets can be seized and the proceeds used to satisfy this debt.

This concept is similar to an individual pledging collateral for a loan, such as allowing an auto to secure an auto note or a home to secure a home mortgage. If the loan is not repaid as agreed upon, the asset may be repossessed and sold to repay the debt.

---

[150] Learn more about money market from Investopedia's extensive tutorial. www.investopedia.com/university/moneymarket
[151] Learn more about the rules concerning money market funds from the SEC. sec.gov/answers/mfmmkt.htm
[152] The types of risks and the returns that are expected from investing are covered more extensively in Chapter 12: Understanding the Risks and Returns of Investing.

Senior debt usually takes the form of notes or bonds. (As an aside, bills, notes and bonds are all debt, but with different time periods to maturity. Bills fall in the short-term category and usually mature in a year or less. Notes are intermediate term and usually mature in between 1 and 10 years. Bonds are long-term and usually mature in a time period greater than 10 years.) Senior debt typically ranks low on the risk scale for default. Because the debt is secured, investors are likely to get repaid.

However, the lower the risk, the lower the return that can be expected (relative to other returns available at the time). With senior debt, investors run three predominant risks:

1. *Purchasing power risk*—even though the rates offered on secured debt are usually higher than what you can earn on money market or bank accounts, you still may net very little real return after allowing for inflation.

2. *Interest rate risk*—this is the risk that interest rates will go up after you have purchased your investment. All "fixed income" securities (and those that behave like fixed-income securities, such as preferred stock) are subject to interest rate risk, even short-term debt to a limited degree. This point leads to the following investment principle:

Bond prices are inversely related to the direction of change in interest rates:
If interest rates go *up*, the value of a fixed-rate bond you currently hold will go *down*.
If interest rates go *down*, the value of a fixed-rate bond you currently hold will go *up*.

Understanding the concept of interest rate risk is so vital to bond holders that an explanation is in order right now before continuing with the third major risk of senior debt.

Why do bond prices move in the opposite direction when interest rates change?

At first glance, this principle seems counterintuitive. These examples help explain why this inverse relationship exists.

Example: When the Prevailing Rates go UP

Let's say you've purchased a bond with a stated rate of 6% per year. Sometime later, the prevailing interest rates go *up*. Now when another company decides to issue new bonds that are of comparable quality and length of maturity as your bond, it must offer a higher interest rate of, say, 7%.

If you decide to sell your bond before it matures, investors compare your old 6% bond to the new 7% bond. All else being equal, they would choose the higher paying 7% bond. So if you really want to sell your bond, you're going to have to *discount* it (mark down the price) to make up for its lower interest rate. If you do not wish to sell your bond and instead hold it to maturity, you will continue to receive the 6% interest payments. In that case, you will not have "realized" a loss from the bond's price going down, but rather, you will have an *opportunity cost*—you've received 6% when you could have had 7% if your money hadn't been tied up.

What is meant by "prevailing rates?" To get an idea of what the current rates are with Treasury, municipal and corporate bonds, pull up the Yahoo Bond Center's Composite Bond

Rates. Debt issues or bonds that are of similar quality and length to maturity will offer about the same interest rates. That's because risk and return are positively related, as explained in Chapter 12. Riskier debt must offer a higher return than other offerings currently available on the market or investors wouldn't purchase it. So debt that falls in the same category, such as 2-year A rated corporate bonds, will all offer just about the same rate of return. A 2-year Treasury, however, is considered less risky, so you'll notice it doesn't have to offer as high a return as do corporate bonds of the same length to maturity.

Example: When the Prevailing Rates go DOWN

On the other hand, if the prevailing interest rates go *down*, you're really tickled because the value of your bond goes *up*. That's because your old bond pays 6% per year, and a newly issued bond comparable to yours pays only, say, 5%. Compared to the newly issued bond, your bond is more attractive. If you choose to sell your bond, investors would be willing to pay you a *premium* because of the higher interest payments on your bond. If you choose not to sell your bond and hold it to maturity, you get to pocket the higher 6% interest payments while other bond investors are stuck with 5%.

So, to sum up this principle, every time the prevailing interest rates change, the prices of already issued bonds or other fixed-income securities change also, but in the *opposite* direction. *The real pain happens when the prevailing rates go UP, because the value of the fixed-rate securities that you already own will go DOWN.*

Now, on to the third major risk of senior debt!

3. *Reinvestment rate risk* — this is the risk that a bondholder will not be able to reinvest the bond's interest payments at the same rate or better than that of the bond itself. This is a particular risk with callable bonds, because bonds are more likely to be called when interest rates are low. Then the investor may be not be able to find another investment that yields as much without taking on greater risk. (Callable bonds are discussed further in this chapter in the section, "How Bonds Work.")

This risk exists for all fixed-income type securities, but it becomes *increasingly more significant the HIGHER the interest rate and the LONGER the period of time that you own the bond.* This brings us to yet another investment principle:

Interest must be reinvested at the same rate in order to earn the compounded return quoted. In order for bondholders to actually receive the quoted *compounded* annual interest rate, each interest payment received must be *immediately reinvested at that same quoted rate.* Otherwise, the return that bondholders actually receive may be higher or lower.

This may not be easy to do, and in actuality, bondholders frequently earn a rate that is different from the stated rate on their bonds or other fixed-income securities. If bondholders *spend* the interest payments or let them languish in a low-return account, their compounded annual rate of return on their investment is usually *much less*. If bondholders *reinvest* the interest payments, the rate of return may be *higher* or *lower*, depending on the investment options available at the time of reinvestment.

At this point, you may be thinking—if a bond pays a certain stated rate per year, how can you *not* be getting that rate? The operative word here is "compounded"[153] annual return.

To explain, let's assume that you have in your portfolio an 8% bond which you just purchased at its $1,000 par value and that it matures in 10 years. If you hold this bond until maturity, you expect to receive $800 in interest ($80 per year x 10 years) plus the return of the $1,000 face value at maturity, for a total of **$1,800**.

If you don't reinvest your interest payments, that's all you get. True, you have received 8% per year, but it's 8% *simple* interest. To obtain an 8% *compounded* rate of return, you must reinvest each payment at the same 8% rate. If you did that, you would end up with a total of about **$2,159** at the end of the 10 years. (In fact, if you receive $40 payments each six months as is typical of bonds, instead of $80 annually, you would end up with about **$2,190**.) The extra top amount on the graph which follows shows the difference between 8% compounded annually and an 8% simple return on a 10 year bond.

Graph 13-A: Comparison of 8% Returns over 10 Years—Simple vs. Annual Compounding.

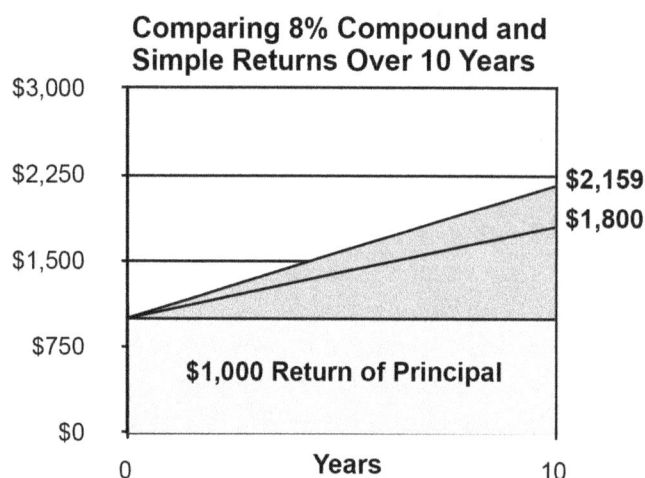

Comparing 8% Compound and Simple Returns Over 10 Years

$3,000	
$2,250	$2,159
	$1,800
$1,500	
$750	**$1,000 Return of Principal**
$0	

0   **Years**   10

The *longer* the time period, the more *frequently* that compounding occurs, and the *higher* the interest rate, the *greater* the reward you will receive from reinvesting the payments and earning a compound rather than a simple return.

Junior or Unsecured Debt

Unsecured debt goes by several names, such as junior debt, subordinated debt or debentures. While all debt carries with it the legal obligation of the company to repay it, unsecured debt is backed solely by the promise of the company and not by any specific asset or assets. Also, in the event of bankruptcy, unsecured debt holders will get paid only if there's anything left after secured debt and any other claims that are in line ahead of them get paid. *Because of this added risk, the interest rate paid on unsecured debt is generally higher than on secured debt.*

---

[153] Read Investopedia's explanation of "compound": www.investopedia.com/terms/c/compound.asp

A company's junior debt is similar in nature to what you may have in your wallet—an unsecured consumer credit card. With your credit card, you know that you have the obligation to repay what you owe and that legal action can be taken against you if you don't, but there is no specific asset that the company can come and repossess. Also, because it's unsecured, the interest rate on your credit card is usually higher than that of any secured debt you may have, such as a home mortgage.

Investing in the unsecured debt of a company involves the same risks as that of investing in secured debt, but in differing degrees. Also, the risk of default becomes more of a concern.

1. *Purchasing power risk*—this risk, while still present, is somewhat diminished. While the rates offered on unsecured debt are relatively higher than the rates on secured debt, they may still not be much higher than inflation. The level of this risk will depend on the prevailing interest rates and the amount of inflation at the time.

2. *Interest rate risk*—as explained above, all fixed-income securities face this risk. However, it becomes even more significant the higher the interest rate, because the price fluctuations will be greater when interest rates change. The real damage occurs if the prevailing rates go UP after you have made your purchase, because the value of your security, should you decide to sell it before maturity, goes DOWN. Therefore, unsecured debt, with its relatively higher interest rates, will be affected more than will secured debt, which typically offers lower interest rates.

3. *Reinvestment rate risk*—this risk is also greater for unsecured debt due to its relatively higher interest rates. That's because the higher the rate, the harder it will be to reinvest the interest received at that high a rate of return. You may have to accumulate your interest payments in a lower-yielding savings account for awhile until you have a large enough amount to purchase another investment.

4. *Financial or credit risk*—this is the risk that the company will be unable to meet its financial obligations. The interest rates on unsecured debt are higher, which makes it more costly for the issuing company to repay. It's also unsecured and backed only by the company's promise to repay, which further increases the risk that the bondholders will not get repaid. This debt will likely receive a lower rating than what the same company would receive on secured debt (ratings are addressed later). The lower the debt is rated, the greater the risk of default.

How Bonds Work

Now that you have seen the placement of various types of debt on a corporate balance sheet, this would be an appropriate time to talk about bonds in general. Bonds are the predominant way that individual investors can invest in debt securities.

A *bond* is a loan, and investors are essentially playing the role of a banker when they purchase bonds. You're loaning your money to the company or whoever issued the bond. This loan is for a stated time period, and at the end of the loan (called the maturity date) investors receive back the face value of the bond (which may be different than what you paid for the bond).

During the term of the loan, bondholders earn interest on their bonds. Most bonds pay a *coupon*.[154] This is simply the interest payment, which is usually calculated at a stated fixed rate and paid twice a year. There are bonds, called *zero coupon bonds*,[155] that do not pay a coupon while you own the bond. However, the interest is still being accrued, and you get it in the end. There are also a few bonds available which pay a *variable interest rate*.[156]

Many bonds are *callable*, which means after a certain time period, the issuer can call or redeem your bond. You'll get back the face value and usually an extra amount, or call premium, as well. Bonds are more likely to be called if interest rates have dropped since your bond was issued, because now the issuer can pay you off and reissue new debt at a lower interest rate. Your challenge is then to find another good investment for your money without taking greater risk.[157]

Par Value

Bonds have a *par value* or *face value*, and for corporate bonds, it's typically $1,000. This means that regardless of the amount the bond was purchased for, whoever owns the bond at maturity will receive back the face amount of $1,000 per bond. Note that government bonds (federal, municipal, etc.) can have various face values, with those of EE Savings Bonds going as low as $50. Also, you may occasionally find corporate bonds with a face amount other than $1,000.

Purchasing Bonds

Bonds can either be purchased when they're newly issued, or they can be purchased later from another investor on the secondary markets (such as the New York Stock Exchange or the Over the Counter (OTC) Market). Because bond prices are affected by changes in the prevailing interest rates, bonds can be purchased for amounts that are greater than, equal to, or less than their face value. Bond prices can also vary because of factors such as supply and demand or changes in the credit quality of the bond.

Due to transaction costs, investors typically purchase several bonds at once, say perhaps a minimum of $10,000 worth of the same issue of bonds. This makes the purchase more cost effective. In fact, there may be a stated minimum number that must be purchased.

Also, be aware that bonds may be more *"thinly traded"* than stocks. Definitely, some issues of bonds are more thinly traded than other issues. This means that at any given time, there may not be a high trade volume. In fact, trades on the secondary markets may be few and far between. If you buy your bond and hold it until maturity, this is not a problem. However, if you wish to sell your bond to someone else before maturity, you may not be able find anybody that wants to buy your bond, particularly for the price that you desire. This can sometimes make the price of your bond quite volatile.

---

[154] The interest on a bond is still called its "coupon" because it used to be that bonds came in a printed certificate form with coupons attached. The bondholder clipped off and sent in each coupon when due in order to receive the interest payments. Many bonds are now issued electronically, without a certificate, and the interest payments are also made electronically into your account where you're holding your bonds.
[155] Zero coupon bonds are discount bonds and are discussed later in the section "Other Types of Bonds."
[156] Zacks presents this interesting article, "Do You Need a Floating Rate Bond ETF?" www.zacks.com/stock/news/66482/Do+You+Need+A+Floating+Rate+Bond+ETF%3F
[157] For more information refer to this SEC article, "Callable or Redeemable Bonds." www.sec.gov/answers/callablebonds.htm

Bond Indenture

Each issue of bonds has its own set of rules, called a *bond indenture*, which spells out the agreement between the bondholder and the company. These rules remain in effect for a given bond issue, even if the company issues other bonds later with different rules.

Example: How Bonds Typically Work

So here's an example of the way bonds usually work: Let's say you just purchased a bond issued by Purple Cow Corp. for $1,000. This bond pays a *coupon*, or annual interest, of 7%, makes semiannual payments, as is typically done, and matures in 10 years.

First, to determine the amount of interest paid annually, multiply the face value by the interest rate to get $70 ($1,000 face value x 0.07). Because this bond pays interest semiannually, divide the annual amount in half to get $35 — this is what you will receive each six months. If you continue to hold the bond until maturity, you will receive $35 every six months for the next 10 years until the very last payment. At that time, you will receive not only the last $35 interest payment, but also the $1,000 par or face value. So over the life of the bond, you will receive a total of $1,700.

Bond Ratings

With all debt, creditworthiness is a prime consideration, but even more so with unsecured debt. As stated previously, *the higher the risk, the higher the expected return demanded by investors*. The credit rating system for bonds helps investors evaluate the level of risk they're taking.

Just as your credit score helps a bank evaluate you as a financial risk and impacts the rate you're offered on loans or credit cards, so it is with debt ratings for companies. However, the rating system for companies is not done with numbers like it is for consumers. Instead, it's an A-B-C system, and just like when you're in school, the more A's, the better!

The agencies which evaluate debt and assign ratings include Moody's, Standard & Poor's, and Fitch. A debt rating represents that agency's opinion of the ability of the company issuing the debt to repay its debt according to the terms of the debt. Ratings can change as time passes, depending on changes in a company's ability (or its perceived ability) to repay its debt.

The abbreviated chart that follows shows the basic bond rating categories. Within a category, the various agencies may further refine the ratings (i.e., add 1, 2, or 3 to the rating or a plus or minus). For a more complete chart, refer to BondsOnline.com.[158]

---

[158] This page shows the more detailed ratings chart. www.bondsonline.com/Bond_Ratings_Definitions.php For more information on bonds, visit the Bondsonline Research Directory. www.bondsonline.com/Fixed_Income_Research/Research_Directory.php

Table 13-B: Chart of Bond Ratings Used by Various Rating Agencies

	Bond Ratings	Moody's	S&P	Fitch
Investment Grade	Highest quality	Aaa	AAA	AAA
	High quality	Aa	AA	AA
	Upper medium quality	A	A	A
	Lower medium quality	Baa	BBB	BBB
Below Investment Grade (also called "junk" or "high-yield" bonds)	Lower quality bonds— the lower the rating, the greater the risk of default.	Ba	BB	BB
		B	B	B
		B	B	B
		Caa	CCC	CCC
		↓	↓	↓
		(various C and D ratings)		

Note that the top four categories above the heavy gray line make up the "investment-grade" ratings. Companies whose debt receives an investment-grade rating are able to issue debt at a relatively lower interest rate, while companies whose debt receives a "below investment-grade" rating must offer a relatively higher interest rate due to the greater risk of default.

That dividing line is especially important for big, institutional investors. They are quite often restricted as to the percentage of their total portfolios that can be invested in below investment-grade bonds, many times no more than 5%. These institutional investors include insurance companies, mutual funds and pension funds, among others. If these big players, who buy vast quantities of bonds and control huge amounts of capital, are allowed to purchase only relatively small quantities of junk bonds, you can understand how this would limit the potential market for below investment-grade bonds.

Companies greatly prefer to have their bonds rated in the investment-grade categories, because they can get by with offering lower interest rates and because the market for their bonds is much less limited.

What causes a company's debt to be rated "below investment" (or "junk") grade?

Anything that might hamper a company's ability to repay its debt can result in a lower rating. This could include companies with the following characteristics:

- Companies with a relatively heavy debt load.
- New start-up companies with a short track record and unproven management.
- Small companies, because they don't have "deep pockets," or large cash reserves to help them weather economic downturns.
- Companies in volatile industries or in newly developing industries.

You can see from this list that just because a company's debt is rated below investment grade doesn't necessarily mean that it's a bad company. The risks of holding its debt are greater, however, but so are the potential rewards. As with any investment, investors must do their homework first, before plopping down their money.

Issuers of Bonds

Bonds come in many varieties and can have a number of features. There are four broad categories of bonds:

1. Corporate Bonds and Other Debt Instruments Issued by U.S. Corporations. Corporate bonds were discussed previously. Note that the returns from these bonds are income-taxable to investors unless they are held within retirement accounts.

2. U.S. Government Bonds. This category often includes:

- Debt securities issued by the **U.S. Treasury** that are backed by the full faith and credit of the U.S. government, such as Treasury bills, notes and bonds.
- Debt securities of **government agencies** whose debt is directly backed by the government, such as Ginnie Mae (Government National Mortgage Association) which provides home mortgage money.
- Debt securities of **government-sponsored agencies** whose debt is sponsored but not guaranteed by the federal government, such as Fannie Mae (Federal National Mortgage Association) and Freddie Mac (Federal Home Loan Mortgage Corporation).[159]

Government agency and government-sponsored agency bonds are progressively a little riskier than bonds issued directly by the Treasury and therefore must offer somewhat higher rates of return. In the past, many investors felt it was a safe bet the government wouldn't allow these agencies to default, and considered the extra risk in holding these securities to be negligible. However, the government's massive bailout of Fannie Mae and Freddie Mac in 2008 caused investors to realize that the level of risk of these securities was greater than they had anticipated.

Interest earnings from Treasury securities are not taxable at the state and local level, but they are subject to federal income taxes. Taxation of government agency bonds and government-sponsored agency bonds may or may not be taxable at the various levels, depending on the particular agency. Of course, whatever is held within a retirement account is not taxable until the money is withdrawn from the account.

3. Municipal Bonds. These are issued by state and local governments for projects such as schools, highways, hospitals, and infrastructure. When you hear about a "tax-exempt" or "tax-free" investment, you can bet it has to do with municipal bonds. Municipal bonds offer a low rate of return compared to other investment offerings. This makes it possible for the state and local governments to finance various projects at a low cost. Investors are willing to

---

[159] This Fidelity page offers more information on agency bonds. www.fidelity.com/bonds/agency-bonds

purchase these low-yielding securities because they don't have to pay income taxes on the interest earned.[160]

Municipal bonds get ratings in much the same manner that corporate bonds do, with AAA being the highest rating for safety. Although it doesn't happen frequently, municipal governments can and do default on their debt payments, which makes for a much greater variation in the level of safety of municipals in general than for federal government debt.

Taxation of Municipal Bonds

Concerning the taxation of munis, there are numerous issues to consider.[161] First of all, the interest earned on some municipal bonds *is* subject to federal income taxes if the federal government feels the project funded by that particular bond issue does not significantly benefit the public as a whole.

However, state and local income taxes are separate issues from federal income taxes. Munis that are not exempt at the federal level may be exempt from state and/or local taxes. Conversely, munis that are tax-exempt from federal taxes may be income taxable at the state and/or local levels if you're holding bonds issued by an entity from another state. This can become a problem for people who own munis and then move to another state where their bonds may be taxable.

Finally, as mentioned previously, if you sell your bonds before maturity, you may have to pay tax on the capital gains. You must keep track of the basis in your bonds to know. Your gain will be taxed differently, depending on whether it's a long-term or short-term gain. If you have a capital loss, you may be able to count it against your other gains. For these reasons and more, investors need to research municipal bonds carefully before purchasing them.

How do you know if you'll be better off purchasing a municipal bond?

It depends on your tax rate, and in general, municipals become more attractive for people who are taxed at higher rates and less attractive for people taxed at lower rates. Because so many people do not understand how to determine if they would be better off with a municipal bond or not, consider the following illustration.

Example: How to Determine if a Tax-Free Bond Will Benefit You

Let's say your marginal tax rate is 25% (assume that only federal income taxes apply), and you're comparing a tax-exempt municipal bond that pays 4% interest per year with a taxable corporate bond of the same quality and length to maturity that pays 6% per year.

With the corporate bond, you'll be surrendering 25% of the return to taxes and be left with

---

[160] While the *interest* on qualified municipal bonds is not federally income-taxable, *capital gains* are. Investors can purchase munis and sell them before maturity. If they sell at a gain, they will have to pay taxes on the gain portion. Also, if you live in a state with a state and/or local income tax, and purchase municipal bonds from a different state, those munis may be subject to your state and local income taxes.

[161] Learn more in this article, "Taxation of Municipal Bonds," presented by Investinginbonds.com. www.investinginbonds.com/learnmore.asp?catid=8&subcatid=60 This page also provides extensive information about municipal bonds: www.investinginbonds.com/learnmore.asp?catid=8&subcatid=53 Look on the right-hand side for the table of contents for this chapter.

75%, for an after-tax return of 4.5% (6% x .75). So in this example, you're better off buying the corporate bond and paying taxes on it. You would only be better off with a municipal if it paid a rate greater than 4.5%. If you broke even after paying taxes on the corporate bond, you would be indifferent between the two.

Formulas for determining if you'll be better off with a municipal bond or not:
You must first find the break-even rate. This is the rate at which you would be indifferent between the two bonds. If you know the rate of return on a taxable corporate bond, the formula to determine your break-even rate on a municipal bond would be:

taxable corporate bond rate x (1 – your marginal tax rate)[162]

If you know the tax-exempt municipal bond rate, the formula to determine your break-even rate on a corporate bond would be:

tax-exempt municipal bond rate / (1 – your marginal tax rate)

Remember, at break-even you're indifferent between the corporate and the municipal, because you would end up with the same return. To tip the tables one way or the other, one of the bonds must yield a greater return on an after-tax basis.

The table below shows the break-even returns for various tax rates. For example, if your total tax rate is 30%, you would need for a corporate bond to return greater than 7.14% for it to be more attractive than a municipal bond with a return of 5%.

Table 13-C: What you must earn on a taxable bond to equal the return on a tax-exempt bond.

Your after-tax return will be:	If your total income tax rate (federal + state + local) is:							
	15%	20%	25%	30%	35%	40%	45%	50%
3%	3.53%	3.75%	4.00%	4.29%	4.62%	5.00%	5.45%	6.00%
4%	4.71%	5.00%	5.33%	5.71%	6.15%	6.67%	7.27%	8.00%
5%	5.88%	6.25%	6.67%	7.14%	7.69%	8.33%	9.09%	10.00%
6%	7.06%	7.50%	8.00%	8.57%	9.23%	10.00%	10.91%	12.00%
7%	8.24%	8.75%	9.33%	10.00%	10.77%	11.67%	12.73%	14.00%

As you can easily see from the table, tax-exempt bonds are much more attractive for people who pay higher taxes. To get the same 5% after-tax return, someone who is taxed at 50% would have to find a 10% taxable bond, while someone who is taxed at 15% would only need a 5.88% taxable bond.

---

[162] Change your tax rate to decimal form. For example, you would change 25% to 0.25 in the formula.

> **Because risk and return are positively related, the person with the higher taxes must take on greater risk than someone with lower taxes in order to be left with the same after-tax return.**

Municipals may well be lower risk investments than the corporate bonds which are offering much higher returns, relative to the current prevailing interest rates.

However, because the word "tax-free" has a nice ring to it, municipals are sometimes heavily marketed to people that will benefit only marginally, or maybe not at all. Those who are taxed at lower rates could be better off with a high quality corporate bond than a muni. And, as mentioned previously, there can be numerous tax considerations with munis, particularly in certain states.

4. International Bonds Offered by Foreign Companies or Governments. Investing internationally adds another layer of risk on top of the risks previously mentioned. (Refer to Chapter 12: Understanding the Risks and Returns of Investing.) These additional risks could include: difficulty in obtaining full financial information on the company or entity, political stability of the country involved and fluctuations in the currency exchange rates, as well as other considerations. If you want exposure to international bonds but don't want to hold them outright, you might consider adding a mutual fund or ETF (exchange-traded fund) to your portfolio which contains the type bonds you desire.

Other Types of Bonds

By now you understand that a wide array of bonds exists. Below are several other types that need to be mentioned.

Discount Bonds

Discount bonds are different by design from regular bonds. Discount bonds are always issued at a discount to their face value and then grow in value through time. They do not pay interest while you own them, but they do pay back the stated face value at maturity. Your reward is the difference between what you paid for the bond and what you receive at maturity.

For example, the paper version of the U.S. Treasury's *EE Savings Bond* which many people still hold was issued in various denominations, and always at a set discount of 50% — you paid $25 to purchase a bond with a $50 face value.[163] Other bonds are discounted by the rate of interest they pay, like *Treasury bills*. Because T-bills mature in one year or less, it doesn't

---

[163] The newer electronic version of the Treasury's EE Savings Bond is issued at face value; you would pay $50 to purchase a bond with a $50 face value. As of January 1, 2012, paper bonds will no longer be sold at financial institutions. You can still purchase a bond for as low as $25, and in exact amounts to the penny. Refer to this page: www.treasurydirect.gov/indiv/research/indepth/ebonds/res_e_bonds.htm
You can defer paying taxes on the interest until maturity if you desire. However, if you choose to pay taxes annually, you must continue to do so, and you must do so for all your savings bonds. For more on savings bonds, refer to Chapter 4: Understanding Your Cash Accounts. Also, this page at the Treasury's web site discusses taxation and other considerations concerning savings bonds.
www.treasurydirect.gov/indiv/research/indepth/ebonds/res_e_bonds_eetaxconsider.htm

make much sense to receive interest payments each six months. (Many have maturities shorter than six months anyway.) You might purchase a 26-week T-bill for $980 and at maturity receive $1,000. The $20 growth in value through time would be the interest you earn.

Zero coupon bonds are another example of bonds always sold at a discount, with the amount of the discount depending on the interest rate being offered. While zeroes usually have longer maturity dates than do T-bills, the idea is the same. You might purchase a zero for say, $600, and in 10 years receive back the face value of $1,000. The bond's growth of $400 would represent an annual interest rate of about 5%.[164]

Note that if zeroes are held in a regular taxable account (rather than in a tax-sheltered retirement account), the interest is *"imputed"* year by year. In other words, the calculated interest amount for the year is chalked up to the bondholder, and the bondholder must pay taxes on the imputed interest year by year, even though he or she receives no actual cash in hand until the bond is either sold or matures.

Also note that zeros are particularly susceptible to interest rate risk. Because they do not pay interest while you hold them, their prices will suffer more than will regular bonds of comparable quality and length to maturity when interest rates go up. Also, longer-term bonds will take a greater hit than will shorter-term bonds.

Why buy zeroes? Some people like to know exactly what they will end up with at the end and not have to worry about finding appropriate investments along the way for any interest payments. Say in 20 years when you retire, you want $20,000 to sail around the world. If you could buy 7% zeros today, you would only have to pay $258.42 for a bond that will mature in 20 years for $1,000. So if you buy 20 of them, it will only cost you $5,168.40 to have the $20,000 waiting for you. However, given your particular situation, there could be better ways to fund your dream. And who knows what your adventure will cost in 20 years? A good financial planner or wealth manager can offer suggestions that are appropriate for your particular needs.

Convertible Bonds

Convertible bonds are like tadpoles — they start out life in one form, and if they survive, they turn into something else. Instead of frogs, however, they can be exchanged for the common stock of the company that issued the bonds.[165]

Like a regular bond, a convertible bond pays interest to the bondholder, usually every six months or one year. Convertible bonds are almost always unsecured debt, and even though this presents a greater risk to the investor, companies are able to issue convertibles at a *lower* interest rate than their nonconvertible bonds.

---

[164] This SEC article discusses zero coupon bonds. www.sec.gov/answers/zero.htm
[165] Investopedia presents more information in this article, "Convertible Bonds: An Introduction." www.investopedia.com/articles/01/052301.asp#axzz1pSzXTwWA

Investors are willing to settle for lower interest, even with the higher risk, because convertibles are issued with the bonus feature that each bond can be converted into a given number of shares of the company's common stock. If the company does well and its common stock share price goes up, there comes a point at which it will be profitable for investors to convert their convertible bonds into stock. Such convertibles are said to be *"in the money."*

Example: How Convertible Bonds Work

Let's say that Big-O Corp. issued convertible bonds with $1,000 face value which pay 4% interest yearly, and each bond can be converted into 20 shares of its stock. If Big-O's stock price is now $3 per share, no one would want to convert their $1,000 bond into $60 worth of stock ($3 per share x 20 shares per bond). Bondholders will be content to simply continue receiving their $40 per year in interest ($1,000 bond x 0.04). However, if the company's stock price were to go up to $50 per share, bondholders would definitely start thinking about converting, because now they can trade one $1,000 bond for $1,000 in common stock ($50 per share x 20 shares).

However, investors may choose not to convert, even though the convertible bonds have reached *parity* with the stock (i.e., can be traded for something of equal value). One reason is that the stock price could go back down and then they would have lost money by converting, as well as having given up the bond's interest payments. Another reason is because when convertible bonds are "in the money," they may trade at an attractive premium to their underlying (or intrinsic) value.

Convertible bonds are more complex than regular bonds and require a greater level of understanding. The risks of investing in convertible bonds include all of those previously mentioned for unsecured debt, but in varying degrees. The financial risk that the company will default in its payments is usually the greatest concern for convertibles.

When the stock markets are volatile and dropping, investors sometimes turn to bonds for a "safe" return. By now you probably understand that no investment is safe and that all investments involve risk. What differs are the types of risks involved and the level or degree of those risks. Bonds certainly have risks, as we have seen. This study of investments will continue in the next chapter, Chapter 14: Investing in Stocks and Funds.

30 Minute LIVING

Suggested Action Plan

- *Consider the current economic climate.* Are the prevailing interest rates currently high or low compared to what they have been in the past? Remember that bond prices move in the opposite direction of interest rates.

- *If interest rates in general are now relatively low,* they are more likely to go up in the future than they are to go down. Purchasing bonds when interest rates are relatively low can be very painful if interest rates go up while you are holding these bonds, because the price of your bonds will go down. If you keep your bonds until maturity, then you are just getting a lower return than you could have gotten if you hadn't sunk your money into these bonds. That's an opportunity cost. On the other hand, if you sell your bonds before maturity, then you are likely to realize a loss on the sale of your bonds.

- *If interest rates in general are now relatively high,* they are more likely to go down in the future than they are to go up. Purchasing bonds when interest rates are relatively high could prove to be quite lucrative if interest rates go down while you are holding these bonds, because the price of your bonds will go up. The higher rate that you have locked in on your bonds will be more attractive than other comparable offerings when the rates go down. Therefore, if you sell your bonds before maturity, you are likely to be able to sell them at a premium and realize a gain. On the other hand, if you just hold your bonds until maturity, you will benefit from receiving higher interest than is available on other comparable offerings. That's nice, too.

- *Time matters.* In general, the longer you have your money tied up in an investment, the greater the return you would expect. Also, the longer the time until maturity on a bond, the more impact a change in the interest rates will have. Prices will fluctuate more on a longer-term bond than on a shorter-term bond from the same company with the same coupon and same credit quality.

- *Compare apples to apples.* When you're comparing bonds and the rates they offer, be sure to compare the same type of bonds of approximately the same length to maturity and credit quality. Otherwise, it's not a fair comparison. For example, you wouldn't compare the return on a one-year Treasury bill with that of a five-year junk bond of a start-up company.

CHAPTER 14

Investing in Stocks and Funds

Don't Invest Your Lunch Money!

It was the first week of Personal Finance class, and on the first day, a young woman named Morgan told the class that she owned some stocks and was into investing. On the second day of class, she announced that she was really upset. The students' tuition bills are due within the first few days of a new semester or they get dropped from the class roster. "I just bought this GM stock a few months ago," Morgan told us, "and now the price is down. I'm going to have to sell my shares at a loss so I can pay my tuition."

Investing is meant to be a longer-term process. The stock markets can be volatile, but over time they usually average an upward trend. However, during a short time period, the markets can certainly go down. You don't want to invest money that you need any time soon, certainly not within the next year or even two years. As a financial planner who presented a guest lecture in one of our classes explained, "You don't invest your lunch money, or you'll go hungry."

Equities have traditionally fueled the engine that's driven long-term portfolio growth. If you expect to obtain a return that beats the negative effects of taxes and inflation, you'll more than likely need to invest a portion of your portfolio in equity securities. This chapter explores the various types of equity investments and the risks involved in holding them.

Equity Securities

So what are equities? *Equity represents ownership of something*, so when you purchase an equity security, you now own at least a tiny sliver of a company. To make it easier to follow the discussion on equities, the corporate balance sheet that was presented in Chapter 13: Investment Overview and Investing in Bonds also appears on the next page.

As a brief review, you'll remember that companies list their assets on the left-hand side of their balance sheets. Their assets are what they use to make money or generate revenues, and they fund their assets with what's on the right-hand side. In other words, their assets are *secured* by their debt and equity.

Most companies will use a combination of debt and equity, but it is possible for a company to be funded entirely by equity and have zero debt. It's not possible, however, for a company to be funded entirely by debt, because someone must own the company.

Also note that while you can purchase the debt not only of corporations, but also that of various levels of the government and government agencies, equity is different. You can purchase ownership only of companies, not of governments. (You already own the government because you're a taxpayer, or maybe it's the government that owns you, but that's a discussion best saved for a political science debate.)

Debt securities were covered in the last chapter, and you saw how the level of risk increases as you travel from the top and go down the right-hand side of a company's balance sheet. In this chapter we will continue on down and cover the equity section.

BALANCE SHEET		
Prepared for: *Big Manufacturing Corp.*	As of: *December 31, 20XX*	
ASSETS	**LIABILITIES (DEBT)**	Lower Risk
Current assets (cash, marketable securities, etc.)	**Current liabilities**—due in 1 year or less (accounts payable, accruals, etc.)	
Other assets (accounts receivable, inventory, etc.)	**Long-term liabilities:** (notes and bonds greater than 1 year)	
Investments (securities of the gov't or other companies)	• Senior or secured debt • Junior or unsecured debt (includes debentures)	
Long-term assets (property, plant, equipment, etc.)	• Convertible bonds	
	Total Liabilities	
	Equity (Ownership)	
	Preferred stock Common stock Retained earnings (this entry is not an investment item)	
	Total Equity	Higher Risk
Total Assets	**Total Liabilities + Total Equity**	

Investing in equities means you have **crossed the line** into the ownership section of a company's balance sheet. Anything in the equity section is considered **inherently riskier** than anything in the debt section. That's because companies have no legal obligation on their equity to either pay dividends or to create capital gains, while they do have the legal obligation to repay their debt.

In the event of a bankruptcy liquidation where the assets of the company are sold to pay the claims against those assets, the owners of the company (that's you if you own the company's stock) stand last in line to receive the proceeds. If the company had difficulty paying its debt obligations before bankruptcy, it's highly unlikely there will be anything left for the owners after bankruptcy.

Because of the inherent level of risk posed by owning a company's equity securities, *it is imperative to do your homework before buying stock!* Of course, you should carefully research *all* investments before you buy them, but people are much more likely to buy stocks on impulse than they are other securities. You don't hear many hot bond tips, but hot stock tips are everywhere, from the beauty parlor to the talking heads on TV. Buying stocks on a hunch rather than basing your decision on sound investment principles is akin to rubbing a lucky rabbit's foot and rolling the dice.

Preferred Stock

Preferred stock will usually be the first item listed in the equity section of a company's balance sheet—if the company even has any outstanding issues of preferred stock. Many companies do not. Like convertible bonds, preferred stock is a hybrid security that rides the fence between debt and equity. It lives in the equity section, but it behaves like debt.

Preferred stock is often referred to as a *"fixed income"* security, because, like debt, it pays a fixed amount each year to its owners. The dividend will be a function of its par value. You may see it stated as either a dollar amount or a percentage (such as $6 preferred or 6% preferred). *The par value of preferred stock is usually $100,* so the dividend in this example would be $6 per year, no matter which way it's stated. That's because 6% of $100 = $6.

Why is preferred stock classified as equity if it pays a fixed amount like debt?

Unlike debt, preferred stock *does not have the legal obligation* to pay its dividend. A company can skip paying its preferred shareholders if needed. However, companies usually don't want to miss a payment, because it sends a bad signal to their creditors that the company is having financial difficulties. Their bond ratings could drop, and it would likely become more difficult and more expensive for them to obtain additional financing in the future. Also, some preferred stock carries the stipulation that if too many dividend payments are missed, the company may forfeit some of the control of the company to the preferred owners. So in general, it's not a good thing for companies to miss a payment.

Does the company have to make up missed dividend payments?

That depends. If the preferred stock is *cumulative,* then the next time the company does declare dividends, it must pay any dividends that are in arrears to the preferred shareholders *before* the common shareholders get paid *any* of their dividends. On the other hand, if the preferred stock is *non-cumulative,* the company is not obligated to pay missed dividends.

So why is it called preferred?

As stated earlier, the preferred shareholders get first claim on any dividends that the company declares. If there's anything left after all the preferred shareholders are paid (including any dividends in arrears), then the common shareholders get to divide the remainder. Remember, companies do *not* have to declare dividends during any given time period, but once they do declare, they are pretty much obligated to follow through.

Also, in the event of a liquidation bankruptcy, preferred shareholders are in line ahead of the common shareholders in the dividing up of the assets. Not that there'll be anything left after all the other claimants are paid. In such cases, it's little consolation being next to last rather than dead last.[166]

How do preferred shareholders profit?

Preferred stockholders potentially have two ways to profit: *current return* from the yearly dividends and a *future return* or capital gain upon the sale of their shares. Of course, preferred stockholders may get no dividends, because the company is not required to declare dividends, and they can suffer a capital loss upon the sale of their shares. There are no guarantees.

What are the risks of owning preferred stock?

The features of preferred stock can be many and varied, so investors must study each individual issue carefully to make sure they understand its complexities and the risks specific to that issue. The general risks to preferred stock investors include these four:

1. *Financial or credit risk* — the risk that the company will be unable to meet its financial obligations. As mentioned earlier, the payments to preferred shareholders can be suspended if the issuing company encounters financial difficulties. Because the company cannot suspend interest payments on its debt without going into default, it logically would quit paying preferred dividends before it would withhold interest payments. Obviously, this makes holding preferred stock riskier than holding the debt of a company.

2. *Interest rate risk* — the risk that interest rates will go up after the investment has been purchased. Because preferred stock pays a fixed dollar amount (unless it's *participating preferred* where shareholders may receive something extra), its share price will respond to changes in the prevailing interest rates in the same manner that debt securities will.

Although the inverse relationship between changes in the prevailing interest rates and the price of fixed-income securities was covered in Chapter 13: Investment Overview and Investing in Bonds, this concept is so important and so frequently misunderstood that a brief review is in order. If the preferred stock you currently own pays, for example, 6% per year and the prevailing interest rates go *up* to, say, 6.5%, your preferred stock's payment does not go up because it's fixed. When other companies issue new debt or preferred stock comparable to what's in your portfolio, they now will have to offer the new, higher rate.

If you decide to sell your preferred stock, investors would choose the new securities instead, which offer 6.5% versus yours which offers 6%, so you will have to *discount* your sales price in order to make up for the lower rate on your preferred stock. If you do not wish to sell your

---

[166] There are several ways corporations may file bankruptcy, and their assets are not always liquidated. Corporations may file bankruptcy under **Chapter 11**, which allows them to reorganize. The company stays in business, but usually is relieved of paying some of its debt or is allowed a longer time period to repay it. If the company's financial or business situation is more serious, the company may have to file **Chapter 7**, where the company essentially goes out of business and its assets are liquidated. This article by the Securities and Exchange Commission entitled, "What Every Investor Should Know," provides more information on corporate bankruptcy. www.sec.gov/investor/pubs/bankrupt.htm

preferred stock, then you do not realize a loss (because there is no sale). Rather, you have opportunity cost, meaning that you're having to settle for less than you could otherwise get if you had not already sunk your money into this investment. All fixed-income securities face this risk.

3. *Purchasing power risk*—the risk that the rate of inflation will be greater than the return on the investment, such that inflation will eat away the investment's purchasing power through time. Once issued, the rate on preferred stock is fixed and will not increase with inflation.

4. *Business risk*—the risk that the company will not be profitable enough to regularly declare dividends or for its equity securities to increase much in value. While this risk goes hand-in-hand with financial risk, it's possible for companies to make enough to service their debt but not enough to ever really flourish, due to factors such as poor management decisions or simply the industry in which the company operates.

As stated earlier, preferred stocks can have many features and complexities. Some can even be convertible into shares of the common stock of the issuing company.[167] Preferred stock can also be callable or redeemable.[168] For more information on the various features and complexities of preferred stock, refer to the sites listed in the footnotes.[169]

Common Stock

Common stock is the predominant way that investors can invest in equity securities. A share of common stock represents a *share of ownership in a company*. Your percentage of ownership depends on how many shares you own compared to the total number of shares the company has outstanding.

Voting Rights

As part owners of the company, common shareholders typically get one vote per share. They cast their votes to make decisions on various issues and to elect members of the company's board of directors, whose job it is to represent the interests of the shareholders.

Truthfully, most shareholders own such a small percentage of the total ownership of the company that their votes do not wield a great deal of power. However, they may sign a *proxy* statement and assign their voting rights to another party, such as the company's management. This other party collects as many proxies as possible in order to vote a large block of stock on various issues.

---

[167] This article from the SEC explains more about convertible securities. www.sec.gov/answers/convertibles.htm
[168] InvestingAnswers explains more about callable preferred stock.
www.investinganswers.com/financial-dictionary/stock-valuation/callable-preferred-stock-59
[169] Here's an article that explains many of the features of preferred stock from The Fool.
fool.com/research/2001/features010424.htm

Par Value

Another feature that common stock can have is a par value. However, unlike the par value of preferred stock or of bonds, *the par value of common stock is not particularly meaningful to investors, and many companies have "no-par" stock*. If a company's articles of incorporation stipulate a par value for the common stock, it's usually a very low amount, such as one cent or one dollar per share. The par value is the minimum amount for which a company can issue a share.

When the company sells new stock, the proceeds from the sale become capital for the company to use, and that amount is added into the equity section on its balance sheet. If the company has established a par value for its stock, then the bookkeeping entry is broken into two parts: the amount which goes toward par value and the remainder which goes into paid-in capital.

Changing the Number of Shares Outstanding

It is important for common stockholders to know that a company can increase the number of shares it has outstanding. It does this by offering a new batch of stock for sale through what's called an *initial public offering*. It's called this regardless of whether the company is a new start-up company issuing publicly traded shares for the first time, or whether it's an existing company issuing a new batch of shares never before traded. Also, the number of shares a company has outstanding will increase when the *stock options* that the company has issued to its executives or employees are exercised.

> When the number of outstanding shares increases, the existing shareholders' percentage of ownership will decrease. Stated another way, the ownership will be diluted.

Conversely, a company can decrease the number of its outstanding shares by *buying back* or *repurchasing* its own shares, either directly from shareholders or on the open market. Stock that has been bought back is no longer part of the total ownership of the company and becomes what is called *treasury stock*. (Picture the company buying back its stock, taking it out of circulation and stuffing it in the office vault or treasury.)

Companies accomplish several things with a stock buyback. They increase the individual investor's percentage of ownership in the company. This increases the company's share price, because the value of the company is now divided among fewer owners. In fact, the price increase may be even more than what you get by doing the math, because the management is often seen as showing confidence in the company and its future prospects by buying back its own shares.

However, companies that are not doing well may also buy back shares because their share price has dropped too low. Many companies prefer that their stock not trade in the single digit range or below a certain level. So-called "penny stocks," which trade at very low prices, are considered more high risk and speculative. Companies can also improve their accounting ratios by repurchasing their own stock, so it's good to research why the buyback is really being done.[170]

---

[170] This article at About.com entitled "Are Stock Buybacks a Good Deal?" discusses the topic further. stocks.about.com/od/understandingstocks/a/Stockbuyb122204.htm

How do common shareholders profit?

Like preferred shareholders, common shareholders can potentially profit in two ways: *current return* from the yearly dividends and a *future return* or capital gain upon the sale of their shares. However, many companies do not pay dividends, and, of course, there are no guarantees that common stock will appreciate in value, either.

Concerning dividends, investors know when they purchase the common stock of a company if that company typically pays dividends or not. Dividends are not like a water faucet that the company turns on and off at will. Usually, when a company starts to pay dividends, their intention is to continue to pay dividends in the future.

If a company that pays dividends stops paying them, it's usually taken as a negative signal that the company is having financial concerns, and its share price will likely drop. In fact, companies may decide to dip into their other assets or even borrow money, perhaps in the form of a bond issue, in order to continue paying their dividends if they have a down year. However, investors should be aware that an increase in debt may put further strain on the company, particularly if their slump continues.

What are the risks of owning common stock?

As owners of the company,[171] common stockholders reap the greatest potential rewards, but they also bear the greatest potential risks. Primarily, these risks are:

1. *Financial risk* — the risk that the company will be unable to meet its financial obligations. Investors wish to purchase the stock of a company that offers the potential for profit, but if it's having financial difficulties, it's obviously also having difficulty making a profit. Even if the company doesn't default on its debt or go bankrupt, the market price of its common stock will suffer. In the event that the company does goes into liquidation bankruptcy, the common stockholders stand to lose the entire purchase price of their stock.

2. *Business risk* — the risk that the company will not be as profitable as expected, usually due to economic or industry factors, or to poor management decisions. Plenty of companies make enough money to pay their bills and stay afloat financially, but they never really flourish. They may be in businesses that are cyclical and not do as well when the economy is down. They may make products that were once hot items but are beginning to go out of favor because of new technology, or out of style because buyer tastes have changed. Also, poor or questionable management decisions can quickly ruin what was once a reputable and well-run company.

Investors will usually want at least a portion of their portfolios invested in common stock because of stock's upside potential. They can either directly hold the stocks of individual companies, or they can hold them indirectly through mutual funds or exchange-traded funds, which are discussed later. However, because share prices can go down as well as up, investors must carefully research their stock purchases *before* investing.

---

[171] While it's true that preferred stockholders are also owners of a company, only a fairly small percentage of the stock that's issued is preferred stock. Preferred stockholders typically do not have voting privileges, either, while common stockholders do. Therefore, the lion's share of ownership in most companies lies with common stockholders.

Building Your Portfolio

Your *portfolio* is simply your collection of assets. You need to think of it as including not only your financial assets, such as stocks and bonds, but also your real assets, such as your home and other items of value. Everything you own is part of your portfolio.

How you put together your collections of assets, or your *asset allocation*, can greatly impact the growth of your wealth. That's because your assets need to complement one another. For example, if you focus only on acquiring real estate, the real estate markets can tank, as we have witnessed in recent years. If you're risk averse and keep all your money in bank accounts, you'll lose purchasing power. Your money won't be able to grow faster than the rate at which taxes and inflation are eating it up. You need a variety of assets in your portfolio so that all your eggs are not in one basket.

As you add to your portfolio, you need to consider what you already have and think about what will help balance out your holdings. If the markets are currently doing well in one area, now may be a good time to consider investing in something else. Remember, the markets for most anything can—and will—go down as well as up. Too many people wait to buy into a certain area until after it's had a long stretch of increasing prices and end up paying top dollar. Then when the price goes back down, they're stuck holding onto their asset in hopes they can recover their purchase amount. That's not the way to create wealth.[172]

Financial Assets

While real assets, such as real estate and collectibles, are definitely part of your entire portfolio, the discussion here will focus on the financial assets in your portfolio. These are generally categorized as cash, bonds and stocks:

- **Cash** includes not only money in your bank accounts, but also everything that can be quickly turned into cash without significant loss in value. A listing of cash-type assets would include money market bank accounts and money market mutual funds, asset management accounts with brokerage firms, as well as any certificates of deposit, Treasury bills and savings bonds that mature within one year. Chapter 4: Understanding Your Cash Accounts discusses these assets further.

- **Bonds** include a variety of debt securities of corporations, governments, and government agencies. While most will pay a regular, fixed stream of income, some may have variable interest rates. Zero coupon bonds don't actually pay out the interest while you hold them, but the amount due is chalked up to your bond periodically. This category is often referred to as the "fixed income" portion of your portfolio. It can also include preferred stock (discussed earlier in this chapter), which pays a regular, fixed dividend. Chapter 13: Investment Overview and Investing in Bonds discusses bonds of various types.

---

[172] The Securities and Exchange Commission offers a "Beginner's Guide to Asset Allocation, Diversification and Rebalancing." www.sec.gov/investor/pubs/assetallocation.htm
This article by SmartMoney, "Perfect Portfolios: Your Next Move in This Market," gives a number of examples of suggested asset allocations for people in various life situations. Scroll to the bottom of the article to click through the pages. www.smartmoney.com/invest/stocks/the-perfect-portfolio-1294688341486/

- **Stocks**, or equities, offer the greatest potential for return but come with the greatest risk. Chapter 12: Understanding the Risks and Returns of Investing discusses the various risks you face when investing and the types of returns that are possible.

Stocks can be classified in a variety of ways, including:

- *Size of the company,* such as small-cap, mid-cap or large-cap.[173] The "cap," or capitalization of a company, is found by multiplying the number of its outstanding shares by the current price per share. Obviously, an individual company's capitalization will vary. The dollar amounts dividing the size categories are not fixed either. As a current approximation, small-cap companies have a capitalization below $1 billion, mid-caps are between $1 billion and $8 billion, and large-caps are greater than $8 billion.[174]

- *Growth or value.* Growth stocks are those of companies that are expected to grow their earnings at a higher rate than most companies. Value stocks are those of companies that analysts believe are undervalued. They feel the company is more valuable than its stock price reflects.

- *Whether the company pays a dividend or not.* Many growth companies pay very small dividends or no dividends at all because they are plowing their earnings back into growing the company. Large, well-established companies and those in certain industries, such as utilities, often pay higher dividends. These may be referred to as "income stocks."

- *Quality and financial stability of the company.* Blue-chip companies are seen as being large, financially sound companies with a proven track record. Most of these companies will pay steady or increasing dividends. Speculative stocks are those of companies that may be new and unproven or in an industry that is particularly volatile. Their share price may trade very low, possibly in the "penny stock" area.

- *Characteristics of the industry.* Defensive stocks are those whose companies are in industries that are less affected by economic downturns. When the economy turns sour, people will still buy food, personal care products, laundry detergent, pet food, utilities, etc., unless they are in very dire circumstances. Actually, some types of companies do better during weak economies, such as debt collection companies. "Inferior" goods also do better. For example, consider less expensive cuts of meat—hamburger, bologna, hot dogs, etc. When people have less money to spend, they buy more of these and less steak. Cyclical stocks tend to move more in tandem with the economy. Autos, real estate and big-ticket items do better in a good economy, but sales often slide in a down economy.

- *Country of origin.* Stocks from international companies can be purchased on the exchanges, as well as those from U.S. companies. An easy way to get at least some international exposure is through purchasing U.S. companies that also have operations in other countries. Another convenient way is through purchasing American Depository

---

[173] The Morningstar Style Box is frequently referred to when evaluating stocks. According to its Glossary, "Large-cap stocks are defined as the group that accounts for the top 70% of the capitalization of each geographic area; mid-cap stocks represent the next 20%; and small-cap stocks represent the balance." Learn more about the Morningstar Style Box at: www.morningstar.com/InvGlossary/morningstar_style_box.aspx

[174] This Yahoo article discusses the size capitalization of companies. finance.yahoo.com/funds/types/article/100613/Large-Cap_and_Small-Cap_Funds_Explained

Receipts (ADRs). These are negotiable certificates issued by U.S. banks and represent a certain number of shares of the stock of a foreign company. The actual stock is held by a U.S. financial institution overseas. ADRs are U.S. dollar denominated and trade on the stock exchanges. They make it much easier and less costly to invest in international companies.[175]

Putting It All Together

How much of your portfolio should you have in each asset category? That depends on the person. A number of factors need to be considered, such as your tolerance for risk, your age, your other assets and how much money you have to invest.

Financial professionals generally recommend a *well-diversified portfolio*. Most people will need some amount in each category of cash, bonds and stocks. Then, within each category, a variety of holdings from various industries is needed to further lessen your investment risks.[176]

While the selection of individual financial securities and the specifics of building a portfolio appropriate for your personal needs are beyond the scope of this book, a number of resources are available for those who want to learn more. This is definitely an area where you may want to consult a financial professional.[177]

One way to attain a well-diversified portfolio is by purchasing shares of an already assembled collection of assets. The remainder of this chapter will address mutual funds and exchange traded funds (ETFs), two widely available types of such collections. Not only are they popular holdings in taxable accounts, but they are also the predominant offering of many retirement plans.

Funds

One of the big problems with purchasing specific securities, such as the common stock of Giant Corp. or municipal bonds issued by the City of Pleasantville, is that it takes a while for most people to assemble a well-diversified portfolio. Also, it's up to the individual to research the specific securities, determine if they are an appropriate fit for his or her portfolio, keep up with them as changes occur and sell them when needed. And note that it's just as important to know when to *sell* a security as it is to know when to *buy* it. In short, purchasing specific securities often exposes the individual to a great deal of unneeded risk.

---

[175] Nasdaq defines ADR: www.nasdaq.com/investing/glossary/a/american-depositary-receipts

[176] Harry Markowitz won the Nobel Prize in Economic Sciences in 1990 for his development of the theory he presented in 1952 that proper portfolio diversification can reduce an investor's risk. His work forms the basis for Modern Portfolio Theory (MPT). Wikipedia presents an overview of his work: en.wikipedia.org/wiki/Harry_Markowitz

[177] As referenced earlier, the SEC offers this Beginners' Guide to Asset Allocation, Diversification and Rebalancing. www.sec.gov/investor/pubs/assetallocation.htm Morningstar's Investing Classroom offers an entire series of free online coursework, which covers Stocks, Bonds, Funds and Portfolios. This link is for Portfolios, but you can click the tabs to view the others as well. news.morningstar.com/classroom2/home.asp?colId=138&CN=COM

Advantages of Investing in Funds

Mutual funds and exchange traded funds offer investors several distinct advantages over holding securities directly. These include:

Instant Diversification

Investors can rapidly attain portfolio diversification with very little money. That's because when investors buy into a fund, they are purchasing a small sliver of every security held in the fund. It's like getting a slice of Neapolitan ice cream, but rather than chocolate, vanilla and strawberry, there's a layer for every security in the fund. This diversification helps lower some of the price volatility, or the ups and downs, of investing.

Professional Management

Investors in funds are essentially pooling their money together and hiring professional money managers to research, select and track individual securities for them. While the fund managers are the ones who make the decisions concerning the funds, they do so in accordance to a fund's *prospectus*. This document is the fund's rule book, and it sets forth the specifics of the fund. It states the types of securities that are to be in the fund, how the fund is to be managed, the expenses of investing, and other relevant information.

Ease of Investing

If individual investors wanted to hold on their own all the securities that a fund owns, it would involve many transactions, and each transaction would incur a cost. Purchasing shares of a fund instead is much easier and more cost effective. It involves only one transaction and one cost. Similarly, when investors wish to sell a fund, it takes only one trade.

Disadvantages of Investing in Funds

Like any investment, funds have their pros and cons. Here are some considerations:[178]

Lack of Control

With ETFs, this is not so much of an issue because many track an index. You know what to expect when you buy into the fund. With actively managed mutual funds, however, the fund managers make the buy and sell decisions concerning the securities to hold within the funds. If you don't like what the manager is doing, you'll just have to take your money and go elsewhere.

Taxes

What the fund manager does may impact your taxes. Every sale within the fund generates a capital gain or loss for you if you're holding the fund in a taxable rather than a retirement account. Again, this tends to be more of an issue with actively managed funds than with those which passively track an index. Index funds, whether they're mutual funds or ETFs, will typically have fewer trades within the fund. Taxes on mutual funds will be discussed later.

---

[178] For more information on the advantages and disadvantages of funds, refer to these articles: www.investorguide.com/igu-article-478-mutual-fund-basics-disadvantages-of-mutual-funds.html
www.investopedia.com/ask/answers/10/mutual-funds-advantages-disadvantages.asp#axzz1tQWeByhi
www.investopedia.com/articles/exchangetradedfunds/11/advantages-disadvantages-etfs.asp#axzz1tQWeByhi
etf.about.com/od/benefitsofetfs/u/etfs_vs_mutual_funds.htm This page contains links to a number of articles discussing the advantages and disadvantages of both ETFs and mutual funds.

Costs

All mutual funds charge yearly management fees, with some being much higher than others. Additionally, load funds charge extra to pay for sales commissions. ETFs typically have much lower yearly fees, but every buy or sell transaction will generate a brokerage cost. Fees and costs will also be discussed later.

The following are a few frequently asked questions concerning funds:

What kind of return can investors expect from funds?

The answer is high, low and anything in between. The return on a specific fund will depend on what's in the fund. On the low-return, low-risk side are money market funds which invest in short-term, highly liquid securities. On the high-return, high-risk side are narrowly focused funds which invest only in certain areas or industries such as energy or employ a certain strategy such as selecting only high-growth stocks. Many other funds, such as balanced mutual funds and market indexed ETFs, offer a well-diversified blend of securities in an effort to earn a reasonable return while holding down the level of risk. By reading the prospectus, investors know what to expect from a specific fund.

What are the risks of owning funds?

After studying cash, stocks and bonds, you may be wondering about a fund's level of risk and where it would fall on the scale illustrated earlier with the corporate balance sheet. The risk of holding a fund would more or less correspond to the risk of the assets held within the fund.

However, with a collection of securities, other factors also come into play. Most mutual funds will have at least some cash, which functions as their operating account for when they bring in new money or make redemptions. While it lowers the total return of the fund, it also serves as a buffer and lowers the risk as well. With blend funds, the mixture of stocks to bonds will vary from time to time. This makes the level of risk vary somewhat as well. And of course, decisions made by fund managers can greatly impact a fund's performance and level of risk.

A number of Web sites provide information on funds as well as on other securities. Enter your fund's ticker symbol, which serves as its unique identifier on the exchanges, and look through the data that's available. If you don't know the ticker, most sites provide a search feature. Morningstar and Yahoo are two comprehensive sites for research.[179]

For whom are funds appropriate?

Funds can serve the needs of many types of investors. As mentioned earlier, people who don't have much money to invest can select a fund that is well-diversified. This gives them instant diversification in the contents of the fund with a small cash outlay.

Funds offer a way for those who have already started their portfolios to "fill the gaps." For example, if they need more bond exposure or more international holdings, a carefully selected fund could be a cost effective way for them to meet such needs.

---

[179] Morningstar: www.morningstar.com/ Yahoo Finance: finance.yahoo.com/

Funds are a convenient way to invest regularly. Many mutual funds allow automatic drafts. For example, an investor can arrange for $100 to be pulled from his or her bank account on the 15th of every month and invested in XYZ Mutual Fund. On the other hand, retirees can select funds which allow automatic withdrawals such that a certain amount is redeemed every month and deposited in their bank accounts for them to use for living expenses.

Funds are especially attractive for people who do not have the time, energy or desire to select individual securities. You choose a fund appropriate for your needs, and the fund handles the day-to-day dealings.

How are funds regulated?
Mutual funds and ETFs are *investment companies*. As such, the *Securities and Exchange Commission (SEC)* oversees their regulation. The SEC provides a wealth of educational materials at its Web site.[180] You can also learn more about the role the Division of Investment Management plays in regulating variable annuities and registered investment advisors, as well as examine the rules and regulations dealing with investment companies.[181]

Mutual Funds

Mutual funds and many exchange traded funds (ETFs) are *open-end* investment companies, one of the three basic types overseen and regulated by the SEC. The other two types are closed-end funds and Unit Investment Trusts (UITs). Closed-end funds generally sell a fixed number of shares at one time in an initial public offering. After that, these shares are typically traded like stock on the secondary markets, such as the New York Stock Exchange. UITs consist of a fixed number of redeemable securities called "units" which terminate and dissolve on a specific date. For the purposes of this chapter, only open-end mutual funds will be discussed.[182]

What are "open-end" investment companies?
With an open-end investment company, there is no set number of shares outstanding. The manager creates new shares when investors send in more money and redeems shares when investors want their money back.

[180] The SEC provides an overview of Investment Companies on this page: sec.gov/answers/mfinvco.htm
The SEC also provides a number of informative articles concerning mutual funds on the page, "Beginners' Guide to Mutual Funds: Online Publications at the SEC." sec.gov/investor/pubs/beginmutual.htm
The SEC provides an overview of Exchange Traded Funds (ETFs) on this page: www.sec.gov/answers/etf.htm
[181] The Division of Investment Management at the U.S. Securities and Exchange Commission regulates variable insurance products and investment companies (such as mutual funds, closed-end funds, unit investment trusts, exchange-traded funds, and interval funds) as well as federally registered investment advisers. This page provides a listing of their services and information on how to contact the SEC. sec.gov/divisions/investment.shtml
[182] Refer to this page for more information on investment companies. www.sec.gov/answers/mfinvco.htm
To learn more about Unit Investment Trusts (UITs), refer to this page. sec.gov/answers/uit.htm
This page provides more information on closed-end funds. www.sec.gov/answers/mfclose.htm

How do mutual fund owners profit?

The profits and losses on mutual funds are passed through to shareholders year by year. It's as if the shareholders hold the securities directly. If the fund receives *current return* on its holdings, such as dividends on stocks or interest on bonds, a proportionate share is passed on to shareholders. When the fund manager sells securities, the *capital gains and losses* are also passed on proportionately to shareholders. Additionally, mutual funds shareholders can have a gain or loss when they redeem shares due to changes in the fund's share price, or its *net asset value (NAV)*.[183]

How are mutual funds taxed?

A short aside into tax accounting is in order at this point to better explain how profits from mutual funds are somewhat different from other investments. Each mutual fund is a separate corporation, and for-profit corporations must pay income taxes. Then, when corporations pay out dividends to their shareholders, the shareholders must include the dividends as income on their personal tax returns. So this money is normally taxed twice—first when the company earns it and then when the shareholder receives it.

Mutual funds hold the securities of other corporations directly and receive their dividends, so normally the funds would be taxed on the income they receive. Then if the mutual fund shareholders were to again be taxed on what they receive, triple taxation would occur.

To avoid this extra layer of taxation, mutual funds are allowed to be classified as *"pass-through entities."* This means a mutual fund cannot keep the income and use it to fund its own operations as a regular corporation would, but must pass at least 95% of its income straight through to the shareholders. The character (such as dividends, capital gains, etc.) of the income remains the same as it passes through, and shareholders must list this income as their own dividends or capital gains or whatever on their tax returns each year (if the fund is held in a taxable account). Fortunately, the mutual fund company usually provides you with much of the information needed for filing your taxes.

Note that it matters whether you hold a mutual fund in a taxable account or in a retirement account. If your fund is in a qualified tax-sheltered retirement account, such as a 401k or regular IRA, you do not pay taxes year by year. You only pay taxes when you withdraw your money, and then it will be taxed as ordinary income (not at the more favorable dividends or capital gains rates).[184]

If you're holding a mutual fund in a taxable account, you need to keep up with what you receive yearly from the mutual fund. Because you're paying taxes on these earnings every year, this adds to your *cost basis* in the fund. When you ultimately sell shares of your fund, the higher your cost basis, the less you'll have to recognize as capital gain on the sale of your shares, and the lower the taxes you'll pay.

---

[183] A mutual fund's net asset value, or NAV, is calculated at the end of each trading day and is simply the current market value of everything the fund holds (its total assets) minus anything owed by the fund (its total liabilities) divided by the number of outstanding shares of the fund. The NAV of a mutual fund is similar to the share price of a stock.

[184] Remember that the Roth IRA is different from other retirement accounts. If you leave your money inside a Roth IRA as required, not only does it grow tax-free, but you will also pay NO taxes on qualified withdrawals.

What are the fees and expenses of holding mutual funds?

As with most investments, there can be both a cost to obtain the mutual fund as well as a cost to keep it.[185] All mutual funds will have some amount of annual operating expenses which are passed on to fund investors, particularly *management fees*. These annual fees cover the costs to operate and manage the fund.

Some funds also charge sales loads while others do not. Funds that allow investors to purchase shares directly from the mutual fund company are called *no-load funds*. There are no fees to purchase these funds, and investors pay the net asset value (NAV) for each share purchased.

Other funds can only be purchased through a third party, such as a broker or financial advisor, who receives a fee for the sale. These are called *load funds,* and the load or sales fee can be charged in various ways, depending on the *class of shares* that you purchase. One fund may offer a variety of share classes and may label them differently from another fund. In general, however, the classes go like this:

- **Class A** shares charge a one-time, front-end sales load at the time of purchase. Some funds have breakpoints on their Class A shares, such that the greater the amount of your investment in the fund, the lower the front-end load.

- **Class B** shares charge a deferred or back-end sales load when you redeem shares.[186] Many times, however, if you hold the Class B fund shares for several years, the back-end load goes away and the B shares convert to Class A shares which have no back-end load and perhaps lower yearly expenses (no front load would apply when the shares are converted).

- **Class C** shares usually charge neither a front-end nor back-end load, or they may charge a load that's lower than the fund's Class A and B shares. However, Class C shares do charge *higher yearly fees*. These are NOT no-load funds. The sales load is included in what is called the *12b-1 fee*, an ongoing annual fee some funds charge for marketing expenses. After a few years, the expense of holding Class C shares may well exceed the expense of either Class A or Class B shares.

Finally, if funds of any type are held in a brokerage account (rather than directly with the mutual fund company), there will likely be a *brokerage transaction fee* for every purchase and redemption.

Example of Sales Loads on Mutual Funds:

Let's say that you invest $1,000 in Blue Chip Mutual Fund which charges 5% loads on both its Class A and Class B shares. If you purchase Class A shares, you pay in $1,000 and $50 goes toward the sales load, so $950 gets invested. If you purchase Class B shares, you pay in $1,000 and $1,000 gets invested. However, if you redeem your shares, you typically

---

[185] For further information on the various fees on mutual funds, refer to the SEC article, Mutual Fund Fees and Expenses. sec.gov/answers/mffees.htm
[186] This may be called a contingent deferred sales load or charge and referred to as a "CDSC," or "CDSL."

surrender 5% of your original investment amount to the deferred sales load.[187] So if your $1,000 investment has grown over time to $1,200 and you cash in all your shares, you'd be charged $50 ($1,000 x 0.05) and you would receive $1,150 ($1,200 – $50).

As mentioned earlier, with many funds their Class B shares convert to Class A after a certain period of time, so the back-end load may go away if you keep the shares long enough. Also, while the Class C shares often charge no front- or back-end loads, their higher annual fees do not go away through time. To repeat — *after several years, the total cost to hold Class C shares often exceeds the cost of either Class A or B shares.*

Which share class should you choose?

Assuming there's a compelling reason for you to purchase a load fund rather than a no-load fund, here are some things to consider:

- If you plan to hold the fund for several years, you would possibly be better off with Class A shares rather than Class C shares, although it would depend on how long you hold the shares and the amount of the front-end load.

- If you plan to hold the fund for only a few years, you'd probably want Class C shares, but again this would depend on the fee structure of the given fund.

- What about Class B shares? Theoretically they offer the best of both worlds for a long-term holding — no front-end load when purchased, and the back-end load falls off if you hold the shares long enough. However, if the investment goes sour and you have to cash out earlier than expected, not only have you lost money on your investment but you have to pay a back-end load to get out of it. Granted, in such an instance you may be no worse off than if you purchased Class A shares, but it stings nevertheless.[188, 189]

Types of Mutual Funds

With the thousands of mutual funds available, selecting the ones that are right for your needs can be challenging. Think about the purpose you are trying to achieve. For example, if you need greater diversification in your portfolio, you might select an index fund that tracks the broad markets. If you need more bond investments, you might select a bond fund or perhaps a balanced fund that contains both stocks and bonds. If you need international

---

[187] Read the mutual fund's prospectus to find out the specifics of a fund's fees. Not every fund is structured in the "typical" manner! And while you may intend to leave your money invested for a long period of time and outlast the back-end load, things can change rapidly in life.

[188] Choose "Mutual Fund Cost Calculators" provided by the Securities and Exchange Commission to help determine the cost of holding specific mutual funds. You will need the mutual fund's prospectus in order to enter that fund's fees. (Many prospectuses can be found online at the fund family's Web site.) sec.gov/investor/tools.shtml The "Fund Analyzer" provided at the Financial Industry Regulatory Authority's (FINRA) Web site allows you to compare expenses of exchange-traded funds (ETFs), mutual funds or share classes of the same mutual fund. The expense information for many funds has already been entered into the calculator, so you just enter the fund family and ticker or keyword for the specific fund. (Find the Fund Analyzer from the home page by clicking Investors and then the tab Tools and Calculators.) apps.finra.org/fundanalyzer/1/fa.aspx

[189] This article at Yahoo Finance explains load and no-load funds and provides an example of the difference these expenses make to the investor. finance.yahoo.com/funds/how_to_choose/article/100601/Load_vs_No-Load_Funds

exposure, you could select a fund that contains only securities from other countries or maybe one that has a mixture of both domestic and foreign securities. If it's liquidity you need, almost every fund family offers one or more money market funds.[190]

The following are several broad categories of funds that are available:

Money Market Mutual Funds

These funds are designed for safety and preservation of principal. They are NOT meant for capital appreciation, as their returns will be very low. Money market mutual funds must operate under special restrictions which mandate that only short-term (one year or less to maturity), highly liquid (easy to turn into cash without significant loss of value), and low-risk (highly rated) securities be purchased.[191] They are appropriate as a store for ready cash if you need liquidity, and they can also serve various needs in portfolio management. Money market funds are discussed in Chapter 4: Understanding Your Cash Accounts.

Bond Funds

Bond funds are composed mainly of bonds and other debt securities. Some bond funds will limit their holdings to only certain types of bonds, like government bonds, or to a certain length to maturity, such as intermediate-term bonds, or to a certain quality, like high yield (which means lower-rated junk bonds that carry higher risk). Other bond funds may hold a variety of different kinds of bonds. Each fund will state its given investment objectives in its prospectus.

While individual bonds can have quite a few complexities, bond funds can have even more. That's due in part to the fund manager having the control, not the individual investor. The fund manager decides what and when to buy or sell, but it's the investor who must realize the gains or losses. Chapter 13: Investment Overview and Investing in Bonds discusses bonds further. The sites referenced in the footnotes also provide a wealth of information on bonds.[192, 193]

---

[190] For more information on the various types of mutual funds, what they invest in, and for whom they are suitable, the Mutual Fund Education Alliance provides an extensive tutorial at its Mutual Fund Investor's Center. mfea.com/InvestingBasics/Default.asp

[191] For more information on money market mutual funds, refer to this article at the Securities and Exchange Commission's Web site: sec.gov/answers/mfmmkt.htm

[192] Investing in Bonds provides comprehensive, easy-to-understand information on all types of bonds. Go to "Learn More." www.investinginbonds.com/learnmore.asp?catid=2&id=62 Start with the Overview, and on the left-hand menu, click your way through their many bond topics. Morningstar has long been recognized as an excellent resource for investment information. Their bond classroom offers classes up to the 500 level! Click on the "Bonds" tab of their Course Catalog to get going. news.morningstar.com/classroom2/home.asp?CN=COM

[193] Yahoo's Bond Center allows investors to screen individual bonds, research bonds, find bond quotes, use calculator tools and learn more about bonds. finance.yahoo.com/bonds Pull up Yahoo's Mutual Fund Center to screen bond funds. finance.yahoo.com/funds

Stock Funds

Stock funds are composed primarily of the common stocks of companies and are often classified according to the companies' characteristics. One of the best known classification systems for stock mutual funds is Morningstar's three-by-three grid of nine investment style boxes,[194] which are arranged like so:

Large-cap Value	Large-cap Blend	Large-cap Growth
Mid-cap Value	Mid-cap Blend	Mid-cap Growth
Small-cap Value	Small-cap Blend	Small-cap Growth

The classifications pertain to an *average of the fund's holdings,* as many funds own a variety of stocks that, if individually held, would not all be classified in the same style box as the mutual fund itself. The grid is arranged such that mutual funds whose average holdings are large-sized companies are on the top row, mid-sized on the middle row, and small-sized on the bottom row.

The measure from left to right has to do with the average *valuation* of companies held in the mutual fund. Funds with a value orientation contain companies that are believed to be undervalued (or whose stock is currently selling for less than it is believed to be worth). Funds with a growth orientation contain companies whose earnings should potentially grow faster than the rest of the market. Obviously, funds that are a blend contain a mixture of both growth and value stocks.

The size of a company is measured by its *market capitalization.* To find an individual company's market capitalization, multiply the number of the company's outstanding shares of common stock by its current market price per share. So if Green Corp. has 2 million outstanding shares of common stock that are currently selling at $40 per share, then the company's market cap is $80 million. While that may seem like a lot to most of us, companies with market caps of less than about one or two billion are considered small cap. To learn more about mutual funds and their Morningstar ratings, click on the "Funds" tab at www.morningstar.com.

Blend Funds

Many funds hold a blend of stocks, bonds, preferred stocks and convertibles and/or money market. The best known of these blended funds are *balanced* funds, which contain a predetermined mixture (such as 60% stock and 40% bonds, with the manager being given some amount of discretion to vary the mix), and *asset allocation* funds which give much more freedom to the manager to do whatever he or she thinks best at the time. *Target* funds, in which the blend changes through time as a retirement target date approaches, would fall into the asset allocation category. Typically, the longer a person has until retirement, the more stocks and fewer bonds held in the portfolio, while as the person approaches and enters retirement, the more bonds and fewer stocks.

---

[194] To learn more about Morningstar's style boxes, pull up this handy guide, "Fact Sheet: The New Morningstar Style Box Methodology." news.morningstar.com/pdfs/FactSheet_StyleBox_Final.pdf

Blend funds offer a greater amount of diversification than do funds composed of all stocks or all bonds. They are particularly useful for investors who are just starting out and those who don't have a lot of money. These funds allow investors to diversify even small amounts of money. If, instead, investors were to buy individual stocks or bonds, it would take them much longer to achieve even a moderate amount of diversification, and the costs of investing, such as brokerage fees, would likely be much higher.

International Funds

Many advisors feel that most investors should have at least some foreign company holdings in their portfolios in order to increase their diversification. Quite a number of mutual funds can provide international exposure in various ways. Funds that hold predominately domestic securities may also include some amount of foreign securities. In fact, funds that hold only U.S. securities often provide the investor with some foreign exposure, as so many American companies also own various foreign operations.

A carefully selected international mutual fund can be an excellent way for investors to achieve better foreign exposure in their portfolios. Mutual funds can help lessen the additional risks that investors face when investing in foreign securities. (For more information on the risks of investing internationally, refer to Chapter 12: Understanding the Risks and Returns of Investing.)

You will see a number of labels for funds holding foreign securities. According to *Smart Money*,[195] *global funds* can invest anywhere in the world, including the U.S. While these funds can offer a great deal of diversity, they may contain a fairly high percentage of U.S. companies. *International funds* hold only a few or maybe no U.S. companies. These funds can be widely diversified across many countries, but others may be more concentrated in only certain regions. *Country-specific funds* invest in only one country or region, which may make them fairly volatile. *Emerging markets funds* invest in countries or regions that are developing. These funds often demand a strong stomach to handle the roller coaster rides.

Index Funds

Many mutual funds are *actively managed*. That means the fund manager makes the decisions concerning the individual securities held within the fund. Index funds are *passively managed*. These funds try to mirror the returns of a market index, such as the S&P 500 (large-cap companies), the Russell 2000 (small-cap companies) or the Wilshire 5000 Total Market Index (all stocks actively traded in the U.S.). While these funds still have managers, their objective is simply to track the returns of the underlying index.[196]

The thinking behind index funds is that few actively managed funds are able to achieve returns greater than the S&P 500 or the Wilshire 5000 anyway. In other words, if you can't beat them, then join them. Also, if the fund simply tracks an index, then there are fewer trades within the fund and fewer decisions to be made. This lowers the management and

---

[195] Yahoo's Mutual Funds Center features this article by SmartMoney.com, "Foreign Stock Funds Explained." finance.yahoo.com/funds/types/article/100615/Foreign_Stock_Funds_Explained
[196] For more information, refer to this SEC article, Index Funds. www.sec.gov/answers/indexf.htm

transactions costs, which serves to increase the returns investors receive. Index funds are often seen as a way to put your investing on auto-pilot.

Note, however, that all index funds are NOT the same. Some will experience much more volatility than others tracking the same index. That's because some will hold all the securities that make up the index they are tracking, while others will hold only a representative sample. Still others will try to achieve their investment objective by using derivatives, such as futures and options. As always, do your research before investing.

Exchange Traded Funds

Exchange Traded Funds, or ETFs, are relative newcomers to the investment world, but they have become very popular. They are similar to mutual funds in that each ETF is a collection of securities. When you purchase a share, you're effectively purchasing a small amount of each security held within the fund. While a few ETFs are actively managed, most passively track some underlying index, such as the S&P 500.[197]

How do mutual funds and ETFs differ?
Mutual funds are open-end companies whose shares are purchased either from the fund itself or through a broker for the fund. Their shares are redeemable, which means investors sell their shares back to the mutual fund rather than to another investor. This also makes the number of outstanding shares of a mutual fund fluctuate, depending on the net purchases and redemptions made by investors.

ETFs can be either open-end companies or unit investment trusts, but according to the SEC, they are not considered to be, nor can they call themselves, mutual funds. Also, there may be several layers to an ETF. The "Creation Units" are usually issued in large blocks (such as 50,000 shares), typically to institutions. The institutional investors may then split these large blocks into smaller shares to sell to individual investors on the secondary markets, such as the New York Stock Exchange.

- *Trading*—because shares of ETFs are bought and sold on the exchanges, they are priced during the day and can be traded much like stocks. Mutual funds, however, are not traded on the exchanges, but as mentioned earlier, they are purchased or redeemed from the fund itself (even if they are held in a brokerage account). The share price, or net asset value, of a mutual fund is officially determined at the close of every trading day. Once the NAV is determined, then the orders for purchases or redemptions are fulfilled. Since their orders are not executed until the end of the trading day, investors won't know in advance the final share price they'll receive.

- *Costs*—because most ETFs passively track an index, their expense ratios tend to be much lower than those of most mutual funds. This yearly savings can really add up, particularly when held for a long period of time. However, because you buy and sell ETFs on the exchanges, each trade will incur a brokerage fee. The key is to find a low-cost brokerage which does not charge yearly fees to maintain your account.

---

[197] For more information on ETFs, refer to these articles. sec.gov/answers/etf.htm
www.nyse.com/pdfs/ETFs7109.pdf   www.nasdaq.com/investing/etfs/what-are-ETFs.aspx

For investors who are building up their portfolios and want to periodically purchase more shares, a no-load mutual fund purchased directly from the mutual fund company could be a better choice than an ETF. While ETFs have lower yearly expenses, having to pay a fee for every purchase could wipe out any savings. Investors can always build up wealth in a mutual fund and then make a large one-time purchase into the desired ETF.

- *Taxes* — remember, every sell order in a taxable account, whether it's a mutual fund or an ETF, has tax implications. Even exchanges between mutual funds that are in the same mutual fund family are subject to taxes. Trades made within a retirement account, however, do not trigger taxes. With an IRA or a 401k, for example, only withdrawals from the account are taxed, and then regular income tax rates will apply (NOT the more favorable capital gains rates).[198]

- *Transparency* — mutual funds are required to disclose the contents of their portfolios only four times a year. By the time the disclosure has been made, the fund manager may have already bought or sold various securities held within the fund. So at any given moment, investors in mutual funds don't know exactly what they own. ETFs, on the other hand, are required to disclose their holdings on a daily basis. That way, if a certain company is having major financial difficulties, you can find out if your fund owns that company and make a more informed decision whether you want to sell shares or not.

Funds, whether they're mutual funds or ETFs, can be a great way for investors to build wealth and get the broad diversification they need to reduce some of the risks of investing. That being said, it's still quite possible for your investment to go down rapidly. Before investing in any fund, you need to understand what types of securities it holds and evaluate the risks involved.

Now that you're on your way to amassing your fortune, you'll want to preserve and protect it for your heirs. Chapters 15 and 16 will cover various topics on estate planning.

---

[198] Remember, withdrawals from Roth IRAs are the exception in retirement accounts. If you abide by the rules, withdrawals from Roths are NOT subject to federal income taxes.

⏱ 30 Minute LIVING

Suggested Action Plan

- *Take a look at the stock market.* Pull up SmartMoney's Map of the Market to see what the market looks like today at www.smartmoney.com/map-of-the-market (it may take a few moments to load). Each rectangle represents a company, and the size of the rectangle corresponds to the company's market capitalization. The returns on the companies are color coded, with green being positive, black being neutral, and red being negative.

- *This is an excellent tool for researching companies.* For example, find the setting for "Show change since" and reset for different time periods. Then choose "Highlight top 5," highlighting first the top five gainers and then the top five losers for each of the time periods. Roll your cursor over the various companies and click on those you're interested in to research them further.

- *Take a look at mutual funds as well.* While you're at SmartMoney, pull up their Mutual Fund Map on this page: www.smartmoney.com/fundmap This map is likely to be much more uniform in color. That's because funds are diversified, with each holding many companies, while the Map of the Market discussed above shows individual companies. The uniformity of the color illustrates how diversification helps lessen the roller coaster ride that you would otherwise get by holding individual companies. Reset the map for various time periods and also view by fund families or by classifications. Scroll over a fund you're interested in and click on it to access additional information.

- *X-ray your portfolio.* Use Morningstar's Instant X-Ray tool to analyze your current portfolio, retirement account or an individual stock or mutual fund. Pull up Morningstar. com, and under the "Tools" tab, scroll down to find "Instant X-Ray."[199] Enter in one item to learn more about each investment. Then enter in all of your investments in your portfolio or account to see how your holdings coordinate with one another.

- *Find the latest investor alerts.* FINRA, the Financial Industry Regulatory Authority, is the largest independent regulator of securities firms in the U.S. Their site provides comprehensive investment information, including the section, "Protect Yourself." Find the most recent investor alerts and well as information on avoiding investment fraud. www.finra.org/Investors/index.htm

---

[199] Visit: portfolio.morningstar.com/RtPort/Free/InstantXRayDEntry.aspx?dt=0.7055475

CHAPTER 15

Planning For Your Estate: Property and Estate Taxes

Don't Be a Spruce Goose!

The fight over billionaire Howard Hughes' estate is one of legend. It finally came to an end in 2010, a long 34 years after his death in 1976. During that time, several parties produced wills that were later declared bogus. California and Texas each claimed to be his state of domicile and attempted to levy taxes, but the courts eventually rejected both. A woman who had claimed she married him but never divorced received a payoff from the estate and later turned her story into a best selling book. A bevy of cousins finally became beneficiaries, after much of the estate's value had been lost to court and litigation costs. The man responsible for the creation of what came to be known as the "Spruce Goose," the largest plane to ever fly, essentially scattered his estate to the wind.[200]

Failing to put proper plans in place for your estate can have unwanted, even disastrous, results, whether you're a billionaire or not. Once you're dead, it's game over. There are no retakes.

Truthfully, however, planning for your estate is optional. You can take comfort in knowing that if you don't get around to doing it, the government already has a plan in place to distribute your assets when you die. If you like that plan, then do no more. Your state's laws of succession will kick in and direct the disposition of what you've worked a lifetime to acquire.

Yes, one way or another, something *will* happen to your wealth and your loved ones after you die. However, if you'd like to have a say, you'll have to have a plan for your estate.

Effective estate planning addresses numerous issues. Beyond leaving directives concerning your material possessions, there are your loved ones to consider, financial and legal documents that your executor will need and people who should be contacted.

Remember, too, there's the possibility you may become incapacitated *before* your death. While you're still alive, others may need to take over your finances or make health decisions on your behalf.

---

[200] The Spruce Goose now resides at the Evergreen Aviation and Space Museum in McMinnville, OR. Learn more about this unique plane: www.evergreenmuseum.org/the-museum/aircraft-exhibits/the-spruce-goose

> Think of estate planning, not in terms of your own death, which is sometimes a painful thought, but in terms of caring for your loved ones. The better the plans you make while alive, the more you can potentially leave them and the less they will have to deal with later. Estate planning is a gift to yourself as well. Putting plans in place not only gives you peace of mind, but also helps you better manage your assets and finances right now. It's truly a win-win for everyone.

This chapter covers estate planning issues concerning your property and provides an overview of how estate taxes work. Chapter 16 addresses planning for yourself and others during the latter part of your life, the legal documents you may need and other important estate planning issues.

Your Estate—Planning for Your Property

Your estate comes into being when you die and consists of the property (or assets) you leave behind. One of the main purposes of estate planning is to put a plan in place to make sure your assets will be distributed according to your wishes.

Obviously, estate planning must be done while you are still alive and in accordance with the laws of the state in which you live. While alive, you have: 1) the option to pass your property to others before your death, or 2) to arrange for it to pass after death. Both of these options can be quite helpful in estate planning and will be discussed below.[201]

Passing Property to Others Before You Die

While you're still alive, you can pass your property to someone else—
*   Directly, by gifting it, or
*   Indirectly, through a trust.

Gifts
Gifts are a direct transfer of assets from one person to another. Things you can gift include any property, such as money, items of value, real estate, the use of income that a property generates, selling something at less than full value, or making an interest-free or reduced-interest loan.

To really be considered a gift, the recipient must receive the property for free or at a discount (which would reduce the dollar value of the gift). Additionally, the transfer must be made with no strings attached. The original owner's ties to ownership must end.[202]

---

[201] This information is meant to be general in nature. While federal laws apply to everyone in the U.S., your state may have additional laws. Also, it's your state's laws which control the disposition of your estate, and your state may impose various taxes. Definitely, you need to consult a professional who knows the both the federal and the state laws that apply in your case.

[202] This IRS page addresses Frequently Asked Questions concerning gifts and gift taxes: www.irs.gov/businesses/small/article/0,,id=108139,00.html

How much can be gifted in any one year without gift taxes being due?

- *Your Spouse* — under current laws, one spouse can give to the other spouse an unlimited amount of property with no gift taxes being due, provided the spouse is a U.S. citizen.[203]
- *Qualified Charities* — an unlimited amount can also be given to qualified charities with no gift taxes being due.[204]
- *Other People* — in addition to these unlimited amounts, each year an individual can give to whomever they choose up to the *annual exclusion* amount ($13,000 as of 2012) to any number of people. If married and both spouses consent, a couple together can give up to $26,000 per year to any number of people without gift taxes being due. Called *gift splitting*, this gifting of a double portion can be from property jointly owned by the couple, or it can belong to only one of them.[205]

Many people who feel like they will leave behind a taxable estate when they die make a point to gift up to the annual exclusion amount every year to family members and/or friends. This helps reduce the size of their estates, which may reduce the amount that will ultimately be lost to estate taxes upon their death.

Trusts

Instead of directly gifting assets or property to someone else, you can give your assets indirectly while you are still alive through a trust. A trust is its own separate legal entity, and the *trustee* of the trust manages the assets on the behalf of others. The person giving the assets to the trust is called the *grantor* or *trustor*, and the person for whose benefit the assets are managed is called the *beneficiary*. And by the way, the grantor can also be the beneficiary if desired. (You would be letting the trust manage your assets for you.)

Types of Trusts — trusts can be established for numerous reasons and be set up in a variety of ways. A trust that's established while the grantor is alive is called an *inter vivos* trust. A trust that is established after a person's death as set forth in his or her last will and testament is called a *testamentary* trust.

Fees on Trusts — state laws (not federal) control trusts, and be aware that costs are involved. There are the attorney's fees to establish the trust, and then there are the yearly fees you pay the trustee to manage the assets. Also, income taxes are assessed yearly against the earnings of the trust, whether these earnings are passed on to the beneficiary or held within the trust. That means you may have to pay someone to prepare the trust's tax returns. Because other people stand to gain from the all the fees generated by trusts, you may be encouraged to establish a trust when truthfully, it may not in your best interest to do so.

---

[203] If your spouse is not a U.S. citizen, there is a limit as to how much you can gift to him/her annually — $136,000 for 2011. Refer to "Instructions for Form 709." www.irs.gov/pub/irs-pdf/i709.pdf

[204] Refer to IRS Publication 526: Charitable Contributions. www.irs.gov/pub/irs-pdf/p526.pdf

[205] For more information, refer to the IRS Publication 950: Introduction to Estate and Gift Taxes. www.irs.gov/pub/irs-pdf/p950.pdf Also helpful are the form used for filing gift taxes, Form 709: United States Gift (and Generation-Skipping Transfer) Tax Return www.irs.gov/pub/irs-pdf/f709.pdf, and the instructions for this form. www.irs.gov/pub/irs-pdf/i709.pdf

Taxes on Trusts—some people mistakenly believe that income taxes can be avoided if a trust is established. Actually, if the earnings are held in the trust and not passed to others, the trust itself must pay income taxes, and the amount of taxes owed can be greater than if passed on to the beneficiary. That's because the rate schedule on taxable income for trusts is different than that for individual tax payers. Income on trusts can very rapidly hit the highest tax rate. For 2011, that rate was 35%, and for trusts, taxable income over $11,350 was subject to that rate. For individuals (those filing as single, married filing jointly, or as head of household), only taxable income over $379,150 was subject to the highest rate of 35%. Also, a separate form must be filed (Form 1041—U.S. Income Tax Return for Estates and Trusts),[206] which can be an added expense if you have to pay a tax preparer or accountant to prepare the return.

Passing Property to Others After You Die

When you pass away and leave behind assets, your estate property can be passed to others by three basic means:

- *Your will*
- *Will substitutes*
- *Your state's laws of intestate succession*

Passing Property Using a Will

A *will* is a written document, or testament, which states how the estate of the person who made the will, or the *testator*, should be distributed upon his or her death. It is important that the will be written in accordance with the laws of the state in which a person lives, or is *domiciled*, because state laws control how property passes upon death. As you might imagine, these laws differ from state to state.

In making your will, you list your property along with who should get what. You name an *executor* (or executrix, if female) to handle the settling of your estate. If you have minor children or other dependents (such as elderly parents), you should name someone to be their *guardian*. If you want to leave property to your minor children, then you will also need to name someone to manage the property until the children come of age. Note that the executor and guardian do not have to be the same person, and it's also good to name one or more backup persons for each role. It could be that the one you've named may die before you do or may no longer have the ability to perform the role when the time comes.

Your will must be signed and witnessed, and you will probably want to hire an attorney to prepare your will for you. Although it is possible to prepare your will yourself, if you have many assets, you want to make sure that your will has been legally prepared according to your state's laws.

---

[206] You may view a Form 1041 here. www.irs.gov/pub/irs-pdf/f1041.pdf To learn more about how taxes for trusts are determined, pull up the accompanying instructions. www.irs.gov/pub/irs-pdf/i1041.pdf Find the tax rate schedule for individuals in the Instructions for Form 1040. www.irs.gov/pub/irs-pdf/i1040.pdf

Even if you don't have many assets, if you have children you certainly want to make sure that they are cared for in the event both parents die prematurely. If you haven't named a guardian, then it's up to the courts to choose one, and it just may not be the person you would have preferred to finish raising your children!

After making your will, it's important to review it every few years because:
- *Situations change* over time, and you may decide you want your property distributed differently than what you originally stated in your will.
- *People change* over time, and the person you named as your executor or the guardian for your children may predecease you, or they may now have diminished mental or physical capacity.
- *Laws change* over time, so it's important that your will stay current.

If you do need to make changes to your will, you may not need to rewrite the whole thing. An amendment, or *codicil*, may suffice if the changes are not extensive. The codicil is added onto the will, and it also must be properly prepared and dated.

How do wills work?

When you pass away, your will is brought before the court and proved to be valid and legal. Usually there's a waiting period, which gives any creditors time to make claims against your estate. After the waiting period is over, the terms of your will are carried out, and your property is distributed. This is called the *probate* process, and property which passes in this manner is called your *probate estate*.

Should the probate process be avoided?

Probate can be avoided if there is nothing which needs to go through the probate process. This can be accomplished through appropriately established trusts and by means of will substitutes (discussed in the following section).

In some states, probate needs to be avoided if possible, because the process is both tedious and costly. Other states have adopted what is called the *Uniform Probate Code*, with the idea being to simplify the process.[207] Still other states have modified this code, so as you can imagine, there is quite a variance from state to state.

Whether you should try to have your estate avoid probate or not depends on the size and complexity of your estate, as well as the laws of your state of domicile.[208] Many people are talked into establishing trusts when it may not be in their best interest to do so. As discussed earlier, trusts cost money to establish and maintain. So bypass the "free" advice that's out there at seminars and dinners, and instead seek the counsel of a competent legal professional who is familiar with your state's laws.

---

[207] To learn more about the Uniform Probate Code and the states which have adopted it, refer to the Web site of the Cornell University Law School. www.law.cornell.edu/uniform/probate.html

[208] The FindLaw Web site provides extensive information on probate and estates, including a bookshelf of online legal texts. To learn more about probate, click through the material presented in Probate 101. estate.findlaw.com/probate

Property which does *not* pass to others by means of probate is called your *non-probate estate*, and the next two sections will discuss how that property passes.

Passing Property Using a Will Substitute

Some types of property pass automatically, regardless of whether you have a will or not. Making use of will substitutes instead of leaving a written will is sometimes called the "poor man's will." That's because people without much property can sometimes arrange to have it all pass without making a will at all. Here are ways that property can pass without a will:

Contracts

Examples of legal contracts which allow property to pass automatically include:

- Insurance policies and retirement accounts on which you have named beneficiaries
- Buy-sell arrangements
- Prenuptial agreements

Property controlled by such contracts does not go through the probate process but passes according to the terms of the contract. In fact, the terms set forth in a will cannot supersede, or override, what has been stipulated in these contracts.

Operation of Law

Several items fall under the operation of law. These include:

1. Titling of property—the ownership of certain types of property (usually large and expensive things, such as land, a home or a car) is established by means of a title to the property. Upon the death of the owner, this property passes according to how it's titled. For example, if a bank account is titled in two people's names and the ownership is stated as joint tenancy with right of survivorship, the entire bank account automatically passes to the survivor when one of the owners dies. It would not go through probate.

2. Property laws of your state—concerning the property of married people, a state is either a *common law state or a community property state*. These laws come into play when the marriage is dissolved, either by death or divorce, and they govern how the property is to be divided. The basic thrust of these laws deals with the surviving spouse—that he or she is legally entitled to at least a certain amount of property, regardless of what the will states or in the event of a divorce or when there is no will.

- In *common law* states, the wife usually receives a *dower* or life estate in one-third of the husband's real property. (If the husband is the survivor, it's called *curtesy* property.)

- In *community property* states, the spouse is entitled to equal rights to all property obtained during the marriage. (Exceptions include separate property acquired before marriage or inherited property.)

Many states have modified these laws, so it is important to understand the property rights laws in the state where you live.

Under *community property* laws, half the real property belongs to each spouse, so each person directs the disposition of his or her half. The will of one spouse cannot direct how the other spouse's half is to be passed on. This means the community property of the deceased spouse may be subject to probate.

The basis for community property laws goes back to Spanish civil law and is found primarily in the states settled by the Spaniards and the French, although other states have adopted it as well. Currently, nine U.S. states are community property states: Arizona, California, Idaho, Louisiana, Nevada, New Mexico, Texas, Washington and Wisconsin. Additionally, Puerto Rico has community property laws, and in Alaska, married couples can accept community property laws by signing an agreement.[209]

The basis for *common law property rights* goes back to the English legal system. The states which are not community property states are common law states, although as stated previously, many states have modified these laws. Particularly in common law states, there seems to be more variance from state to state as to how property is to be divided. You will need to search your state's Web site or find someone familiar with the laws of your state to learn more about your particular state.

Alimony paid to a former spouse is more prevalent in common law states, due to an attempt by the court systems to even out the distribution of the property. However, in either type of state, it may be impossible to "disinherit" a spouse (barring criminal activity or extenuating circumstances), because these laws were specifically designed to protect the property rights of both spouses.

3. Trusts and gifts established while alive — arrangements can be made *before* you die to have certain property pass automatically to others *after* you die without having to go through probate. Such arrangements can be made by means of a *living* or *inter vivos trust* which you establish while alive. Your assets which you use to fund the trust are then managed by the trustee according to the terms stipulated in the trust. When you pass away, the assets are distributed as set forth in the trust.[210]

Accounts that are set up as *Payable on Death (P.O.D.)* are another common means of arranging for property to pass automatically at death. While you are still alive, the money in the account is yours to use as you wish, and the beneficiary does not have access to the money. At your death, what's left in the account goes to the named beneficiary.[211] These accounts are known by various names, including Totten trust, Transferable on Death (T.O.D.) and revocable trust accounts.[212]

---

[209] For more info, see: www.answers.com/topic/community-property Be sure to scroll down and see the many entries that are there. Also consult the Law Library of Congress at memory.loc.gov/ammem/awhhtml/awlaw3/property.html for more on "Property Law," and at memory.loc.gov/ammem/awhhtml/awlaw3/property_law.html concerning "Married Women's Property Laws." This article entitled, State Laws Dictate Division of Joint Property, is also informative: www.investopedia.com/articles/pf/08/community-common-law-property.asp?partner=answers#axzz1vJUk2sGa

[210] For more information on living trusts, pull up the pamphlet, "Do I Need a Living Trust," presented by the State Bar of California. calbar.ca.gov/LinkClick.aspx?fileticket=7xX4AesY230%3D&tabid=1341

[211] Be sure to ask your bank about the specifics of any such account that you establish.

[212] A good legal reference site is www.findlaw.com. Type in a term, such as *payable on death account* or *probate*, to find the definition and a list of articles on that topic.

Passing Property Using Your State's Laws of Intestate Succession

If you have a valid will in place at your death, you have died *testate* and left your last will and testament as a declaration or testimony of your wishes to be carried out upon your death. If you die without a valid will in place, you have died *intestate*. Because you haven't stated your wishes (in a manner recognized by your state's laws), any of your property that doesn't pass automatically, such as by contract or operation of law as mentioned previously, will pass according to the intestate succession laws of the state in which you live. The court will appoint an *administrator* (because if you don't have a will, then you haven't named an executor) to oversee the settling of your estate.

In essence, if you don't write a will, *the state writes one for you and determines who gets your property and selects the guardian for your minor children.*

Also called *statutes of descent*, or *rules of descent and distribution*, most states' laws of intestate succession place the surviving spouse first in line to receive the assets of the deceased. However, in some states, the spouse doesn't receive *all* the assets but must share them with the children. If the children are minors, then the court must appoint a trustee to represent the interests of the children. This means if you're the surviving spouse, not only have you suffered the loss of your mate, but you also have to deal with the courts and a third party in your life until your children become of age.

In some states, if the deceased has no children but does have a surviving spouse *and* a surviving parent(s), then the parent(s) gets a portion of the estate along with the spouse. The laws vary quite a bit from state to state, and it's likely that what the state has in mind for your property is not exactly what you would desire. However, the most important thing to remember is:

Regardless of the property you may or may not have—*if you have minor children and both you and the other parent die without a will, the COURTS must decide who will be the guardian of your children.*[213] Don't let that happen! Create your will.

What happens if the state cannot find any of your relatives that are on its list of who should get your property in the event you die intestate? Then your property *escheats* to the state. Even if you don't know what that word means, you can probably guess from the context that your state of domicile will get your stuff.

The next major discussion concerns estate taxes. Because some of the terminology may be new or used in unfamiliar ways, a brief explanation of commonly used terms is in order before proceeding.

---

[213] For more information on various estate issues, visit the Estate Planning Center at estate.findlaw.com

Estate Terminology

Estate — the assets or property (everything you own) that you leave behind at your death.

Executor or Executrix — the person (male or female) that you appoint in your will to handle the settling of your estate. The court can also appoint an *administrator* to fulfill this role if you did not name someone, or the person(s) you named in your will is not able to serve.[214]

Estate Tax — a tax that may apply to your taxable estate at your death. Your taxable estate is your gross estate less allowable deductions.

Gross Estate — the sum total of all your property you leave behind at your death.

Probate Estate — the part of your property that must be distributed by your will. In the absence of a valid will, your state's laws of intestate succession determine how it will be distributed. This property must go through the probate process.

Non-Probate Estate — the part of your property that is distributed automatically by contract or operation of law. For example, if you name your son as the beneficiary of your retirement account, it will pass to him at your death and not have to go through the probate process. However, the value of this account may still be part of your gross estate and possibly subject to estate taxes, regardless of whether it had to go through probate or not.

Probate — the legal process of proving that the will is a *valid* will and that it is the *last* will and testament of the one who passed away. The steps in the probate process include bringing the will before the court, presenting a list of the deceased person's assets along with the values of the assets, paying claims against the estate such as debts and income taxes, and distributing the remaining assets according to the terms of the will. When all the deceased person's assets have been distributed, then the estate no longer exists.

Taxable Estate — the value of your estate's property that is subject to estate taxes. Certain amounts can be subtracted off the value of your estate before taxes are calculated. This reduces the taxable estate and lowers the amount of estate taxes due. Such items include claims paid against the estate (like debts you owe) and property left to a surviving spouse or to a qualified charity.

Marital Deduction — current laws allow an unlimited amount of property can be left to one's spouse without estate taxes being due on this amount. Special rules and limitations apply if the spouse is not a U.S. citizen.[215]

Charitable Deduction — current laws allow an unlimited amount of property to be left to a qualified charity without estate taxes being due on this amount.

---

[214] For more on the duties of an executor, refer to IRS Publication 559: Survivors, Executors and Administrators. www.irs.gov/pub/irs-pdf/p559.pdf

[215] If your spouse is not a U.S. citizen, there is a limit as to how much you can gift to him/her — $136,000 for 2011. Refer to "Instructions for Form 709." www.irs.gov/pub/irs-pdf/i709.pdf

Unified Credit — an amount applied against gift or estate taxes owed in order to reduce taxes. If you use up some of this credit against taxable gifts you make while alive, then you have less to apply toward estate taxes owed after you pass away.

Annual Exclusion Amount — while alive, you can give any number of people up to the annual exclusion amount each year without gift taxes being owed. The annual exclusion amount is currently $13,000 (as of 2012). If the total of the gifts made in any one year to any one person is less than this annual exclusion amount, you do not use up any of your unified credit.

Exclusion Amount for Estate Tax Purposes — after death, only estates whose taxable amount is greater than this exclusion amount are subject to estate taxes. For years 2006, 2007, and 2008, this exclusion amount was $2 million, and the unified credit amount was $780,800. That means in those years, taxable estates of $2 million or less did not owe estate taxes. The estate taxes that otherwise would have been owed on a taxable estate of $2 million would have totaled $780,800. The unified credit forgave that amount of estate taxes owed, so taxable estates of $2 million or less owed no estate taxes.

For the year 2009, the exclusion amount was $3.5 million. If, by chance, you happened to die in 2010, no estate taxes were due, no matter the size of your estate. However, another law was passed later for 2010 deaths that gave executors a choice of using the 2010 rules or the 2011 rules. The difference had to do with how the basis of inherited property was treated, so the executor was able to pick the most beneficial. A return may have had to be filed for certain estates, and gift taxes may have applied.

For those who died in 2011, estates of $5 million or less were exempted from federal estate taxes, and in 2012, that amount increased to $5.12 million. Currently, if Congress doesn't act, in 2013 the laws revert back to what they were in 2001. Because these laws seem to be in constant flux, you must check the IRS Web site for the latest revisions.

Deceased Spousal Unused Exclusion (DSUE) — each person's estate is allowed the exclusion amount, so a married couple could potentially have a total of twice that amount excluded. In the past, however, if your spouse died and did not use all of his/her exclusion amount, it was lost. Now, with this new DSUE provision which came into effect beginning in 2011, his/her unused portion may be added onto your estate's basic exclusion amount. In order to be allowed this extra amount when you die, your deceased spouse's estate must have made this election when his/her Form 706 was filed.

Estate Taxes

As stated earlier, your estate consists of the property you leave behind when you die. While you worked during your lifetime to acquire those assets, you paid an assortment of taxes — sales taxes, property taxes, income taxes — depending on the type of property. Unfortunately, if you were too successful in acquiring property and leave behind too large an estate, it may also be subject to death taxes.

Death taxes include estate taxes at both the federal and the state level. Then, at the state level, your state may have either a state estate tax or an inheritance tax or both, or a variant of these taxes, depending on the state in which you live.[216] While the structure for federal estate taxes is presented in the IRS tax code, there is no such uniformity for state estate taxes. Therefore, only federal estate taxes will be discussed here.

How Estate Taxes Work

Your estate has a finite life. It comes into being upon your death and ceases to exist when all your assets have been appropriately distributed. During the period of time your estate exists, if your assets continue to earn income (such as rental income on property or interest on bank accounts), the estate itself may have to pay *income taxes* on these earnings. In fact, your executor may have to file estate income taxes for several years, depending on how long it takes to get your estate settled.

For the year in which you die, your executor may need to file two income tax returns on your behalf—your final 1040 for the portion of the year you were alive, and a 1041 for income earned on your estate for the remainder of that year.

How much will your estate owe in taxes?

The Economic Growth and Tax Relief Reconciliation Act of 2001, along with later revisions, was the law in effect until the end of 2010. A brief review of this complex law will be presented, as it affects estates that came into being during that time that may not yet be settled.

The federal estate taxes owed depend on the amount of your estate subject to taxes (shaded area on the flow chart in Table 15-A which follows on the next page) and the year in which you die. The table which follows shows the size of an estate on which taxes were due, along with the highest estate tax rates:

Year of Death	Size of Estate	Highest Rate
2006	$2,000,000	46%
2007 and 2008	$2,000,000	45%
2009	$3,500,000	45%
2010	(it depends; executor can choose between the 2010 and 2011 rules)	

For years 2011 and beyond, the law was set to revert back to what the exclusion amount and tax rates were in 2001. However, Congress passed a short-term patch for this law for the years 2011 and 2012. Now, once again, the law is set to revert back to 2001 levels in 2013 and beyond unless Congress acts.

---

[216] Examine the various tax burdens of different states at the Retirement Living Information Center: www.retirementliving.com/RLtaxes.html Use this map provided by the Federation of Tax Administrators to go to your state's tax Web site: www.taxadmin.org/fta/link/default.html

Year of Death	Size of Estate	Highest Rate
2011	$5,000,000	35%
2012	$5,120,000	35%
2013 and beyond	$1,000,000 (reverts back to the 2001 amount)	55%

So, in answer to the original question, it is very difficult to anticipate how much your estate may owe in taxes.

How is the estate tax calculated?

The abbreviated flow chart which follows presents the basic outline for how estate taxes are determined. The actual process can be much more involved, depending on the complexities of your estate. Should you or your loved ones have to deal with estate taxes, you need to consult legal and tax professionals concerning the given situation. Like the warning on television commercials – don't attempt this on your own.[217]

Table 15-A: Estate Tax Calculation

Gross Estate

– Debts of the estate, funeral expenses, administrative expenses and other allowable expenses and deductions

– Amounts left to surviving spouse and qualified charities

Tentative Taxable Estate

– State death tax deduction

(calculated using another tax table; note that various states handle state estate taxes differently)

Taxable Estate

+ Adjusted taxable gifts (gifts made during life that were greater than the annual exclusion amount)

Estate Tax Base—(This is the number you take to the estate tax tables and use in determining the tentative estate tax due—next number below.)

Tentative Estate Tax

– Gift taxes paid during life

– Unified Tax Credit

(in 2011, that was $1,730,800 based on the exclusion amount of $5 mil.)

– Credits for foreign death taxes and tax on prior transfers

Federal Estate Tax Due

(Note: Your total estate taxes = federal estate tax + state death tax.)

Aren't you glad this is the abbreviated version? The actual tax return is many pages long. Note that you must add back in any *taxable* gifts the person made while alive to determine the estate tax base. Any gift taxes he or she may have paid are subtracted later.

---

[217] Estate taxes are filed with the IRS on Form 706: United States Estate (and Generation-Skipping Transfer) Tax Return. www.irs.gov/pub/irs-pdf/f706.pdf For further information, refer to the form itself, to the instructions to Form 706 www.irs.gov/pub/irs-pdf/i706.pdf and to Publication 950: Introduction to Estate and Gift Taxes. www.irs.gov/pub/irs-pdf/p950.pdf

Why is the taxable gift added back in, even if gift taxes were paid while alive?

The tax credit an estate receives is *unified* between gifts made while alive and the value of the estate passed on after death. Even though any gift taxes paid while alive are later subtracted from the tentative estate taxes due, it's not a wash. By requiring the taxable gifts to be added back, the estate tax base is now larger, resulting in higher taxes and possibly pushing the taxable estate into a higher tax bracket than was used in calculating the gift taxes at the time the gift was made.

If all this sounds complicated, that's because it is. Various estate tax calculators are available on the Internet to help you estimate estate taxes. However, these are not likely to be totally accurate, given the state where you live and your particular situation, but they should give you a good idea based on the information you enter.[218]

Tax Considerations for Various Types of Property Passed

Two basic types of taxes come into play when property is passed at death to one's heirs:

- *Estate taxes* based upon the value of the taxable estate left behind.
- *Income taxes* on the property or assets held in tax-sheltered accounts.

Many people do not consider the income tax implications, *yet it's likely that income taxes impact more estates than do estate taxes*. That's because tax-sheltered accounts (retirement accounts and annuities) are used by so many people to accumulate wealth.

Whether the original owner is alive or dead, when the money comes out from under the tax shelter of these retirement accounts and annuities, the party's over. Income taxes will be owed at regular tax rates (not at the more favorable capital gains rates).

However, it may be possible for the heir or beneficiary to postpone taking the money from the account for a time period, or to take the money in a series of smaller withdrawals to be made through the years. Because U.S. income tax rates are progressive (the higher the income, the greater the percentage taken), a large wad of money taken out in one year is likely to be subject to a higher tax rate than would be smaller amounts taken out year by year.

The following list summarizes the various types of accounts and property and how they are subject to income taxes. Note that this is merely an overview. These are often complex matters and the laws can and do change. You definitely may need to consult a tax professional.

Here is a generalization of how income taxes work:

> As a rule of thumb, it's the government's position that your income *should be taxed*. So when money goes into a tax-sheltered account (retirement accounts and insurance annuities), if it wasn't taxed going in the door, it will be taxed coming out.

---

[218] Here are several estate tax calculators available on the Internet: willsandprobate.com/calculator.htm www.smartmoney.com/taxes/estate/?link=SM_topnav_taxes (Click on the Estate Tax Calculator tool.) www.banksite.com/calc/estate

On the other hand, if you paid taxes on the money contributed (that is, you made contributions with after-tax dollars), then those same dollars should not be taxed coming out the door. However, the *growth or earnings* on those dollars will be taxed (Roth IRAs are the notable exception).[219]

1. Assets and Property NOT Held in a Tax-Sheltered Account

These assets could include land and other real estate as well as financial assets, such as stocks and bonds. These assets have a *basis* (usually the purchase price, adjusted for any yearly income on which you have paid income taxes). If you leave these assets to your heirs upon your death, they receive a *"step-up in basis,"* meaning that the basis is reset to the value of the property at the time you died rather than what you paid for it. Then later, when your heirs sell the property, they pay capital gains tax only on the property's increase in value, if any, since you passed away.[220] Of course, the value of the property is still part of your estate and subject to estate taxes — if your total estate is enough to warrant the payment of estate taxes.

If you *gift* this property instead to loved ones *while you are still alive*, under current laws they will not receive a step-up in basis. Later, when they sell the property, they will owe capital gains tax on the property's increase in value since the time you purchased the property way back when. So they may be better off inheriting the property after your death versus you giving it to them while you are still alive.[221]

2. Assets in a Tax-Sheltered Account—Tax Deductible Contributions

These assets would include traditional deductible IRAs, 401(k)s, 403(b)s, etc. Because income taxes have never been paid on these assets, they are subject to *both* income taxes on the amount withdrawn as well as estate taxes on their total value. These assets suffer the greatest "shrinkage" when passed to your loved ones due to the double tax whammy. Rules govern how withdrawals can be made from these accounts by your beneficiaries, so it may be possible for them to spread out the withdrawals over a period of years to lessen the income tax bite somewhat.

3. Assets in a Tax-Sheltered Account—Contributions NOT Tax Deductible

These assets would include traditional nondeductible IRAs and insurance annuities purchased with after-tax dollars (but NOT the Roth IRA, which is in a category by itself).

On a tax-sheltered account in which income tax was paid on the money contributed to the account, withdrawals from the account by your heirs after you pass away will be split. The portion that is considered *return of principal* (or money you put into the account) is not subject to income tax, because you paid income tax on that money already in the year you earned it. The portion that is considered growth or earnings *will be subject to income tax at regular income tax rates.* (The lower capital gains rates do not apply.)

---

[219] Refer to IRS Publication 590: Individual Retirement Arrangements (IRAs). www.irs.gov/pub/irs-pdf/p590.pdf
[220] Investopedia gives the meaning and an example of how the step-up in basis works. www.investopedia.com/terms/s/stepupinbasis.asp
[221] Refer to IRS Publication 551: Basis of Assets. www.irs.gov/pub/irs-pdf/p551.pdf

As an example, let's say that you contributed a total of $100,000 of after-tax dollars to one of these type accounts. When you passed away, the account was valued at $200,000. If the money is then taken out, half would be considered a return of principal on which you had already paid income taxes, and half would be considered growth. The growth portion would be subject to regular income tax rates (not the more favorable capital gains rates).

4. Assets Held in a Roth IRA

Roth IRAs are precious jewels for anyone's investment portfolio, and they sparkle like the true treasures they are whether you are alive or dead. Many financial planners feel they are too good to be true, so get them while you can before the government does away with them.[222]

Contributions to Roth IRAs are made with after-tax dollars—you do *not* get to deduct your contributions on your tax return. Currently, your income must be under certain limits in order to be eligible to make contributions. (They weren't designed for the mega-wealthy.) Roths offer flexibility and various options during the years they are accumulating wealth, but their uniqueness lies in the fact that zero dollars ($0) of income taxes will be due on withdrawals, if made in accordance with the rules concerning Roths.

What you may not know is that a Roth IRA is also an excellent vehicle for passing on wealth to your loved ones upon your death. That's because when your heirs withdraw money from the account, *they will not owe any income taxes either!* Now remember, income taxes and estate taxes are two separate deals, and your Roth IRA, as part of your estate, may be subject to estate taxes along with the rest of your assets. But at least your heirs will not experience the shrinkage due to income taxes as they would with other types of retirement accounts.

> In general, you want to use up your Roth IRA assets *last* in retirement, because your loved ones will be better off inheriting a Roth IRA versus other types of assets subject to income taxes.

5. Insurance Annuities

Insurance annuities are products sold by insurance companies (not to be confused with company retirement benefits). Once money gets inside an annuity, it is allowed to grow tax free until withdrawn. Annuities can be held either inside or outside of retirement accounts.[223]

- If an insurance annuity is held *inside* a qualified retirement account and contributions were made with *before-tax* dollars, then *all* the money withdrawn is subject to *regular income taxes* because none of the money has ever been taxed. In this case, the "double shrinkage" mentioned earlier can occur due to the possibility that it may be subject to both income *and* estate taxes if your heirs receive such an annuity.

---

[222] Pull up these Web sites for more information on Roth IRAs.
www.irs.gov/pub/irs-pdf/p590.pdf   www.rothira.com   www.fairmark.com/rothira/inherit.htm
[223] Please note: This discussion is merely a generalization. Annuities can be very complex and there can be many variations. Refer to these two IRS publications, as well as search the IRS Web site for further information.
Publication 939: General Rule for Pensions and Annuities: www.irs.gov/pub/irs-pdf/p939.pdf
Publication 575: Pension and Annuity Income: www.irs.gov/pub/irs-pdf/p575.pdf

- If the annuity is held *outside* a qualified retirement account and contributions were made with *after-tax* dollars, then a distinction is made between the principal (the money you put in) and growth portions of the money withdrawn. Only the growth or earnings portion is subject to income taxes.

So when you take money out of this type annuity, how do you know if it's considered principal or growth? It depends on if you have *annuitized* your annuity or not. Annuitization is a rather formal and usually irreversible agreement you enter into with the insurance company. Typically, when you annuitize your annuity, which is also called your *annuity starting date*, you start taking a series of regular distributions or payments. If you have annuitized, each payment you receive will be considered part principal and part growth. Only the growth portion will be subject to income taxes, because the principal was already taxed before you put it into the annuity. Fortunately, the insurance company will usually determine this for you according to IRS regulations.

However, many people choose not to annuitize or start these types of annuities for various reasons. In such cases, if you make a withdrawal, the first dollars out are considered growth or earnings and are taxed as gross income at regular income tax rates. If you withdraw more than your annuity has earned, then the remainder is considered return of principal and that portion is not subject to income taxes.

With annuities, as with retirement accounts, if you withdraw money before age 59 ½, an additional early withdrawal penalty of 10% may apply. Tax treatment of annuities can get complicated, and you may need to consult a tax professional.

6. Smaller Assets

Smaller items are not usually named in the will, like who should get Grandmother's china, your jewelry, the artwork, a special collection or whatever. Designate who should get these things and place the list in your *Important Information* file. Some people choose to include this list in a *Letter of Last Instructions* along with other information and directives.[224] Concerning taxes of smaller assets, the executor would need to consult with the attorney, accountant and other professionals who are helping the family settle the estate.

The laws concerning estate taxes have been works in progress for the past several years. This makes planning very difficult. People can establish a plan while they are still of sound mind, but unfortunately they may not be aware of the changes in the laws that may occur later.

Particularly as we age, professionals become even more important to help us keep on top of things. And here's something you may want to consider — find trustworthy professionals, such as attorneys, accountants, wealth managers and physicians, who are *several decades younger than you are*. That way they are much more likely to still be alive and fully engaged

---

[224] The University of Florida IFAS Extension provides an extensive list of suggestions concerning what to include in a Letter of Last Instructions. edis.ifas.ufl.edu/FY537

in their professions when you need them the most later in life and when you pass away. This tip came courtesy of a long-lived gentleman who finally wised up after outliving so many of his contemporaries!

Other estate planning concerns are addressed in Chapter 16: Planning for Your Estate: Yourself and Your Loved Ones.

30 Minute LIVING

Suggested Action Plan

- *Review your property.* Make a list of what should be included in your estate, both the real property and your financial assets. You'll also need to have a list of your debts as well as any life insurance policies that you may have. If you worked through the other chapters in this book, you should be able to find this information easily by looking at the financial statements that you completed in Chapter 2: Evaluating Your Current Position, the Debt Worksheet in Chapter 6: Managing Your Debt, and the insurance inventory sheet provided at the end of Chapter 8: Insuring Your Life.

- *Review the titles and beneficiaries.* On all of your property, check how it's titled and who the beneficiaries are, if applicable. If you were to die today, would all your property and accounts pass to the people or charities that you desire? If not, you need to immediately change what needs to be changed.

- *Review your will.* If you have a will, make sure it's still relevant. If you don't have a will, find an attorney and schedule an appointment to have one prepared.

- *What about your spouse, parents or other loved ones?* If you are able, try to find out what arrangements your loved ones have made concerning their property and accounts. If they have a will, ask where it's kept, the name of their attorney and other relevant information.

- *Consider which assets to spend first in retirement.* Assess the types of accounts that you have. For any which may be tax-sheltered, consider not only your current need to minimize income taxes, but also if you want to maximize what you pass on to your loved ones. Then make a plan for which assets to spend first in retirement. If your loved ones inherit an account in which taxes were not paid on the money you contributed, they will owe income taxes in addition to any estate taxes that may apply. If they inherit a Roth IRA, they will not owe income taxes (estate taxes may still apply if your estate is large enough) and be able to keep more of the money.

- *Curious about the wills of other people?* Read the wills of famous people at this Nolo site: www.willsandtrustslawfirms.com/famous-wills

  This list of 10 unusual wills makes for interesting reading: listverse.com/2008/08/23/10-unusual-last-wills-and-testaments

  Finally, here's another list of 10, this time of famous people who died without a will: www.legalzoom.com/legal-headlines/celebrity-lawsuits/10-famous-people-who-died

CHAPTER 16

Planning For Your Estate: Yourself and Your Loved Ones

If you love them, plan for them!

Chad was a remarkable young man. He was only in his second year of junior college, but he had a truck that he had paid for himself and was busy planning his wedding with his fiancée. Together, they had enough money set aside so that their wedding would be paid for without incurring debt. When asked how he had accomplished this, Chad was quick to credit his father who had passed away several years ago.

It seems Chad's father had a health condition and knew from a young age that he would not live a normal life span. He had explained this to Chad's mother, who decided she wanted to marry him anyway. Together, they managed to have three children before he passed away.

During his all too brief life, Chad's father made the most of his limited time to help provide for his family's future. Not only had he made saving and investing a priority, but he also worked to teach his young family how to manage money wisely. By the time he passed away, he had enough set aside to help supplement his wife's income for several years as well as provide a college education for all three of his children. More importantly, he showed his family by the example of his life the value of planning for those you love.

Estate planning often gets pushed to the back burner because people tend not to want to think about the end of their lives. This reluctance can have unintended consequences for the people they love the most. Their families are often left scrambling to find important papers and access bank accounts to keep the bills paid. Their loved ones may also be left with too little money such that their quality of life suffers.

What if someone else had to take over?

Estate planning covers much more than how to distribute your property upon your death (those topics were covered in Chapter 15 — Planning for Your Estate: Property and Estate Taxes). It also includes planning for the later years of your life as well as planning for those you care about.

With life expectancies being longer, many people will likely spend quite a few years needing some type of assistance and may need to turn their bill paying and decision making functions over to others. It's also important to have plans in place, regardless of your age, because unexpected occurrences, such as debilitating accidents or illnesses, can happen at any time.

This chapter covers the following important planning issues:
- Planning for your loved ones: children, family, friends and charities
- Planning for your finances: powers of attorney, important documents and important people
- Planning for your health: living will, medical power of attorney and issues concerning your health
- Paying for elder care: savings, long-term care insurance, Medicaid and Medicare
- Planning your final disposition: people to contact, burial instructions, etc.
- Creating an estate planning checklist

Planning for Your Children, Family, Friends and Charities

How can you know for sure that your family and other loved ones will be cared for, or that your special interests will be continue to be funded once you're no longer in the picture? You can't, unless you create a plan—and then fund that plan!

Minor Children
Many people think they don't have enough money or other assets to worry with making a will, or that they have titled their property to pass automatically. Regardless, if you have minor children, you absolutely need a will. It is essential that you name a guardian for your children, and don't think that if you're not around, your children's other parent will care for them. It's not all that uncommon for children to lose both parents before they reach adulthood, sometimes in a single accident. *If you don't name a guardian in your will, then the courts will decide who will finish raising your children!*

As mentioned in Chapter 15, you need to name a backup guardian or two as well. It's a big responsibility for someone else to step in and finish raising your children. Your number one choice may no longer be physically or mentally capable. They may, in fact, have predeceased you. Or, they may not be willing or financially able to take on the challenge when actually faced with the job of caring for your children.

Other Dependents
Many people also have adults in their lives who are their dependents. If this is the case for you, make sure that they will be cared for should something happen to you.

- *Children with special needs* may need to be provided for all the way to the end of their natural lives. In fact, some may live for many years after their parents have passed away.[225] Their future oversight often falls to a sibling or other relative. Special planning should be done in such cases, and if at all possible, the resources put in place for their

---

[225] The Special Needs Alliance provides numerous resources at its site. www.specialneedsalliance.com/resources The Montana State University Extension Service presents this article entitled, "Estate Planning for Families with Minor and/or Special Needs Children," which also addresses the needs of children by a previous marriage. msuextension.org/publications/FamilyFinancialManagement/MT199117HR.pdf

care. Also be sure and discuss your plans with whoever will assume responsibility for your child.

- *Parents or other elderly loved ones* often become dependents in their later years. Should this situation arise in your life, remember that even though you may be younger and normally would outlive them, caregivers can and do pass away before the ones who are being cared for. Think about what would happen to them should you die first. Make provisions for them, and again, be sure and discuss your plans with whomever you would like to take over should this occur.

Your Spouse

Don't leave things to chance concerning your spouse. The laws vary from state to state concerning the property one spouse receives when the other one dies. Be sure you understand how property passes in your state, because your parents or siblings could stand to receive some of the assets that you might assume would go to your spouse. As discussed in Chapter 15, only non-probate property passes automatically. If you don't leave a will, any probate property you may have would pass according to your state's laws of intestate succession.

Friends

Those whom we care about but who are not related to us must be specifically named. That's because only those who are related by blood or legal adoption are part of the lineup to receive assets in the event you die without a will. Unless your friend also happens to have a financial claim against your estate, the courts will likely leave him or her out entirely.

Unmarried partners also fall into this category and must be specifically provided for. Particular care must be given to the titling of property so that, for example, one partner is not without a home should the other one die first.

Charities and Special Interests

Likewise, charities are not in one's lineage, either. If there's a cause that you feel strongly about, you need to specifically make plans for those charities, schools, hospitals or other special interests to receive part of your estate. You also need to discuss your desires with your children or other loved ones so that no one feels slighted when they learn that part of the inheritance will be going to another entity.

What means can be used to pass property?

Various means can be used to pass your property to your loved ones or charities. Of course, you can always specifically name them in your will. You can also use a will substitute as mentioned in Chapter 15, such as naming them the beneficiary of your IRA or life insurance policy, for example. However, depending on your needs and your given situation, it may be better to establish a trust for their benefit.[226] There are many types of trusts, so be sure and consult with a competent legal professional who knows the laws in your state.

---

[226] SaveWealth provides information on charitable remainder trusts as well as retirement and estate planning. www.savewealth.com/planning/estate/charitabletrusts

Planning for Your Finances

It can be a huge task for someone else to take over your finances should you become incapacitated or pass away. Their biggest challenges are typically:

- Being able to *find your financial documents*, and
- Having the *proper authority to access your accounts* so others can take care of your business.

To address the issue of you becoming incapacitated due to accident or illness while alive, the following suggestions should prove helpful.

Organize Your Finances

Try to imagine if someone else were to take over your day-to-day bill paying activities. What would they need to know? Would they be able to find your records and your bills? Of course, some bills still come in the mail, but others are electronically delivered. How would someone else know what bills are due when?

Important Information File

Create an *Important Information* file folder for the purpose of instructing someone else about your finances. What should go in the folder depends on your situation, but here are some suggestions:

- A copy of the *budget* you prepared in Chapter 3: Planning Your Future Expenditures would be a good place to start, because it shows what bills you normally pay. Beside each expense, you could write in what day of the month each bill comes due. If you keep your finances on a computer program, you might print off a report of your last year's expenses organized by category.

- Make a list of any *automatic bill payments* that are made from your bank accounts. Detail how much is drafted, from which account, and when the draft normally occurs. It's important to keep enough money in your accounts to cover these drafts when they come due.

- A copy of your *personal balance sheet* that you prepared in Chapter 2: Evaluating Your Current Position would also be good to include. This provides a list of your assets as well as your debts. Beside each asset (or on a separate sheet), you could write in how the asset is titled and where the title or other related documents are located. Beside each debt you could write in relevant information, such as the name of the lender, when the debt will be paid off, location of the loan documents, etc.

- *Insurance* is very important in emergency situations, so make a list of all your policies — life, health, auto, home, etc. — along with how to contact each company or agent. Then consider how you pay the premiums on each policy, whether the amount is automatically drafted out of your bank account or you write a check. If the premiums are due quarterly, semi-annually or annually, be sure to make a special note about these. *Billings that only occur occasionally tend to slip through the cracks.* The last thing you or your family needs while you're incapacitated is for your insurance to get cancelled.

- The *location* of valuable or important items will be especially crucial. If your will or insurance policies, for example, are in a bank box, list out who has access to the box. If you've hidden something somewhere, you need to tell someone while you still remember where you put it. Contractors have been known to find stashes of cash in the walls of homes or behind cabinets when remodeling, long after the rightful owners have passed away and the home sold. Even worse are the safes that people may have buried in their back yard! Many of those may never be found.

- If you do *not* receive Social Security but *are* on Medicare and have both Part A and Part B, be sure to let others know how you pay for your Medicare. Because Social Security payments are so common, others may assume that your payments for Medicare are being automatically withheld from Social Security and not recognize (and hence not pay) the bill that comes in the mail. This can be the case, for example, with teachers who taught in school districts that did not pay into Social Security and receive teacher retirement payments instead.

Make a List of Important People

Also place in your Important Information file folder a list of important people along with their contact information. Depending on your circumstances, your list could include:
- Family members and friends that you would like notified in the event of an emergency.
- If you have granted someone your power of attorney (discussed below), be sure to list this person along with his or her contact information.
- Others that your spouse or agent may need to get in touch with, such as your doctors, attorney, accountant, financial advisor or supervisor at work.
- If you have a special situation, such as you own your own business or have rental property, list out people who may need to be contacted and include any instructions that need to be carried out.

Consider Creating a Power of Attorney

Creating a power of attorney is a good idea for everyone, because you just don't know what the future holds. However, it's even more crucial if:
- You have health problems or potential health concerns.
- You don't have a spouse, or your spouse is unwilling or unable to handle the finances.
- You're traveling to a foreign country.
- You engage in risky or dangerous activities, either for sport or in your job.

A *power of attorney* is a legal document that gives another person the authority or power to act on your behalf. Various options exist when drawing up this document as to the extent of the power given, under what situations the power can be used and for how long.

For financial planning purposes, you would probably want a *durable power of attorney*, but this is something you would need to discuss with an attorney familiar with your needs and with the laws of your state.

A durable power of attorney is indeed a powerful document. Your *agent* whom you have named will be able to perform activities for you, such as sign documents, access your bank accounts, or buy and sell your property. Obviously, this person needs to be someone that you fully trust.

As mentioned previously, you need to state who has your power of attorney in your Important Information file so that he or she can be notified and pay your bills for you or do whatever is needed. Again, a competent attorney can advise you as to what would be appropriate in your given situation, such as who should keep possession of the document and if it should be publicly recorded or not.[227]

Planning for Your Health

Depending on your age and health, several documents may be in order. The information given below is general in nature, as these documents may vary from state to state.[228]

Living Will

With a living will, you are able to state your wishes concerning how you would like to be treated in the event you become terminally ill or injured. Different states allow various stipulations, but basically it has to do with your desire concerning whether life support should be continued or not, should you become permanently unconscious with no detectible brain activity and unable to live without life-sustaining treatment.

This document is as much for the comfort and peace of mind of your loved ones as it is for your own. Even though you may have verbally stated your wishes on numerous occasions, having this document reassures your family that they are indeed doing what you would want. It also affirms your wishes to the attending physicians.

Think of your living will as a gift to your family, relieving them of the burden of having to make that life-or-death decision on their own. Sometimes there will be a family member who wants every means possible used to keep a loved one alive, regardless. The situation they create can make this decision guilt laden and absolutely gut wrenching. Your living will helps the doctors and decision makers know they are doing what you would have liked.

Durable Medical Power of Attorney

This document goes by several names, including health care proxy and health care surrogate. With it, you name someone to make medical decisions for you in the event you are unable to do so.

While the living will deals with the end-of-life decision, a durable medical power of attorney is for when you are unconscious or otherwise not legally competent to make your own medical decisions. Examples of when this document would come into play could include occasions such as accidents which render you unconscious or comatose, advancing dementia, or decisions that must be made during surgery while you are under anesthesia.

Other Health Care Directives

You may need other documents or instructions concerning your care, depending on the state in which you live and the specific institutions involved, such as hospitals or nursing homes.

---

[227] The Web site of the American Bar Association provides extensive information on estate planning issues, including the power of attorney. In the Estate Planning FAQ section, scroll down to "Power of Attorney." americanbar.org/groups/real_property_trust_estate/resources/estate_planning/estate_planning_faq.html
[228] Scroll down on the above referenced site to the section, "Living Wills, Health Care Proxies and Advanced Heath Care Directives."

People of advanced age or with terminal illnesses sometimes file *"Do Not Resuscitate"* orders. Those with certain moral or religious convictions may specify for or against various treatments and medications. Discuss your medical treatment options and concerns with your physician or health care professionals and then take the appropriate actions.

Remember, without health care documents or directives in place, you won't have a say in your treatment should you become incapacitated or otherwise unable to make competent decisions. The burden will lie on your loved ones and physicians, all of whom may have conflicting opinions.

Paying for Elder Care

Most people need some type of extra assistance as they get older, which usually creates additional expenses. Most people will use a combination of some or all of the following means of paying for those added costs.

Savings

Your savings, investments, retirement accounts and pensions will likely be your first line of defense in paying for your expenses later in life. With any luck, they'll last as long, or longer, than you do. Often, they are used to supplement some of the other items that follow.

Long-term Care Insurance

Long-term care insurance (LTC) is an option that's become available in the last several decades and was discussed in Chapter 9: Insuring Your Health. To get this insurance, you have to plan ahead and purchase it while you are young enough and healthy enough to afford the premiums. This means you'll likely be paying those premiums for years, all the while not knowing if you're going to have to use the insurance or not. However, if you wait until you actually need the insurance to try to buy it, you probably won't be allowed to purchase it. The cost becomes prohibitive at advanced ages, and most companies will not issue a policy at all if you're past a certain age.

If you already have a policy, you'll probably want to continue with it. If the premiums become a burden, it may be to your family's advantage to step in and help pay for your policy. The cost of the premiums is likely to be far less than the cost of the care that the policy will provide for later.

Be aware that there are many considerations with LTC policies, particularly those that were issued a number of years ago. Some of the earlier policies only covered care in the nursing home, not care needed to keep you in your own home. Many were issued to cover a set amount per day (for example, $50) and did not allow for rising costs. That amount may be totally inadequate years later when the coverage is actually needed. Policies which do allow for inflation riders to be purchased may make for such an increase in premiums that the cost becomes unmanageable. If you're considering purchasing LTC, be sure and research your choices carefully.[229]

---

[229] The Texas Department of Insurance provides "A Shopper's Guide to Long-Term Care Insurance." www.tdi.texas.gov/pubs/consumer/cb032.html

Medicaid

You may have heard or read about Medicaid planning as a means of obtaining government assistance in paying for nursing home care. Medicaid is a federal program for people of low economic means that is administered at the state level. Your state may provide additional funding as well. Different states handle Medicaid differently, so only general information can be provided here. You will need to get specific information from the state where you live.

Medicaid pays the nursing home expenses for those who qualify, and it used to be that people would simply give their assets away. Because so many people resorted to this self-induced impoverishment, a law was passed that required a three-year look-back period. Assets that were given away in the past three years would be counted as still belonging to the individual for the purpose of paying for their care.

More recently, however, *the look-back period has been changed to five years*, making it even more difficult for people to qualify for Medicaid until they have spent down their own assets. Exceptions are made for those who have a spouse or certain other dependents still living in the community (that is, not living in an institution). In such cases, more assets and income can be kept in order to prevent the spouse or other dependent from becoming impoverished.[230]

Another problem with Medicaid is the issue of *control*. If you qualify for nursing home care under Medicaid, you may be sent to the next available bed in your area or region. This may not be convenient for your loved ones, and it may not be the nursing home you would choose. To learn more about Medicaid, you definitely need to find someone who is familiar with how it works in your state and region. If possible, you don't want Medicaid to be your primary means for providing elder care.[231]

Medicare

Medicare is the government health insurance program for people age 65 and older, and it consists of several parts:

- *Part A* — for those who have lived and worked in the U.S., Part A is typically free and covers some amount of expenses for inpatient care in hospitals, skilled nursing facilities, home health care or hospice.[232]

- *Part B* — this part is optional and typically covers outpatient care expenses and doctors' fees. Many people pay for Part B by having the premiums deducted from their Social Security payments. Those who don't receive Social Security must pay for it out of pocket. Also, if you have other insurance and become eligible for Medicare, many policies will

---

[230] This article in Aging Well magazine addresses Medicaid planning issues. www.agingwellmag.com/archive/083109p26.shtml

[231] Find contact information for your state's Medicaid offices: www.cms.gov/apps/contacts/ This page provides links to the state Medicaid websites: www.medicaid.gov/Medicaid-CHIP-Program-Information/By-State/By-State.html Here's another site with helpful Medicaid links: www.colorado2.com/medicaid/states.html

[232] Refer to this page for more information on what Medicare covers. Scroll down to 'What does Medicare Part A cover?" www.medicare.gov/what-medicare-covers/index.html

no longer pay for what Parts A and B cover. That means if you don't choose to pay for Part B, you'll be paying out of pocket for the costs it would otherwise cover. Be sure and find out how any other insurance you may have will coordinate with Medicare.[233]

- *Part C* – if you desire, you can join a Medicare Advantage Plan. Also called "Part C" or "MA Plans," they are offered by private companies that are approved by Medicare. These plans provide all of your Part A and Part B coverage, and may offer extra coverages, such as vision, hearing, dental, etc. Most will also include Part D, the Medicare prescription drug coverage. Costs for these plans vary, and you may have restrictions (for example, the doctors and facilities you can use). You also must choose a plan that's available in your area.[234]

- *Part D* – this part covers prescription drugs. The costs vary by the plan you choose, the drugs you require and other factors. When you're first eligible for Part D, carefully consider whether you want to sign up or not. If you do not have other creditable prescription drug coverage, or you don't receive certain types of extra help, you may have to pay a late enrollment penalty to join later.[235]

Medicare covers many things with no expense to the individual, but on others you may be required to pay a percentage of the cost or a co-payment to your provider. Many people also choose to purchase a supplemental insurance plan in order to have more complete health care coverage.

What does Medicare NOT cover?

While it's important to know what Medicare covers, it's even more important to know what it does not cover in order to plan for how to meet those needs. A short list follows, but you will need to consult the Medicare handbook or Web site for more specific information.[236] Currently (as of 2012), Medicare does not cover:

- Long-term care
- Routine dental care and dentures
- Cosmetic surgery
- Acupuncture
- Hearing aids and exams for fitting hearing aids

Also note that Medicare covers very little nursing home care. It will cover up to 100 days per benefit period in a skilled nursing facility if you need to recuperate further from a hospital stay. Even so, if you qualify, only 20 days are paid outright. For days 21–100, you would pay $144.50 per day. Then, after day 100, you would have to pay all the costs (as of 2012).

---

[233] Refer to the above Medicare page. Scroll down to 'What does Medicare Part B cover?"
[234] Learn more about Medicare health plans on this page. www.medicare.gov/sign-up-change-plans/medicare-health-plans/medicare-health-plans.html Use the Medicare Plan Finder to search for plans available in your zip code. https://www.medicare.gov/find-a-plan/questions/home.aspx
[235] Learn more about Medicare Prescription Drug Coverage on this page. www.medicare.gov/part-d/index.html
[236] Pull up the Medicare Web site at: www.medicare.gov Consult the Medicare handbook for more information. www.medicare.gov/Publications/Pubs/pdf/10050.pdf

Planning for Your Final Disposition

For most families, this is not a topic that comes up frequently at the dinner table. It would probably be better if it did, because the discussion would likely be more casual in nature and less emotionally charged. Unfortunately, once someone has passed away it's too late to have that conversation. You'll be doing your family a favor if you at least tell them verbally what you would prefer concerning your final disposition. It would be even better if you wrote it all down and put your instruction sheet in that Important Information file mentioned earlier.

Those who have been faced with the untimely death of a loved one know how overwhelming making all these decisions can be. So here are some points to address:[237]

1. *Do you wish to donate your organs to others, or perhaps your body to a medical school?* You need to make this known ahead of time or it's not likely to happen. Some states now list if you're an organ donor on your driver's license. Many people have surprisingly strong opinions, one way or the other, on this matter.

2. *Do you wish to be buried or cremated?* This is something else about which many people have very strong opinions. If you don't tell someone that you want your ashes scattered over Tahiti, you might get stuck in a coffin and buried beside the cousin you never liked.

3. *Where would you like to be buried (if that's your choice)?* If it's under the old oak tree at the family farm, better start working now to get the burial site approved according to the laws of your state. Also consider that the family farm could be sold someday, which might make it difficult for your loved ones to access the property in the future. Surviving spouses may also have a hard time deciding whether you would prefer to be buried back where you grew up or in your current home town that's closer to him or her.

4. *What arrangements have you already made?* If you have already purchased a burial policy or a cemetery plot, your family definitely needs to know this and where everything is located. Also let them know about any other arrangements you may have made.

5. *What type of memorial service would you prefer?* Maybe you want it to be meaningful and uplifting to your loved ones. Perhaps you want it to be a gala event or just a simple graveside service. Some people like to name their pallbearers, the songs and other particulars for the service, and even the clothes they would like to be buried in. Whatever your desires, let your family know. Also remember to leave them some extra cash to take care of things. Funerals can be surprisingly expensive. (If you leave life insurance, it usually takes time for the check to arrive. However, your beneficiary may possibly be able to get a loan against the policy fairly quickly, which they can pay off later when the policy proceeds arrive.)

It really helps to have these and any other instructions or wishes that you have for your family written down where they can easily find them. They will likely be under a great

---

[237] Download the Personal Funeral Planning Guide here:
webconnect.funeralplan.com/umbraco/aurora/pdfs/personalplan.pdf

deal of stress and will have to make arrangements fairly quickly. And, by the time you pass away, your family may already be physically and emotionally exhausted, possibly having gone without sleep for an extended period of time.

Even though this is not one of the fun topics in personal finance, think about the plans and preparations you make ahead of time as a parting gift to your loved ones. They will thank you many times over, particularly if some relative comes along with a strong opinion that's counter to what you would have wanted. The arguments that ensue can turn bitter, and the hurt can last for years. If you've left your wishes, it's case closed!

Estate Planning Checklist

The following checklist can be used as a guide for your estate planning. You'll want to add whatever else may be appropriate for your given situation. It can also serve as an excellent resource for you to use in your day-to-day planning and will help you organize your finances.[238]

This information also needs to go in your Important Information file. You may have already assembled much of it as you worked through the various aspects of your financial planning. You may want to record it in a computer file so that you can save it, print it out for your Important Information file, modify it later, e-mail it to your family members, etc.

1. *Personal information*—include your full legal name (as well as maiden, if applicable), birth date and birthplace, Social Security number and any other relevant personal information. Copies of documents, such as your birth certificate, marriage license(s), divorce paper(s), citizenship papers, etc., would be good to include in your folder. Be sure to state where the actual documents are located.

2. *Family information*—list all the personal and relevant information for your spouse and children, as well as that of any ex-spouse(s) and children by prior marriages. Be sure to include information on any other loved ones that you deem relevant, such as your parents, grandparents, special needs sibling that you help care for, etc.

3. *Employment information*—include information on your current employer, such as name, address, your position, your supervisor, contact numbers and e-mail addresses, any benefits or insurance that you get through your employer and how to contact the benefits office. If you receive benefits from former employers, or if you are retired from an employer, be sure to provide any relevant information on them, as well as list the benefits and insurance you get through them.

4. *Business information*—if you are a business owner, list relevant information such as any partners, buy-sell arrangements, insurance or other pertinent information concerning the ownership of the business, employees in charge of the various operations, attorneys, accountants, location of documents, etc.

---

[238] This more extensive estate planning checklist is made available by the Webb and Webb law firm. www.webbwebb.com/estateplanningchecklist.pdf

5. *Military information* — if you served in the military, include your service dates, a copy of your discharge papers, and any other relevant information.

6. *Insurance information* — list out the policy numbers and contact information for all your insurance, such as life, health, disability, long-term care, auto, home, umbrella or other liability coverage. If you become incapacitated or pass away, insurance becomes a prime concern — determining the coverages you have, what is applicable for the situation and filing timely claims. Remember that insurance companies tend to be very picky about whom they talk to, so whoever has your power of attorney will probably have to submit it before they will be able to find out from the company any information on your policy or to act on your behalf.

7. *Your assets* — be sure to include copies of property deeds and titles and/or instructions as to where these items are located or publicly recorded. Also include copies of recent property tax statements and other information (if it's not already included on other documents), such as when the property was purchased, from whom, current estimated value, etc.

    a. Real estate owned — your home, land, business or commercial properties. List the locations and legal descriptions. (Look on your deeds for this information.)

    b. Vehicles — include relevant information along with copies of the current registration, proof of insurance, titles, etc.

    c. Other tangible properties — this would include boats, RVs, business property (other than real estate), etc.

    d. Financial assets — list out bank accounts, brokerage accounts, retirement accounts, etc. Include the account numbers and contact information, particularly for the person or department that you deal with. Copies of your recent statements would be very helpful.

    e. Bank boxes — include their location and bank contact information, name of everyone who has a key, where your key is located, contents of the box, when and how the box rent is paid, etc.

8. *Your debts* — list out any loans or mortgages you may have, including account numbers, terms of the loan, amount of the payments and when due, contact information for the person who helps you at the bank, etc. Also, list out your consumer debt information (credit cards, store cards, gasoline cards, etc.) — whether you have a balance or not — so that you have all that information together, particularly the customer service numbers. This also comes in really handy should your cards get lost or stolen.

9. *Tax returns* — copies of your returns for the last two years and W-2 and/or 1099 forms. If you file electronically, print out a copy of the files. If you use an accountant, include his/her contact information. Filing taxes on your behalf is an important part of what someone else may have to do for you, so try to gather everything together that they may need.

10. *Legal and other important documents*—either provide copies or list the location of important documents such as your will, trusts that have been established, powers of attorney (for your finances as well as your medical power of attorney if you have one), living will, health care directives, business documents, etc. These are things your agent will need to access.

11. *Other directives*—burial instructions, arrangements that may have already been made and/or paid for, your Letter of Last Instructions, friends and important people to contact and anything else you deem important.

As your net worth grows over time, various aspects of estate planning may become more complex. Try to find competent professionals to help you with the documents you will need and the decisions you must make. Estate planning is not something you want to leave to chance. Even though the future is an unknown, today you do have the opportunity to put appropriate plans in place so that you will have a say in what happens.

Planning for your estate provides the added bonus of helping you set your financial house in order in the here and now. Going through this process will enable you to better track your finances, and you'll be surprised at how quickly you will be able to accomplish your financial goals.

30 Minute LIVING

Suggested Action Plan

- *Determine your needs.* Do you have dependent children? What about elderly parents or a special needs sibling? Consider the people in your life that you would like cared for in the event that you are no longer around, and start planning for them. You may need to consult an attorney and/or financial advisor.

- *Start collecting information.* It takes time to assemble your Important Information file, but you can start today by doing at least a portion. As you pay bills during the month, make notes in your file concerning which items come in the mail, are automatically drafted from your bank account, etc.

- *Which documents do you already have, and which do you still need?* Think about the different documents you need and make arrangements with your attorney to have them prepared. If you already have appropriate documents, make notes in your Important Information file as to where these documents are located.

- *Talk with your loved ones.* Think about what you would prefer for your final arrangements and discuss these issues with your family. Such decisions are easier to make before you become ill or incapacitated. It may cause undue anxiety to your loved ones for them to have to make these decisions later on their own.

- *Begin working through the estate planning checklist.* In connection with your Important Information file, work through the points on the checklist to make sure you have included as many of these items as apply to your situation.

About The Author

Marilynn E. Hood is a financial educator and writer who has taught the principles of personal finance to thousands. She draws upon her own personal learning journey and years of teaching experience in presenting *Money For Life*.

Marilynn holds an MBA from Texas A&M University, where she later joined the faculty in the Department of Finance of the Mays Business School. She currently holds the CERTIFIED FINANCIAL PLANNER™ certification, the designation of Chartered Retirement Plans Specialist™ and is licensed with the Texas Department of Insurance as a general lines agent. She has previously been a mortgage loan officer with the Texas Department of Savings & Mortgage Lending and has held the Series 7 and 63 securities licenses for stockbrokers.

Marilynn is the owner and creator of 30MinuteLiving.com. She currently resides in College Station, Texas, along with her husband, David Hood.

www.ingramcontent.com/pod-product-compliance
Lightning Source LLC
Chambersburg PA
CBHW081809200326
41597CB00023B/4195